WALT WHITMAN'S
LANGUAGE EXPERIMENT

WALT WHITMAN'S LANGUAGE EXPERIMENT

James Perrin Warren

THE PENNSYLVANIA STATE UNIVERSITY PRESS
University Park and London

Library of Congress Cataloging-in-Publication Data

Warren, James Perrin.
  Walt Whitman's language experiment / James Perrin Warren.
    p.   cm.
  Includes bibliographical references.
  ISBN 0–271–00688–9
  1. Whitman, Walt, 1819–1892. Leaves of grass. 2. Whitman, Walt, 1819–
  1892—Knowledge—Language and languages. 3. Whitman, Walt, 1819–
  1892—Language. 4. Experimental poetry, American—History and
  criticism. I. Title
PS3238.W39   1990
811'.3—dc20   89–37353

It is the policy of The Pennsylvania State University Press to use acid-free
paper for the first printing of all clothbound books. Publications on
uncoated stock satisfy the minimum requirements of American National
Standard for Information Sciences—Permanence of Paper for Printed
Library Materials, ANSI Z39.48–1984.

For Yolanda, Sylvia, and Eline

Contents

Acknowledgments

Along the road that led to this book, I incurred more debts of gratitude than I can name here, but certain individuals and institutions deserve special mention. My deepest thanks go to Ward Allen, Marie Borroff, and Richard Brodhead, who taught me as much as I could learn. I also thank Hans Aarsleff, Ed Folsom, Arthur Golden, and Carroll Hollis for their advice, criticism, and encouragement during the writing of the book. I thank Washington and Lee University for providing financial support in the form of John M. Glenn Summer Research Grants, and the research libraries at the University of Virginia, Duke University, and the Library of Congress Manuscript Division for making their Whitman holdings available to me. For editorial support, I am especially grateful to Philip Winsor and Cherene Holland of The Pennsylvania State University Press. I am also grateful to the editors of *Walt Whitman Quarterly Review* and *ESQ* for permission to use essays I published in their pages. Dale Mantautas deserves special credit for indexing the volume.

Finally and most important, I wish to thank my entire family for their love and for their confidence in me, but I especially thank the three ladies to whom I dedicate this work.

Abbreviations

CRE   *Leaves of Grass: Comprehensive Reader's Edition*, ed. Harold W. Blodgett and Sculley Bradley (New York: New York University Press, 1965).

DBN, III   *Daybooks and Notebooks*, III, ed. William White (New York: New York University Press, 1978).

Grammar   Randolph Quirk, Sidney Greenbaum, Geoffrey Leech, and Jan Svartvik, *A Grammar of Contemporary English* (New York: Longman Group, 1972).

Outlines   Christian C. J. Bunsen, *Outlines of the Philosophy of Universal History, Applied to Language and Religion* (London: Longmans, 1854).

Philology   Maxmilian Schele de Vere, *Outlines of Comparative Philology* (New York: Putnam's, 1853).

PW   *Prose Works 1892* (vols. 1 and 2), ed. Floyd Stovall (New York: New York University Press, 1964).

Rambles   William Swinton, *Rambles Among Words*, rev. ed. (New York: Ivison, Blakeman, Taylor, 1872).

SOED   *The Shorter Oxford English Dictionary on Historical Principles*, ed. C. T. Onions, 3d ed. (Oxford: Clarendon Press, 1973).

Variorum   *Leaves of Grass: A Textual Variorum of the Printed Poems*, ed. Sculley Bradley, Harold W. Blodgett, Arthur Golden, and William White (New York: New York University Press, 1980).

Introduction

Books are like men—the best of them have flaws.
Thank God for the flaws![1]

Whitman's equation of books and men raises the question, at the very beginning of this work, as to how the critical reader can best approach the book *Leaves of Grass* and the poet Walt Whitman. We may think, first of all, of the poet's last essay on his book, published just ten days after he made the above remarks to Horace Traubel. In "A Backward Glance O'er Travel'd Roads," Whitman offers one of his clearest warnings:

> "Leaves of Grass," indeed (I cannot too often reiterate) has mainly been the outcropping of my own emotional and other personal nature—an attempt, from first to last, to put *a Person*, a human being (myself, in the latter half of the Nineteenth Century, in America,) freely, fully and truly on record. I could not find any

1. Horace Traubel, *With Walt Whitman in Camden*, I (Boston: Small, Maynard, 1906), 176. The date of this statement is 18 May 1888; Whitman made the remark concerning the flaws in the various editions of *Leaves of Grass*, even in the Osgood edition of 1881.

similar personal record in current literature that satisfied me. But it is not on "Leaves of Grass" distinctively as *literature*, or a specimen thereof, that I feel to dwell, or advance claims. No one will get at my verses who insists upon viewing them as a literary performance, or attempt at such performance, or as aiming mainly toward art or aestheticism.[2]

The figurative equation now becomes a definite distinction between the two italicized terms, "*a Person*" and "*literature.*" And Whitman clearly warns us to disregard his book as *literature* and to see it, instead, as the "outcropping" of *a Person*.

But it is difficult to take the poet at his word. Even the word "outcropping," for instance, gestures toward the figurative nature of poetry. The word originates in the discourse of mining and geology, but by 1856 the verb "outcrop" carries the figurative sense of "to come out casually."[3] In "A Backward Glance," both senses play a part in creating the texture of Whitman's language. And this dual quality of language—the ability to signify two distinct yet related "things" at the same time—contradicts the poet's call for an "either-or" approach to *Leaves of Grass*. This is to say, then, that the paragraph from "A Backward Glance" undercuts its own assertion, for the language of the paragraph qualifies it as *both* a personal utterance and a literary performance.

At the outset of this study, I would like to make the same claim for all of Whitman's writing—that it is surely an attempt to put *a Person* on record, and that we would err if we were to regard *Leaves of Grass* as aiming primarily at "aestheticism." But this does not mean that *Leaves of Grass* and Whitman's prose are somehow *not* literary performances, for they certainly are. Rather than accept the distinction between *a Person* and *literature* as absolute, I would argue that the two are by no means mutually exclusive. Whitman's warning in "A Backward Glance" simply means that we should not ignore the personal elements of the book in favor of the literary elements. Nor, however, should we ignore the literary elements in favor of the personal.

The history of Whitman criticism revolves around the distinction

2. "A Backward Glance O'er Travel'd Roads," in *CRE*, pp. 573–74.

3. *SOED. The Dictionary of American English on Historical Principles*, ed. Sir William A. Craigie and James R. Hulbert (Chicago: University of Chicago Press, 1938–44), notes that "outcropping" is first used in American English in 1853 but gives no figurative meanings of the word. The related noun "outcrop," defined as "in *geology*, to come out to the surface of the ground; *applied to strata*," appears in Noah Webster's *American Dictionary of the English Language* (Springfield, Mass.: G.&C. Merriam, 1847).

between the personal and the literary, and it would appear that Whitman's warning has carried a great deal of weight with his readers in this century. As Donald Kummings points out in "The Contours of Whitman Scholarship," much of the early work on Whitman involved biographical studies, the establishment of specialized journals, and the launching of a new collected edition of his writings. In the late 1960s and through the 1970s, various versions of a psychobiographical approach to the poetry held sway, and these have "continued in abundance." But the "emphasis in recent years has centered more and more on the artist's poetry and less and less on his personality or doctrines."[4] It would seem, then, that Whitman scholarship has gradually moved from a naive form of hagiographical criticism to an eclectic blending of approaches.

This study is rhetorical or formalist in its critical leanings, and the argument I carry through the book could probably be labeled "poststructuralist" or, more specifically, "deconstructive," though it differs sharply from much deconstructive criticism in that I do not necessarily argue for a "decentered" poetic self. In any case, I do not intend to give here a critical pledge of allegiance, since my main purpose is to pay attention to the language of Whitman's poetry and prose, to allow the language to shape my argument. In that way I have attempted to remain loyal to the literature—and to the personal outcroppings of literature—rather than to any critical approach or line of argumentation.

Although recent criticism has begun to center upon the performative quality of Whitman's poetry, very little is known about the poet's theory of language and how it relates to his poetic practice. My double concern—both with language theory and with Whitman's literary performances—has led to a two-part structure in this book. In the first three chapters, I explicate Whitman's theory of language as he developed it from around 1854 to 1856, and I then attempt to show how the theory applies to the diction and syntax of the first two editions of *Leaves*. In the next three chapters, I show how Whitman changes the focus of his theory of language between 1856 and 1892, and I then analyze the style of the last four editions of *Leaves*, showing how the diction, syntax, and organization of the poetry reflect Whitman's changing theoretical concerns. Throughout the six chapters of the book, I have tried to avoid any distinction between theory and practice. Whitman's vision of language is so fundamental to his vision of his own poetry, and vice versa, that the poems are as "theo-

---

4. Donald D. Kummings, *Walt Whitman, 1940–1975: A Reference Guide* (Boston: G. K. Hall, 1982), pp. ix–x.

retical" as they are "practical," just as Whitman's pronouncements concerning language are as performative and rhetorical as the poems. Similarly, I have tried to avoid the distinction between extrinsic, contextual criticism and intrinsic, formalist criticism by treating Whitman's poetry and prose within the context of his interest in historical linguistics and American English. Whitman demands that we focus on the language of literature as a distillation of the language at large, and both of these are the verbal embodiments of American culture—past, present, and future. My argument lies at the boundaries of these various concerns.[5]

The scope of the study is large, since I attempt to account for Whitman's literary style from 1855 to 1892. And any project of such scope will necessarily reveal some rather glaring gaps and blemishes. For instance, in this book featuring a host of close readings of Whitman's greatest poems, I offer no interpretation, as such, of "Song of Myself." This is not critical cowardice, however, but a conscious decision. Since most of my published work on Whitman's style has focused upon his masterpiece, I chose to use that text, and my previously published analyses of it, as a point of departure for many of the readings I offer in these pages. Though the reader may search in vain for a blocked-out interpretation of the poem, I believe the reading is implicit in the first three chapters of the book. That is only one example, of course, and I choose it because I can defend the apparent gap in my argument. Doubtless there are other gaps, other flaws. And doubtless they will be pointed out. But I hope to remember that a book is like a man, and even the best book has flaws.

Thank God for the flaws!

---

5. The distinction between extrinsic and intrinsic criticism is presented in fullest form by René Wellek and Austin Warren, *Theory of Literature* (New York: Harcourt, Brace, 1949), pp. 65ff. Interestingly, John Burroughs makes a similar distinction concerning Whitman's art in *Whitman: A Study* (New York: Houghton Mifflin, 1902), pp. 101–67. Two recent studies—Wynn Thomas's *The Lunar Light of Whitman's Poetry* (Cambridge, Mass.: Harvard University Press, 1987) and Betsy Erkkila's *Whitman the Political Poet* (New York: Oxford University Press, 1989)—show the strengths of a contextual approach to the poetry. For a representative deconstructive reading of Whitman, see Joseph G. Kronick, *American Poetics of History* (Baton Rouge: Louisiana State University Press, 1984), pp. 90–123.

PART 1

1

The "Thought of the Ensemble": Whitman's Theory of Language

This subject of language interests me—interests me: I never quite get it out of my mind. I sometimes think the Leaves is only a language experiment—that it is an attempt to give the spirit, the body, the man, new words, new potentialities of speech—an American, a cosmopolitan (the best of America is the best cosmopolitanism) range of self-expression. The new world, the new times, the new peoples, the new vista, need a tongue according—yes, what is more, will have such a tongue—will not be satisfied until it is evolved.[1]

Although Whitman made this statement late in life, it indicates that "this subject of language" is fundamental to his poetic vision of America in the latter half of the nineteenth century. According to the poet, the "new potentialities of speech" embodied in *Leaves of Grass* should somehow meet the needs of "the new world, the new times, the new peoples, the new vista." Whitman's theory of language implies a theory of literature; even more, it implies a way of interpreting humankind's place in the temporal flux of the natural world. By incorporating his vision of "the new vista" into his theory of language, Whitman provides himself with a theoretical basis for conducting the "language experiment" of *Leaves of Grass*.

It is hardly surprising that Whitman's theory of language has not received the attention it warrants, for the poet published only two essays on language during his lifetime. The first, "America's Mightiest Inheritance," appeared in the 12 April 1856 issue of *Life Illustrated*,

1. Walt Whitman, *An American Primer*, ed. Horace Traubel (Boston: Small, Maynard, 1904), pp. viii–ix.

a "family magazine" owned by Fowler and Wells. The second, "Slang in America," did not appear until November 1885, in the *North American Review*. The only other linguistic work by Whitman to reach the general reading public was *An American Primer*, a series of notes edited by Horace Traubel and published in 1904. Recently, however, several unpublished manuscripts have come to light, the most important of which is the notebook *Words*. Finally, the most coherent expression of Whitman's theory of language is contained in *Rambles Among Words*, a popular book on English etymology, signed by William Swinton and first printed in 1859.[2]

Scholarship of the last ten years indicates that the "subject of language" occupied an important place in the literary culture of nineteenth-century America. The chapter "Language" in Emerson's *Nature* and the entire essay "The Poet" spring immediately to mind. Thoreau's philological extravagances in *Walden*, the linguistic focus on representation in such novels as *The Scarlet Letter* and *Moby Dick*, and poems like Dickinson's "Many a phrase has the English language" (#276) follow quickly.[3] In addition to these canonized texts, we can find numerous articles on language in English and American journals of the period, and the decade 1850–60 saw a host of books published on the "new science" of historial linguistics.[4]

"America's Mightiest Inheritance" suggests the intensity of Whitman's interest in the subject of language. He makes the grandiose claim that the English language "subordinates any perfection of politics, erudition, science, metaphysics, inventions, poems, the judi-

2. For a useful bibliography of articles on Whitman and language, see Sherry G. Southard, "Whitman and Language: An Annotated Bibliography," *WWQR* 2:2 (1984): 31–49. Three book-length studies deserve special mention here: John E. Bernbrock, S.J., "Walt Whitman and 'Anglo-Saxonism,'" Ph.D. diss., University of North Carolina, 1961; Michael R. Dressman, "Walt Whitman's Study of the English Language," Ph.D. diss., University of North Carolina, 1974; and C. Carroll Hollis, *Language and Style in "Leaves of Grass"* (Baton Rouge: Louisiana State University Press, 1983).

Fowler and Wells published *American Phrenological Journal, Water-Cure Magazine*, and the first two editions of *Leaves of Grass*. "America's Mightiest Inheritance" is reprinted in *New York Dissected*, ed. Emory Holloway and Ralph Adimari (New York: Rufus Rockwell Wilson, 1936), pp. 51–65.

"Slang in America" was reprinted in *November Boughs* (1888) and appears in *PW*, II, 572–77. All references to Whitman's prose works are to this two-volume edition and are cited in my text as *PW*, with volume and page numbers.

3. The most important study of the subject, though it does not treat Whitman and Dickinson, is Philip Gura's *The Wisdom of Words* (Middletown, Conn.: Wesleyan University Press, 1981).

4. For a highly readable account of the numerous publications in England, see Hans Aarsleff, *The Study of Language in England, 1780–1860* (Princeton University Press, 1967; reprint University of Minnesota Press, 1983), pp. 162–263.

ciary, printing, steam-power, mails, architecture, or what not."[5] By placing language ahead of all the cultural and technological advances of the nineteenth century, Whitman suggests that the "language experiment" of *Leaves of Grass* creates more than simply "new potentialities of speech"—it creates the "cosmopolitan . . . range of self-expression" necessary for "any perfection" of culture whatsoever.

This claim for the all-encompassing nature of the English language is similar to Whitman's view of its history. After giving a retrospective treatment of the Indo-European languages and of the "composite" history of English, Whitman asserts that "the history of language is the most curious and instructive of any history, and embraces the whole of the rest. It is the history of the movements and developments of men and women over the entire earth. In its doings every thing appears to move from east to west as the light does" (p. 57). The westward migrations of prehistoric Indo-European tribes become an analogue for the westward expansion of the United States. This implied argument for the doctrine of Manifest Destiny becomes clear in a later passage of the essay:

> The English language seems curiously to have flowed through the ages, especially toward America, for present use, and for centuries and centuries of future use; it is so composed of all the varieties that preceded it, and so absorbs what is needed by it. (p. 59)

The chronological structure of the sentence takes us from retrospect to prospect, from the history of the English language to the "new vista" of English in America. In addition, Whitman's history emphasizes the active qualities of the English language. Flowing, composing, and absorbing, language takes on the characteristics of a self-directed, purposive entity, while in the earlier passage language is figured as a natural being, one that "appears to move from east to west as the light does."

These passages from "America's Mightiest Inheritance" are, like Whitman's view of the history of language, both "curious and instructive." They indicate that language—particularly the English language in America—gives Whitman an enthusiastic and enabling vision of "the new vista."

An early manuscript essay, "Our Language and Literature," originally titled "Our Language, and Future & Literature," shows Whit-

---

5. "America's Mightiest Inheritance," p. 55. All further references to this essay appear in my text, cited by page number.

man's characteristic concern for the "vista" of future linguistic developments, and it couples that concern with the specific role of literature in encouraging "new potentialities of speech."[6] The manuscript begins with terms that strongly echo "America's Mightiest Inheritance." Whitman calls the English language "our most precious inheritance—greater than arts, politics, religions or greater than any wealth or any inventions" (p. 809). The catalogue of cultural advances is more general than that of the published essay, suggesting that "Our Language and Literature" contains draft material used in "America's Mightiest Inheritance."

The remaining pages of the manuscript connect the history and future development of American English with the differences between British and American literary language. And in this regard the manuscript displays connections with the August 1856 "Letter" to Emerson. For example, in the manuscript Whitman asserts that "the life-spirit of These States must be engrafted upon their inherited language:—indeed I see the beginning of this already and enjoy it. As for myself I love to go away from books, and walk amidst the strong coarse talk of men as they give muscle and bone to every word they speak" (p. 811). In the 1856 "Letter," the play among past, present, and future is more fully developed:

> To poets and literats—to every woman and man, today or any day, the conditions of the present . . . are the perfect conditions on which we are here, and the conditions for wording the future with indissuadable words. These States, receivers of the stamina of past ages and lands, initiate the outlines of repayment a thousand fold. . . . Always America will be agitated and turbulent. This day it is taking shape, not to be less so, but to be more so, stormily, capriciously, on native principles, with such vast proportions of parts! As for me, I love screaming, wrestling, boiling-hot days.[7]

The rhetoric of the last sentence, with its "as for me," recalls the "as for myself" of the manuscript passage. More important, the passage from the "Letter" develops Whitman's call for an "engrafting" of the American "life-spirit" upon the English language by announcing the "conditions for wording the future with indissuadable words." Whitman portrays America as the perfect "receiver" of the past, possessing

6. "Our Language and Literature" appears in *DBN*, III, 809–11; all further references to the manuscript appear in my text.

7. *CRE*, p. 738.

in its present the "perfect conditions" for "wording the future" through its literature. In the last three sentences, the sequence of past participles, adverbs, adjectives, and present participles marks those conditions as, above all, dynamic and active. So Whitman's vision of America would seem to call for a dynamic and active language to match the dynamic and active "life-spirit."

This cluster of texts suggests that in 1856 Whitman was preoccupied with the "subject of language," and it argues for a close relationship between the poet's view of American English and his view of American literature. In both general and specific terms, the texts indicate that the "language experiment" of *Leaves of Grass* should reveal Whitman's strategies for unlocking "new potentialities" in the speech and spirit of nineteenth-century America. But they do not present, in any focused argument, the theoretical underpinnings of Whitman's hortatory and polemical assertions. Unless we are willing to allow the poet a large measure of jingoistic bombast, we must examine the theory of language underlying his bravado.

Whitman's theory emerges in three texts dating from 1855 to 1859: the notebooks *Words* and *Primer of Words*, and the last two chapters of *Rambles Among Words*, which Whitman authored.[8] In "The Growth of Words," the penultimate chapter of *Rambles*, Whitman places himself within a specific tradition of language theorists. He takes as his epigraph a quotation from Wilhelm von Humboldt:

> An idiom is an organism subject, like every organism, to the laws of development. One must not consider a language as a product dead and formed but once: it is an animate being and ever creative.[9]

8. The *Primer* notes appear in *DBN*, III, 728–57. *Words* appears in *DBN*, III, 664–727. All citations of Whitman's *Primer* and *Words* notebooks refer to *DBN*, III.

For an account of Whitman's role in the writing of *Rambles Among Words*, see my "Whitman as Ghost-Writer: The Case of *Rambles Among Words*," *WWQR* 2:2 (1984): 22–30. Selections from *Rambles* have been published recently in *Notebooks and Unpublished Prose Manuscripts*, ed. Edward F. Grier (New York: New York University Press, 1984), V, 1624–62. Grier's introduction to the selections is helpful, but it was written before the publication of my essay, and Whitman's authorship is presented as more problematic than it in fact is. All references to Grier's edition appear in my text, cited as *NUPM*.

9. *Rambles*, p. 265. As Grier points out, all three of the editions of *Rambles* are identical except for prefatory material (*NUPM*, V, 1624). Because I do not always cite material excerpted by Grier, I have chosen to refer to *Rambles Among Words* by short title and original page numbers; this will also serve to distinguish the printed book from Whitman's unpublished manuscript notes and notebooks. In editing *Rambles* for

Humboldt is a major figure in the tradition of "organic," or transcendental, language theory. Throughout the early years of the nineteenth century, the transcendentalists attempted to alter the empiricist theory of language as an arbitrary set of conventional signs designed by human beings to further communication.[10] Countering the theory of language as a means of communication, the transcendentalists proposed a theory of language as an expression of the spirit, whether individual or collective. For the transcendental theorists, language is essentially an activity of the spirit, functioning to unify sense-data and concepts. Language is an "organism," in Humboldt's view, in a metaphorical sense: It is the process of spiritual formation through which the subjective and objective poles of being are joined. The "organic" or transcendental theory stresses the "laws of development" inherent in language because these laws reveal the development of the human spirit. As Humboldt phrases the point, "Language is the formative organ of *thought. Intellectual activity*, entirely mental, entirely internal, and to some extent passing without trace, becomes, through *sound*, externalized in speech and perceptible to the senses. Thought and language are therefore one and inseparable from each other" (p. 54).

The organic theory of language relates directly to the rise of historical Indo-European linguistics in the nineteenth century. Faced with a seemingly chaotic welter of unrelated languages, the transcendental theorists were forced to ask whether the truth formulated in

---

inclusion in *NUPM*, Grier provides the page numbers of the original edition, so in most cases the interested reader can easily find the cited passage.

The quotation from Humboldt is a translation of the second sentence of Section 11, "The Form of Language," in the introduction to the Kawi work. The title of the introduction is "Uber die Verschiedenheit des menschlichen Sprachbaues und ihren Einfluss auf die geistige Entwicklung des Menschengeschlechts" (1830–35). An English translation of the introduction is now available: *On Language*, trans. Stephen Heath (New York: Cambridge University Press, 1988). All quotations from Humboldt refer to this translation.

10. My discussion of transcendental language theory has been aided by the following works: Oswald Ducrot et al., *Qu'est-ce que le structuralisme?* (Paris: Seuil, 1968), pp. 16–34; Oswald Ducrot and Tzvetan Todorov, *Encyclopedic Dictionary of the Sciences of Language*, trans. Catherine Porter (Baltimore, Md.: Johns Hopkins University Press, 1979), pp. 3–14; Ernst Cassirer, *The Philosophy of Symbolic Forms. Volume One: Language*, trans. Ralph Manheim (New Haven, Conn.: Yale University Press, 1955), pp. 117–67; Holger Pedersen, *The Discovery of Language: Linguistic Science in the Nineteenth Century*, trans. John Webster Spargo (Bloomington: Indiana University Press, 1962); Hans Aarsleff, *The Study of Language in England, 1780–1860*, and *From Locke to Saussure* (Minneapolis: University of Minnesota Press, 1982); and Michel Foucault, *The Order of Things: An Archaeology of the Human Sciences*, trans. Alan Sheridan (New York: Pantheon, 1970).

Peking was the same as the truth formulated in Bombay, in Berlin, or in ancient Athens or Rome. The aim of comparative philologists like Bopp, the Schlegels, Grimm, Humboldt, and Schleicher was to find the historical "laws of development" that would reveal a unity underlying both the diversity of languages and the temporal changes within any given language. Humboldt makes this point in the first section of the Kawi work: "The *comparative study of languages*, the exact establishment of the manifold ways in which innumerable peoples resolve the same task of language formation that is laid upon them as men, loses all higher interest if it does not cleave to the point at which language is connected with the shaping of the *nation's mental power*" (p. 21).

In the analogies existing between Sanskrit and most of the ancient and modern European languages, the transcendental comparatists were provided with an important first clue to the unity of languages.[11] The similarities among certain languages led to the idea that kinships existed among them and that they were descendants of a single mother tongue, primitive Indo-European. The apparent differences among languages melted away in the light of a common ancestry. But the comparatists were still faced with the problem of relating other families of languages to the Indo-European family. Was Chinese related to Latin, German, or English?

The transcendentalists solved this larger problem of linguistic unity by proposing a typology of languages, classifying them as Isolating, Agglutinating, and Inflecting.[12] The typology is based upon the ways lexical elements (the base, or root) and grammatical elements (inflectional endings, particles, and affixes) relate to one another. The root is the material unit of signification, while the grammatical elements mark the formal relation of roots to one another. Such isolating, or Monosyllabic, languages as Chinese simply employ monosyllabic units for designating objects. Agglutinating languages employ grammatical markers, but these markers bear no direct relation to the internal form of the root. Inflecting, or Organic, languages unify lexical and grammatical elements according to morphological rules.[13]

11. Sir William Jones's address to the Asiatick Society in Calcutta on 2 February 1786 began the work developed most fully by Franz Bopp in *On the Conjugational System of the Sanskrit Language, in Comparison with that of the Greek, Latin, Persian, and Germanic Languages* (Frankfurt, 1816). See Aarsleff, *Study*, pp. 115–61, and Foucault, *Order*, pp.280–300.

12. Many versions of the typology exist in the discourse of nineteenth-century comparative philology. See, for example, Humboldt, *On Language*, pp. 100–108.

13. See Otto Jespersen, *Progress in Language* (New York: Macmillan, 1894), pp. 1–16.

In the three types of language we see a philological version of Hegel's dialectic. The Monosyllabic languages merely designate the empirical given. In the clash between lexical and grammatical elements, the Agglutinating languages represent the opposition between the empirical given and *a priori* forms. Finally, the Organic languages represent the synthesis of the empirical given and *a priori* forms in the act of thought expressing itself in language. Thus the Organic languages represent the unity of subject and object, and it so happens that the Indo-European languages form that class.[14]

The cultural bias of linguistic typology is immediately apparent. Moreover, the Hegelian dialectic is interpreted by linguists like August Schleicher as a temporal, historical fact, so that the Organic languages are seen as more "developed" or "evolved" than those of the other two classes. And this view eventually leads to the idea that the "organism" of language is like any other natural organism, obeying the Darwinian laws of evolution.[15]

Humboldt's response to the problem of linguistic unity is more complicated, for he never views language as an organism subject to natural laws of evolution. Instead, Humboldt's treatment of the problem leads in the direction of pure spirit. And because the spirit is, like language, a never-ceasing activity, the principle of linguistic unity can never be fully grasped:

> If we are not to forego all discovery of a connection between phenomena in the human race, we still have to come back to some independent and original *cause*, not itself in turn conditioned and transitory in appearance. But we are thereby most naturally led to an inner life-principle, freely developing in its fullness, whose particular manifestations are not intrinsically unlinked because their outer appearances are presented in isolation. This viewpoint is totally different from that of the purposive theory, since it does not proceed towards a set goal, but from an admittedly unfathomable cause. (p. 26)

The "inner life-principle" is Humboldt's formula for the creative power of the language-making mind, and it functions as a noumenal, *a priori* principle of unity underlying the "outer appearances" of par-

14. Ibid.
15. Schleicher's view is set forth clearly in his introduction to *A Compendium of the Comparative Grammar of the Indo-European, Sanskrit, Greek and Latin Languages*, trans. Herbert Bendall (London: Trübner, 1874), pp. 1–5. For the most extreme statement concerning linguistics as a natural science, see Schleicher, *Die Darwinsche Theorie und die Sprachwissenschaft* (Weimar: Hermann Böhlau, 1863).

ticular languages. The "inner life-principle" also allows Humboldt to distinguish his own theory from a "purposive theory," one which would employ the concept of communication as the primary purpose of language.

The "inner life-principle" recalls Whitman's idea of an American "life-spirit" announced in "Our Language and Literature," but in neither case is the concept as monolithic as it would first appear to be. Humboldt's unifying principle is not necessarily the same in all languages, and each language incarnates the spirit of the nation which speaks the language. The only feature the various languages necessarily have in common is that the inner principle of each is equally mysterious:

> All *becoming* in nature, but especially of the organic and living, escapes our observation. However minutely we may examine the preparatory stages, between the latter and the phenomenon there is always the cleavage that divides the something from the nothing; and this is equally so with the moment of *cessation*. All comprehension of man lies only between the two. In languages, a period of origination, from perfectly accessible historical times, affords us a striking example. We can follow out a multiple series of changes that the *language of the Romans* underwent during its decline and fall, and can add to them the minglings due to invading tribesmen: we get no better explanation thereby of the origin of the living seed which again germinated in various forms into the organism of newly burgeoning languages. An inner principle, newly arisen, rebuilt the collapsing structure, for each in its own fashion, and we, since we always find ourselves situated among its effects only, become aware of its transformations only by the multitude thereof. (p. 43)

Humboldt's solution to the problems of linguistic unity and variety depends upon a radical "cleavage" between spirit and matter, for he bases his interpretation of linguistic change and variety on the unknowable, noumenal origin of an endless unfolding of forms. Moreover, this linguistic idealism entails an optimistic view of language, since Humboldt sees in all languages "the *endeavour* to secure being in reality for the idea of *linguistic completeness*" (p. 27). The "endeavour" can and does take varying forms, but the comparative philologist searches for the constant and uniform structures underlying apparently diverse manifestations of the ideal of "linguistic completeness." The "endeavour" is another term for the "inner life-principle" or "living seed" of language, and each language is the spontaneous, involuntary expression of this noumenal and inexplicable principle.

Humboldt gives the abstract theory of the "inner life-principle" a concrete focus when he considers the three classes of languages. He argues that "all spiritual progress can only proceed from an internal emission of force, and to that extent has always a hidden, and because it is autonomous, an inexplicable basis," and he then proceeds to offer linguistic typology as an example:

> For it now follows at once that where enhanced appearances of the same endeavour are perceivable, we cannot, unless the facts imperatively demand it, presuppose a *gradual progress*, since every significant enhancement appertains, rather, to a peculiar creative force. An example may be drawn from the structure of the Chinese and Sanscrit languages. One might certainly suppose here a gradual progression from the one to the other. But if we truly feel the nature of language as such, and of these two in particular, if we reach the point of fusion between thought and sound in both, we discover there the outgoing creative principle of their differing organization. At that stage, abandoning the possibility of a gradual development of one from the other, we shall accord to each its own basis in the spirit of the race, and only within the general trend of linguistic evolution, and thus ideally only, will regard them as stages in a successful construction of language. By neglecting the careful separation here proposed of the calculable stepwise progress and the unpredictable, immediately creative advance of human mental power, we banish outright from world-history the effects of *genius*, which is no less displayed at particular moments in peoples than it is in individuals. (pp. 31–32)

Here Humboldt attempts to discredit the temporal, evolutionary view of the three types, but he still wishes to preserve an ideal model of "stages in a successful construction of language." Thus he can deny any "stepwise progress" of Monosyllabic languages toward the Organic languages, but he will still argue, in a later chapter on linguistic typology, that the "so-called agglutinating languages do not differ in type from the inflectional ones, as do those which reject all indication by means of inflection; they deviate only to the extent that their obscure endeavour in the same direction is more or less of a failure" (p. 107). This is to say, then, that Humboldt's vision of language as an organism is teleological but not evolutionary.

Humboldt's Kawi introduction marks an important chapter in the history of linguistics, for the transcendental comparatists had arrived at a crossroads in the treatment of language as an organism. In later interpretations of the problem of unity and variety, theorists like August Schleicher treat language as a self-contained entity that develops according to general laws; in their view, language is a natural organism that, prior to the utilitarian concern for communication, evolves in the same ways that plants and animals evolve.[16] Thus theorists like Schleicher employ a diachronic, evolutionary model of language in order to posit a principle of unity underlying linguistic variety and change. In Humboldt's account of language as an organism, on the other hand, the "inner life-principle" is a synchronic, atemporal principle of unity. The influx of spiritual, creative energy into a nation is registered in the unfolding forms of the nation's language, but this "spirit of the race" is not part of a gradual evolution.

The distinction between the synchronic and diachronic approaches to language has been made familiar by the work of Ferdinand de Saussure, but it is a distinction that many nineteenth-century linguists did not recognize. It fits within Saussure's larger purpose of arguing for the arbitrary nature of the linguistic sign, an argument that directly counters the nineteenth-century view of language as an organism. Thus, for instance, Saussure argues against the idea of language as a purposive organism that evolves toward a necessary system of forms, and he insists that language be regarded as form only, not as substance.[17] Perhaps the best way to appreciate Saussure's point is to consider what would happen if a theory were to combine an evolutionary, diachronic account of linguistic change and diversity with Humboldt's idealist, synchronic account. The result could be called a theory of "spiritual and linguistic evolution" or "the evolution of the national spirit." According to such a view, the "spirit of the race" would be temporally revealed in the three stages

16. In order to make this argument, Schleicher divides human history and physical nature into separate categories. *Philology* is the study of the spiritual being of a people, and it concerns itself with *history* as the sphere within which the human will operates. *Linguistics*, by contrast, is the study of the unconscious necessity of language, and it concerns itself with *nature* as the sphere of immutable (phonetic) laws. See Schleicher, *Die Sprachen Europas* (Bonn: H.B. König, 1850), pp. 1–39. For an analysis of the distinction, see John Arbuckle, "August Schleicher and the Linguistics/Philology Dichotomy: A Chapter in the History of Linguistics," *Word* 26 (1970), 17–31.

17. Ferdinand de Saussure, *Course in General Linguistics*, trans. Wade Baskin (New York: McGraw-Hill, 1966), pp. 79–100, especially pp. 83–87. For a clear account of Saussure's argument within the context of nineteenth-century linguistics, see Jonathan Culler, *Ferdinand de Saussure* (Harmondsworth, U.K.: Penguin, 1977), pp. 36–63.

of language, so that the languages of the more "evolved" races—those of the Indo-European family—would reveal a more highly developed spirit through more highly developed forms.

By invoking Humboldt at the beginning of "The Growth of Words," Whitman confronts the problem of finding unity within linguistic diversity and change. His response is precisely the theory of spiritual evolution that results from giving a diachronic interpretation of Humboldt's synchronic idealism. One reason for the response is that Whitman's knowledge of Humboldt stems from his reading of Christian C. J. Bunsen's *Outlines of the Philosophy of Universal History* and Maxmilian Schele de Vere's *Outlines of Comparative Philology*, both of which present the combination of the two approaches in a fully articulated account of language as an organism.

Bunsen's evolutionary theory of language permeates the text of *Outlines*. In the chapter "Mutual Relation of the three Forms of Language, progressive and retrogressive," for example, Bunsen reacts to Humboldt's argument against the idea of "gradual progress" with a combination of consternation and disbelief:

> After this lucid statement of the gradual growth of grammatical forms, it is extraordinary that Humboldt should still have doubted a possible historical transition between the different forms. Professor Boethlingk's words on this point deserve to be quoted together with Humboldt's. "It is inconceivable," he writes, "how, with such a view on the origin of inflection, any one can doubt for a moment about the possibility of two such languages as Chinese and Sanskrit having the same origin."[18]

Bunsen's solution to the problem of unity is precisely the theory of "gradual progress" that Humboldt wishes to avoid. That is, Bunsen views Chinese as simply a less developed version of Sanskrit. Because Sanskrit has already passed through the Monosyllabic and Agglutinative "stages," it reveals a higher development along the scale of spiritual evolution.

Bunsen's account of Humboldt's theory influenced Whitman's view of language considerably, and we can see that influence in two entries Whitman made in the notebook *Words* concerning Humboldt. In the first, Whitman quotes directly from Bunsen's summary of Humboldt's Kawi introduction: "Language is the outward expression of what he calls the spirit or individuality of a nation" (*DBN*, III, 721;

18. *Outlines*, I, 283. All quotations refer to this edition and are cited in my text as *Outlines*.

cf. *Outlines*, I, 282). In the second note, Whitman summarizes Bunsen's account of Humboldt's three classes of language:

Von Humboldt

"Language expresses originally objects only, and leaves the understanding to supply the connecting form—afterwards facilitating and improving the connections and relations by degrees. (*DBN*, III, 721)

The first part of the passage—from the quotation mark to the dash—is a direct citation of Bunsen's version of Humboldt's discussion of linguistic typology. Humboldt bases his discussion of the three classes of language on the dual function of any word: "For to the act of designating the *concept* itself there is allied also a special operation of the mind which transposes that concept into a particular *category* of thought or speech; and the word's full meaning is the simultaneous outcome of that conceptual expression and this modifying hint" (p. 100). Bunsen simplifies Humboldt's ideas by making designation depend upon the correspondence of word to *object* rather than word to *concept*. More important, Whitman's summary of the passage transforms Humboldt into a diachronic, evolutionary theorist. The adverb "afterwards" shows Whitman's temporal interpretation of Humboldt, while the verbs "facilitating" and "improving" reveal the poet's evolutionary view of changing grammatical forms. And Whitman's first note suggests that this evolution is not merely linguistic, since the language is the "outward expression of . . . the spirit or individuality of a nation."

A second major source for Whitman's theory of spiritual evolution is Maxmilian Schele de Vere's *Outlines of Comparative Philology*.[19] Schele de Vere's admitted purpose is "to state briefly, in a popular manner and with a view to give rather suggestive than complete information, what Comparative Philology is, and what it has done" (*Philology*, p. 3). At numerous points in the book, Schele de Vere shows that he adheres to the transcendental theory of language and that, like other popularizers of the theory, he merges the synchronic and diachronic treatments of language. For example, in the chapter "Methods of Comparative Philology," Schele de Vere repeats the idea of language as a living expression of the national spirit:

19. A copy of *Philology*, with "Wm. Swinton, Greensboro, North Carolina," inscribed on the flyleaf, was part of Whitman's library at the time of his death. See C. Carroll Hollis, "Walt Whitman and William Swinton: A Cooperative Friendship," *American Literature* 30 (1959), 436.

Languages appear, then, no longer mere mechanical structures, but, in their higher vocations, as enveloping and embodying specific national notions. . . . Modern science . . . sees even in the caprices and fancies of an idiom only so many crystallized expressions of that mind of the nation which works unceasingly at the loom of its language, and weaves the fine texture of its idiom. (*Philology*, pp. 212–13)

Schele de Vere clearly follows Humboldt's idea of the "inner life-principle" of language, but the evolutionary interpretation of the "mind of the nation" is not so clear here as it is in Bunsen. In the chapter "The Three Great Classes of Language," however, he seems to agree with Bunsen's evolutionary interpretation of linguistic typology:

The intimate connection between the mental life and culture of a nation and its language, explains why these most perfect and most highly developed idioms are found to be the work of those nations which have been or are now the best representatives of the progress made by man. The races that have successively ruled the world, have also possessed the languages that show the highest development, in expressing most, and that most best. To this third class of inflectional idioms [i.e., the Organic] belong, therefore, the Indo-European languages. (*Philology*, p. 233)

Schele de Vere's ethnocentrism is obvious enough, and the progressivist assumptions underlying such phrases as "most perfect and most highly developed idioms" and "the best representatives of the progress made by man" do not require clarification. He differs from Bunsen, on the other hand, in his rejection of the idea that "every language had to pass through each of these three classes, as through so many stages of gradual development, progressing from a monosyllabic expression of the idea only to a mechanical combination of two sounds, in order finally to accomplish the organic union of inflected words" (p. 234). Schele de Vere's view of language, then, appears to be much like Humboldt's: Because languages are created prior to our knowledge of them, we cannot assert that all languages passed through the three stages (p. 235).

Schele de Vere's version of spiritual evolution emerges from his discussion of the so-called decay of modern Indo-European languages, and his treatment of language is as evolutionary as Bunsen's. The idea of linguistic "decay" arose from the observation that highly inflected languages like Sanskrit, Greek, and Latin had developed into analytic languages, which employ word order rather than inflectional endings to signal the grammatical function of a word. To some theorists, this process seemed to signal the reversal of language making, since the Organic languages appeared to be reverting to the stage of the Monosyllabic languages.[20] But Schele de Vere asserts that this "decay" is only apparent, that "it is, in reality, a progress and improvement." To support that assertion, he invokes the principle of least effort:

> Language, being a spiritual manifestation of the mind, tries, like the mind itself, to rise above matter; it has a tendency, ever active and ever progressive, to strip off all forms with which thought is encumbered; it strives to free itself more and more. (*Philology*, pp. 238–39)

In Schele de Vere's view, the process of "leveling," by which synthetic, inflected languages move toward analytic, uninflected languages, is a progressivist process of spiritual evolution. Through leveling, language can cast aside the encumbering "body" of grammatical forms in order to move toward the expressive freedom of pure spirit and thought. Language, as a purposive, evolving organism, "strives to free itself more and more," and the striving is a form of spiritual evolution. Moreover, Schele de Vere calls this "the same law which governs language as well as all organic nature" (p. 240). Thus Schele de Vere shows himself to be a less naive evolutionist than Bunsen, but he is nonetheless an evolutionist. In both of these popular introductions to the new science of comparative philology, Humboldt's synchronic idealism becomes a diachronic, evolutionary account of the linguistic organism.

The shifts I have described in the history of transcendental language theory are reenacted in the last two chapters of *Rambles Among Words*. Whitman begins with the synchronic, philosophical aspect of the organic theory, but he moves to a diachronic treatment of language as a temporally evolving organism. In "The Growth of Words," the poet begins with the idea that language is "begotten of the blended love of spirit and of matter," but he finds that in his search for a unifying principle he must state the idea of unity again and again: "Language is begotten of a lustful longing to express, through the plastic vocal energy, man's secret sense of his unity with nature"

20. Schleicher affords clear examples of this view throughout his work, while Schele de Vere devotes a chapter to a survey of the problem in *Philology*, pp. 236–41.

(*Rambles*, p. 266). One reason for this restatement is the persistence of "lustful longing"; another is that the human sense of unity with nature is "secret." Whitman cannot actually prove the unity of spirit and matter; he can only state and restate his "secret sense," which is itself never completely known or completely expressed.

If Whitman's philosophy of language seems close to the transcendental idealism of Humboldt, the parallel is even more striking in the next two paragraphs:

> This vitality of speech manifests itself in a two-fold manifestation: in the possession of a distinctive personality and identity—in material elements and formal laws that stamp it with the stamp of linguistic individuality; and, further, in that other characteristic of every living organism—in the exhibition of growth, progress, decay—in the ongoing processes of absorption, assimilation and elimination—in the inworking and outworking of the creative energy.
>
> And it is in this sense that the English language is alive—as displaying successive processes of growth and development within the limits of its linguistic individuality. (p. 266)

Here Whitman states his two laws of language, which correspond to the twin problems of linguistic diversity and linguistic change. Like Humboldt, Whitman perceives language as a never-ceasing dialectic between the finite forms of linguistic individuality and the formless flux of linguistic change. But unlike Humboldt—and like Bunsen and Schele de Vere—he proposes an evolutionary solution to the opposition. He therefore combines the two signs of linguistic vitality in "successive processes of growth and development." For Humboldt the influx of spiritual energy into a language is inexplicable, a part of the "inner life-principle." For Whitman, on the other hand, the influx is part of the inherent, organic development of a language through time, and it can be understood by grasping the evolution of a language through history. So Whitman responds to the metaphysical problem of the "secret sense" of unity by translating it into progressivist terms of "growth and development."

Whitman's shift from metaphysics to evolution is accompanied by a move from the individual spirit to the national spirit. He hints at the movement by specifying that the *English* language is alive, and he proceeds to direct his attention to the evolution of English as an organism:

Shooting its deep tap-root into eldest antiquity, drawing from the pith and sap of that grandest of all families of races and tongues—the Indo-European stock; receiving living grafts from France and Italy and Scandinavia, this divine tree of the English Speech has grown up into its sublime proportions nurtured by the history of a thousand years. (p. 267)

As in "America's Mightiest Inheritance" and "Our Language and Literature," Whitman's grandiose claims for the English language are based on an evolutionary interpretation of its history. The Indo-European languages are the "grandest of all families of races and tongues," and English has become a "divine tree" of "sublime proportions" because the spirit of English-speaking nations is the most highly evolved in history. As Whitman asserts in the same paragraph, "the History of a Language is measurable only in terms of all the factors that have shaped a people's life" (p. 267). From "America's Mightiest Inheritance" we know that those factors would include the "perfection of politics, erudition, science, metaphysics, inventions, poems, the judiciary, printing, steam-power, mails, architecture" (p. 55). We can therefore see that an evolutionary account of language entails an evolutionary account of the national spirit.

In order to support the organic metaphor of English as a "divine tree," Whitman turns to the history of the language, a turn similar to the chronological argument of "America's Mightiest Inheritance." And it is here that the "thought of the Ensemble" comes sharply into focus:

A History of the English Language, rising out of a full appreciation of the Philosophy of Speech (to which must go that large hospitality and impartiality that flows from the thought of the Ensemble), answering the requirements of modern research, and after the broad, free methods America lets down, has yet to come. (*Rambles*, p. 268)

This involved sentence raises several important points. First, the diachronic "History" of language and the synchronic "Philosophy of Speech" merge in the flow of Whitman's "thought of the Ensemble." Second, while referring to objective concepts like "History," "Philosophy," and "Ensemble," Whitman's language emphasizes the subjective, personal "appreciation," "hospitality and impartiality," and "thought" of an unnamed thinker, a thinker who must also be modern, scholarly but freely methodical, and American. Third, in the main clause of the sentence Whitman denounces the present lack of the "History," but in the three qualifying phrases he defines the formula for its future realization. His rhetoric mixes the present and future in much the same way that his theory mixes the synchronic and diachronic approaches to language.

This threefold merging provides a glimpse into the workshop of Whitman's theory. In the three phrases qualifying "History of the English Language," style overrides logic, emphasizing a progressive, evolutionary "flow" within which the boundaries between opposites blur and very nearly dissolve. That tendency in Whitman's thought is particularly clear in the concept of "Ensemble," which he defines later in *Rambles Among Words*: "The totality as distinguished from the details. A noble word with immense vista" (p. 283). When Whitman thinks the "thought of the Ensemble," he disregards "details" of difference in order to perceive a "totality" underlying linguistic diversity and change.

The concept of the "Ensemble" is, without doubt, what we would now call a totalizing figure. And the etymology of the word, from the late Latin *insimul*, meaning "at the same time," suggests a synchronic, timeless notion of totality. But in defining the word himself, Whitman links this totalizing figure to the figure of "vista." In Whitman's vocabulary, "vista" indicates the temporal flow toward the future. In "By Blue Ontario's Shore," for example, the poet proclaims that "others take finish, but the Republic is ever constructive and ever keeps vista."[21] Similarly, in the dialogue with Traubel concerning *Leaves of Grass* as a "language experiment," the "new vista" corresponds to the progressivist spirit of America that "will not be satisfied" until its "new potentialities of speech" are "evolved." Thus the word "vista" evokes a diachronic, evolutionary view of both language and spirit, while "ensemble" evokes a synchronic, idealist view of totality and unity. And Whitman will keep neither the two ideas nor the two approaches separate from one another. "Ensemble" and "vista" merge in the poet's evolutionary perception of an America that is "ever constructive," both in its language and in its national "life-spirit."

The evolutionary merging of "ensemble" and "vista" develops more fully when Whitman repeats his "appreciation of the organic laws of the English Language in its historic unfolding," an appreciation that is "inseparable from considerations that embrace the en-

21. Line 19. Unless otherwise noted, all quotations from *Leaves of Grass* refer to *Variorum*. The printed text of the *Variorum* is the same as *CRE*, which follows the 1881 edition.

semble of Languages" (*Rambles*, p. 268). The only "ensemble of Languages" Whitman actually considers is the Indo-European (he also refers to it as the Japhetic, or Iranic, family), for it contains the "noble and highly developed languages" that reflect the Indo-European mind, the highest product of the evolutionary process: "Science was born in that mind, the intuition of nature, the instinct for political organization and that direct practical normal conduct of life and affairs" (p. 269). The poet's embrace of the Indo-European "ensemble" leaves no room for any pessimism associated with the "decay" of languages:

> From this mind, too, flowered out the grandest and most spiritual of languages. The Japhetic or Iranic tongues are termed by the master-philologers the Organic Group, to distinguish them from the Agglutinative and Inorganic speech-floors that underlie them in the Geology of Language. They alone have reached the altitude of free intellectual individuality and organism. To them belongs the splendid plasticity of Sanskrit, Greek, German, English! (pp. 269–70)

This passage registers the combined impact of Bunsen and Schele de Vere. Bunsen provides the evolutionary slant that Whitman gives to the three classes of language, while Schele de Vere provides the emphasis he places on the ever-increasing spirituality and "free intellectual individuality" of the Indo-European languages. Whitman's four examples of "splendid plasticity"—Sanskrit, Greek, German, and English—are arranged in a rough chronological order, from most ancient to most modern. Even more important, however, is the order according to the process of leveling: Sanskrit is the most synthetic of the four languages, while English is the most analytic. In Schele de Vere's terms, English is more spiritually evolved than the earlier languages and modern German because it has freed itself from the encumbering forms of inflectional endings. Once again, therefore, Whitman interprets the "ensemble" of Indo-European languages by their progressive evolution toward the "free intellectual individuality and organism" of English. And the geological metaphor that controls the passage implies that the evolution is ancient, inevitable, and ongoing.

In the remaining pages of "The Growth of Words," Whitman develops the implication that the English language exhibits the world's highest "altitude" of spiritual evolution. Taking the fall of the Roman Empire as his historical locus, he contrasts the "vigorous, individual, egotistic German" to the "decaying Latin." The "Teutonic genius" acts on the Latin language, "breaking up the crystalline structure of the classic mould, freeing the grammatical forms from their absorption in the terminations of nouns and verbs, and erecting them into independent prepositions and auxiliaries" (*Rambles*, p. 271). The poet's example recalls Humboldt's account of the new "living seed" that rebuilt the crumbling structure of late Latin, and his assessment of the phenomenon of leveling, the "passage from synthesis to analysis" (p. 271), is, like Schele de Vere's, overwhelmingly optimistic.

Whitman's optimism extends to the composite character of modern English, which forms an "ensemble" of diverse linguistic sources. Instead of bemoaning the fact that the "Teutonic genius" of Old English has been conquered by linguistic invasions from classical and modern civilizations, Whitman praises "the genius of the English race, which is unequaled in absorption and assimilation, in receptive and applicative power" (p. 272). Once again the historical discussion is cast in evolutionary terms: Anglo-Saxon is the heart and spine of English, but Norman French was needed for the Anglo-Saxon to grow into the English tongue, for without it the Anglo-Saxon could never have freed itself of "those useless and cumbersome forms" of inflection (p. 274). The classical contributions, which Whitman attributes exclusively to the Renaissance, "furnished the spiritual conceptions, and endowed the material body of the English speech with a living soul" (p. 277). The evolution—from Saxon to French to Greek and Latin—is always in the direction of increased spirituality, even though the late "inoculations" of classical words would seem to be more materialistic because of their "cumbersome forms." Moreover, Whitman ignores the process of "elimination" in his treatment of English as an organism. In terms reminiscent of "America's Mightiest Inheritance," he asserts that "every addition to practical civilization, every scientific generalization, commerce in all its branches, foreign literary influence, diplomacy, religion, philosophy, sociology are the perpetual agents of linguistic increase" (p. 280). Because Whitman's concept of "ensemble" is irrevocably tied to the "vista" of future progress, the English "ensemble" is figured as perpetually growing and increasing.

The poet's progressivist vision of the "vista" of American English clearly structures the last two chapters of *Rambles Among Words*. "The Growth of Words" moves from the philosophical, synchronic concern for "man's secret sense of his unity with nature" to the "historic unfolding" of language as it evolves into a more and more highly spiritualized organism. From an attempted explanation of the metaphysical origins of language, Whitman moves to a spiritual genealogy of the English language. And in the last chapter, "English in America," the genealogy moves into the present and, inevitably, into the future.

In "English in America" Whitman focuses upon the English language as "the speech of the Modern," expressing "the spirit of the modern, breaking up the crystalline structure of the classic mould—the splendid newness, the aspirations of freedom, Individualism, democracy" (p. 286). The American spirit will act on the English language, which "expresses aristocracy and monarchy among the rest" of the spiritual influences shaping it, in exactly the same way that the "Teutonic genius" acted upon late Latin—"breaking up the crystalline structure of the classic mould." American English, then, expresses the "genius of a new age," and it will be subject to specifically American "agents of linguistic increase." The "mind of the ages" has thrown off aristocracy and monarchy, and it is not by accident that English has been transported to the new and vaster arena of America:

> Of course the English Language must take on new powers in America. And here we are favored by the genius of this grand and noble language, which more than all others lends itself plastic and willing to the moulding power of new formative influences. Was it supposed that the English Language was finished? But there is no finality to a Language! The English has vast vista in it—vast vista in America. (*Rambles*, p. 287)

Whitman's progressivist vision is signaled by the single word "vista." Although the English language is an "ensemble" of the past's formative influences, it must take on new powers if it is to express the new democratic spirit of America. For that reason Whitman turns to "future expansions" of American English, expansions that "follow the divine indications" the history of the language provides.

Whitman takes as a "spinal fact" of that history the "composite character of our language" (p. 288) because the composite "ensemble" of the English language is a divine indication of the "spirit of the Language—moulded more and more to a large hospitality and impartiality" (p. 289). Because America is made up of diverse individual spirits from diverse nations and races, American English must express the "immense diversity of race, temperament, character" in "free, rich growths of speech." And America must never be content to crystallize its spirit in one "mould," for then the organism would cease to grow:

Land of the Ensemble, to her the consenting currents flow, and the ethnology of the States draws the grand outline of that hospitality and reception that must mark the new politics, sociology, literature and religion. (p. 288)

For Whitman, linguistic diversity and linguistic change are mutually supporting processes of spiritual evolution. The "ensemble" must flow into "vista," and the "vista" must contribute to the receptive hospitality of the "ensemble." The poet applies the progressivist theory of spiritual evolution to the special case of English in America, where the English language and American social conditions coincide exactly. Each has absorbed and assimilated diverse elements from diverse lands, and each reflects the union of those elements in the "vista" of a totalized and evolving "ensemble."

Whitman's entire account of language has as its basis the process of spiritual evolution, and the goal of the process is, in his eyes, the "spontaneous expansions" of American English and American "lifespirit." As the poet nears the end of his account, the evolutionary nature of his theory leads him to consider how these future "spontaneous expansions" are to be encouraged. Opposing his own theory of "hospitality and reception" to the "theory of repression" that stresses ethnic and linguistic uniformity, Whitman calls for a new "American literat," a figure whose principal qualities will be "large knowledge of the philosophy of speech" and "rich aesthetic instincts" (pp. 289–90). The first of these qualities recalls Whitman's requirement for a history of the English language (p. 268), and the two qualities taken together raise the question of why the poet's evolutionary theory of spirit and language must imply a theory of literary expression.

One answer would focus upon the poet's inability to distinguish between his theoretical and practical interests, between historical linguistics and *Leaves of Grass*. A second, perhaps better, answer would focus on Whitman's sense of the relationship between language at large and the uses language is put to in literature. The coda to "English in America" hits upon that very relationship:

Over the transformations of a Language the genius of a nation unconsciously presides—the issues of Words represent issues in the national thought. And in the vernal seasons of a nation's life the formative energy puts forth verbal growths opulent as flowers in spring. (p. 291)

The "genius of a nation" and "the formative energy" are virtual synonyms here, and they combine to represent American English as an unconscious and necessary expression of "national thought." The passage recalls Humboldt's view of an "inner life-principle," and it suggests that the "formative energy" of American English will seek expression in vernal/verbal "growths."

The idea of language as an unconscious expression of the national spirit is important for Whitman's theory of literature because he gives the idea his characteristic evolutionary twist. In a passage from *Rambles Among Words* that clearly echoes "America's Mightiest Inheritance," Whitman transfers the "inner life-principle" of language to the lips of the democratic people:

> And the vast billowy tendencies of modern life, too—the new political, social, scientific births—are making new demands on the English idiom. It is for America especially to evoke new realizations from the English speech. Always waiting in a language are untold possibilities. On the lips of the people, in the free rich unconscious utterance of the popular heart are the grand eternal leadings and suggestions.
>
> Of all the heritages which America receives the English language is beyond all comparison the mightiest. Language of the grand stocks, language of reception, of hospitality, it is above all fitted to be the speech of America. There is nothing fortuitous in language. It is for reasons the English idiom is here. In the English, more than all others, was concentrated the spirit of the modern, breaking up the old crystalline classic mould. No language has, no language ever had, such immense assimilation as the English. Freely it absorbs whatever is of use to it, absorbs and assimilates it to its own fluid and flexible substance. This rich copious hospitable flow is to be encouraged. (p. 12)

The function of literature is to encourage the "rich copious hospitable flow" of both American English and the American "spirit of the modern." The spirit is always present in the "free rich unconscious utterance" of the people, but literature can take the "popular heart" toward "the grand eternal leadings and suggestions." That is, literature encourages the evolution of the "popular heart" toward spiritual fluidity and flexibility. Whitman envisions literature as the expression of "untold possibilities" in the twin realms of language and spirit, for it evokes "new realizations" that match "the new political, social, scientific births," and those realizations carry the "popular heart" from material to spiritual "leadings and suggestions." Literature points the reader in that direction by employing an exemplary "language of reception," a "fluid and flexible substance."

Democratic Vistas shows how fundamental the theory of spiritual evolution is to Whitman's vision of American politics, society, and literature.[22] The theme of "the grand experiment of development," of "the law over all, and law of laws . . . the law of successions" (*PW*, II, 380–81), runs throughout the poet's attempt to reconcile democracy and the individual, but it is crystallized in one particular passage. Faced with the ruptures of the "Secession War" and the corruptions of postwar American government and business, Whitman calls for America to "attain harmony and stability by consulting ensemble and the ethic purports, and faithfully building upon them." His account of the "ensemble" is, as in *Rambles Among Words*, based upon the "vista" of linguistic and spiritual evolution. There are, says Whitman, three stages of development in America:

> The First stage was the planning and putting on record the political foundation rights of immense masses of people. . . .
> The Second stage relates to material prosperity, wealth, produce, laborsaving machines. . . .
> The Third stage, rising out of the previous ones, to make them and all illustrious, I, now, for one, promulge, announcing a native expression-spirit, getting into form, adult, and through mentality, for these States, self-contain'd, different from others, more expansive, more rich and free, to be evidenced by original authors and poets to come, by American personalities, plenty of them, male and female, transversing the States, none excepted— and by native superber tableaux and growths of language, songs, operas, orations, lectures, architecture—and by a sublime and serious Religious Democracy, sternly taking command, dissolving the old, sloughing off surfaces, and from its own interior and vital principles, reconstructing, democratizing society. (*PW*, II, 409–10)

Whitman divides the three stages according to their position in time: The first is referred to in the past tense, the second in the present, and the third in a combination of present and future. Of course, the third stage exists only in Whitman's rhetorical act of "promulging" it. But without it, the first two stages would be incomplete, for the third stage bears the promise that the principles embodied in the

22. *Democratic Vistas* (New York: J. S. Redfield, 1871). The eighty-four-page pamphlet combines two previously published essays: "Democracy" and "Personalism," both in *The Galaxy* in 1867 and 1868. See Gay Wilson Allen, *The New Walt Whitman Handbook* (New York: New York University Press, 1975), pp. 128–32.

Declaration of Independence and the federal Constitution will give rise to more than "laborsaving machines."

The third-stage mixture of present and future tenses recalls Whitman's simultaneous criticism and prophecy concerning the "History of the English Language" (*Rambles*, p. 268), and both passages typify the rhetoric of what Sacvan Bercovitch has called the "American jeremiad," in which the prophetic speaker fixes his eye both on the present failings of his people and on the future promise of their destiny. Modeled on the American Puritan political sermon, the American jeremiad fuses secular and sacred history in the same way that Bunsen, Schele de Vere, and Whitman fuse the diachronic and synchronic approaches to language. As Bercovitch explains, the progressivist theory of spiritual evolution is the basic assumption behind the American jeremiad, just as it is the underpinning of Whitman's theory of language and literature:

> The American Puritan jeremiad was the ritual of a culture on an errand—which is to say, a culture based on a faith in process. Substituting teleology for hierarchy, it discarded the Old World ideal of stasis for a New World vision of the future. Its function was to create a climate of anxiety that helped release the restless "progressivist" energies required for the success of the venture. . . . The future, though divinely assured, was never quite there, and New England's Jeremiahs set out to provide the sense of insecurity that would ensure the outcome. Denouncing or affirming, their vision fed on the distance between promise and fact.[23]

In *Democratic Vistas*, which Bercovitch calls "a work of symbolic interpretation" (p. 198), Whitman uses the theory of spiritual evolution to fill the gap between the ideals of American democracy—the symbol *America* itself—and the material results of democratic society. Whitman's ideal is a "Religious Democracy" in which the same American "growths of language" he called for in *Rambles Among Words* will be realized. His rhetoric does not present the ideal simply as a utopian dream; rather, it places the ideal in an evolving present, so that the ideal is "getting into form" in the act of the prophet's "announcing." By adding the "Third stage, rising out of the previous ones," Whitman returns America to a spiritual dimension he sees immanent in the Declaration and the Constitution. Nor is it an accident

---

23. Sacvan Bercovitch, *The American Jeremiad* (Madison: University of Wisconsin Press, 1978), p. 23.

that the first and the third stages are characterized by verbal arti-
facts: In both, words are supposed to embody "interior and vital principles;" in both, matter and spirit, thing and word, are one.

Whitman's symbolic interpretation of America bears a remark-
able similarity to the popularized versions of linguistic typology we
have seen in Bunsen and Schele de Vere. The first stage represents
the primary unity of spirit and matter, thought and word, embodied
in the Declaration and the Constitution. The second represents the
opposition of spirit and matter, where there are no words or thoughts
at all—only "laborsaving machines." The third represents the re-
union of spirit and matter in the synthesis of the previous two stages,
in which material progress and spiritual progress are mirror images,
both reflecting the "native expression-spirit."

For Whitman, literature is the "mightiest original non-subor-
dinated SOUL" (*PW*, II, 413) that will lead America beyond mere material progress, beyond "the growing excess and arrogance of real-
ism" (p. 417). The meaning of literature lies not so much in what it
says or does but in what it leads to, and Whitman places his faith in
the idea that it contributes to the evolution of a future American "Religious Democracy." For the poet, the promise of both language and
literature is the promise of the spirit that "lies sleeping, aside, unrecking itself, in some western idiom, or native Michigan or Tennessee repartee, or stump speech—or in Kentucky or Georgia, or the
Carolinas—or in some slang or local song or allusion of the Manhattan, Boston, Philadelphia, or Baltimore mechanic" (pp. 412–13). Literature functions to awaken that spirit, but it can do so only when
its language answers to the constantly evolving national spirit:

> Prospecting thus the coming unsped days, and that new order
> in them—marking the endless train of exercise, development,
> unwind, in nation as in man, which life is for—we see, fore-
> indicated, amid these prospects and hopes, new law-forces of
> spoken and written language—not merely the pedagogue-forms,
> correct, regular, familiar with precedents, made for matters of
> outside propriety, fine words, thoughts definitely told out—but a
> language fann'd by the breath of Nature, which leaps overhead,
> cares mostly for impetus and effects, and what it plants and in-
> vigorates to grow—tallies life and character, and seldomer tells
> a thing than suggests or necessitates it. In fact, a new theory of
> literary composition for imaginative works of the very first class,
> and especially for highest poems, is the sole course open to these
> States. Books are to be call'd for, and supplied, on the assump-
> tion that the process of reading is not a half-sleep, but, in highest

sense, an exercise, a gymnast's struggle; that the reader is to do something for himself, must be on the alert, must himself or herself construct indeed the poem, argument, history, metaphysical essay—the text furnishing the hints, the clue, the start or framework. Not the book needs so much to be the complete thing, but the reader of the book does. That were to make a nation of supple and athletic minds, well-train'd, intuitive, used to depend on themselves, and not on a few coteries of writers. (pp. 424–25)

According to Whitman's theory, literature does not provide clearcut, well-defined forms in which the spirit of the reader can rest. To do so would be to sink into the inactivity of a "crystalline mould." Instead, literature must employ a language that "suggests or necessitates" a direction for the reader's waking spirit. By raising the unconscious power of American English to the level of conscious literary form, Whitman asserts, the "new law-forces of spoken and written language" will ensure the future spiritual progress of American readers. Just as the English language is America's "mightiest inheritance," therefore, so American literature is its "mightiest . . . SOUL," a soul that is as progressivist and evolutionary as Whitman's vistalike "thought of the Ensemble."

2

The "Real Grammar": Loan Words and Word Formations in *Leaves of Grass*, 1855–1856

Whitman's twin theories of language and literature find a variety of concrete expressions in the first two editions of *Leaves of Grass*. In the 1855 Preface, for example, the poet devotes one of his final paragraphs to the subject of American English:

> The English language befriends the grand American expression—it is brawny enough, and limber and full enough. On the tough stock of a race who through all change of circumstance was never without the idea of political liberty, which is the animus of all liberty, it has attracted the terms of daintier and gayer and subtler and more elegant tongues. It is the powerful language of resistance—it is the dialect of common sense. It is the speech of the proud and melancholy races, and of all who aspire. It is the chosen tongue to express growth, faith, self-esteem, freedom, justice, equality, friendliness, amplitude, prudence, decision, and courage. It is the medium that shall wellnigh express the inexpressible. (*PW*, II, 456–57)

As in *Rambles Among Words*, Whitman joins language and literature by joining the English language and "the grand American expression." In conferring awesome powers upon the literature of American English, moreover, Whitman echoes Humboldt's interpretation of language as an expression of a national spirit. Thus the second sentence of the paragraph asserts that the English language has "attracted the terms of daintier and gayer and subtler and more elegant tongues" and engrafted them "on the tough stock of a race." This sentence elliptically refers to the history of the English language. The "tough stock" alludes to Anglo-Saxon, while the "more elegant tongues" refer to later borrowings from French, Latin, and Greek.[1] Whitman gives this one-sentence history his characteristically evolutionary interpretation: American English is "the chosen tongue," and there can be no question of accident or random change. Instead, the "grand American expression" must embody, first and foremost, "growth," and in doing so it will grow toward the condition of well-nigh expressing the "inexpressible," or pure spirit.

Several poems from the 1855 and 1856 editions show that Whitman's concern with language is more than passing. In "By Blue Ontario's Shore," the paragraph from the 1855 Preface is taken up and altered in several significant ways:

> Language-using controls the rest;
> Wonderful is language!
> Wondrous the English language, language of live men,
> Language of ensemble, powerful language of resistance,
> Language of a proud and melancholy stock, and of all who
>   aspire,
> Language of growth, faith, self-esteem, rudeness, justice,
>   friendliness, amplitude, prudence, decision, exactitude,
>   courage,
> Language to well-nigh express the inexpressible,
> Language for the modern, language for America.
>
>   (159[1]–[8])

Although much of the stanza is a verbatim repetition of the 1855 Preface, the fourth and eighth lines echo key points made in *Rambles*

---

1. The botanical imagery of "tough stock" arises in part from Whitman's reading of *A Hand-Book of the Engrafted Words of the English Language* (New York: Appleton, 1854), which is treated in detail by Bernbrock, "Whitman and 'Anglo-Saxonism,' " pp. 41–51.

Among Words. "Language of ensemble" recalls the phrase "that large hospitality and impartiality that flows from the thought of the Ensemble" from "The Growth of Words" (p. 268). And "language for the modern, language for America" directly parallels passages in both the introduction and the conclusion of the philological treatise: "In the English, more than all others, was concentrated the spirit of the modern, breaking up the old crystalline mould. It is for America grandly to use this grand inheritance" (p. 12). "By a combination of circumstances the English language became the speech of America. There was nothing fortuitous in this. For English is eminently the speech of the Modern" (p. 286). In *Rambles* as in "By Blue Ontario's Shore," Whitman's evolutionary view provides America with a linguistic and spiritual inheritance. It would seem, then, that Whitman's meditation on the "Many in One" is as much concerned with American English as it is with American democracy, for both are composite, vistalike ensembles.

Whitman's linguistic and spiritual "thought of the ensemble" resurfaces in two poems from the 1855–56 *Leaves*. In "Great Are the Myths" (1855), the poet calls language "the mightiest of the sciences" (29), a phrase that anticipates the title of the 1856 essay, "America's Mightiest Inheritance." The connection to the idea of linguistic legitimation becomes evident in the lines that follow:

> Great is the English speech—what speech is so great as the
>   English?
> Great is the English brood—what brood has so vast a destiny as
>   the English?
> It is the mother of the brood that must rule the earth with the
>   new rule;
> The new rule shall rule as the Soul rules, and as the love,
>   justice, equality in the Soul rule.
>
> (32–35)

By leaving the terms of inheritance unstated, the poet combines reticence and brashness. It is nonetheless clear that the "English brood" is portrayed as the linguistic "mother" of the American brood, which "must rule the earth with the new rule" of linguistic democracy. Further, the "new rule" is equated with the soul, so that the process of linguistic legitimation entails an evolution toward pure spirit. In the closing section of the poem, this movement is rephrased in more general terms, where life leads inevitably to death: "Has Life much purport?—Ah, Death has the greatest purport" (49).

Even more important than "Great Are the Myths" is the 1856

"Song of the Rolling Earth," which was originally titled "Poem of the Sayers of the Words of the Earth." Here Whitman takes language to the boundaries of signification, to a place where language does "well-nigh express the inexpressible." He begins paradoxically, by approaching things as words:

> Earth, round, rolling, compact—suns, moons, animals—all
>   these are words,
> Watery, vegetable, sauroid advances—beings, premonitions,
>   lispings of the future—these are vast words.
>
> (1[1]–[2])

The two lines place the figural equation of things with words within a cosmically vast context. It is as if the "vast words" of prehistoric "sauroid advances" formed the origins of human language. Whitman's metaphorical etymology leaps the gap between the silent past and the "lispings of the future" just as it bridges the gulf between things and words.

The problem with this double leap is, of course, that the poet cannot escape the confines of metaphor itself. There is no direct, unmediated relation between words and things, since language is itself the mediator. Whitman attempts to evade the mediating influence of language by proclaiming the things of the earth to be the words of a cosmic language:

> Were you thinking that those were the words, those upright
>   lines? those curves, angles, dots?
> No, those are not the words, the substantial words are in the
>   ground and sea,
> They are in the air, they are in you.
>
> Were you thinking that those were the words, those delicious
>   sounds out of your friends' mouths?
> No, the real words are more delicious than they.
>
> (2–6)

In complementary rhetorical movements, Whitman first denies the existence of printed words as language and then replaces "those upright lines" with "substantial words" or "real words." The substantial or real words would join the two poles of things and words in a vocabulary of pure presence or substance. The rhetoric is self-contradictory, to be sure, but it is also powerful, for Whitman's strategy is to employ figuration in order to deny the basically figural, for-mal quality of all language.[2]

One of the most basic figural strategies in the poem is personifi-cation. After naming "amelioration" as "one of the earth's words," the poet illustrates his progressivist vocabulary with personifications of the earth (17–43), motion (44–47), reflection (48–53), hours (54–62), days (63), and nights (64). The initial personification of the earth as "the eloquent dumb great mother" (41) controls the next five figures, all of which become instances of the "earth's words," which "never fail." The control is clear in the female personifications of motion as "the interminable sisters" and of reflection as "she whom I too love," a self-absorbed figure who sits "holding a mirror day and night tire-lessly before her own face." These two images contrast sharply with one another, as do the abstractions they personify, but the contrast is subsumed within the context of femaleness, a type of sisterhood. In-deed, the two females are really versions of the original earth image: The stanza on motion focuses upon "the beautiful sister we know," while the stanza on reflection suggests the self-contained impartial-ity of the earth in the phrase "inviting none, denying none" (52). Whitman's strategy is to create a humanlike kinship between logi-cally opposed ideas, for both motion and reflection are necessary to his poetic vocabulary of amelioration. Moreover, the terms are akin to the opposition of "vista" and "ensemble," and Whitman shows his overwhelming bias in favor of temporal change in the stanzas person-ifying the concrete concepts of hours, days, and nights.

The figure of amelioration is, without doubt, both temporal and progressivist. Whitman gives a special turn to the figure in the last stanza of Section 1, where he abandons personification and refers to the earth as "the divine ship" that "sails the divine sea." The image of the ship implies a goal or purpose for the ship's journey, and the poet hints at that goal when he says that the earth is "still inheriting" the "soul's realization and determination" (67). The imagery of kinship or inheritance again establishes an analogical connection between op-posites, in this case between the material world and the soul. Thus

2. This rhetoric is analyzed in Paul de Man's seminal essay, "Semiology and Rhetoric," in *Allegories of Reading* (New Haven, Conn.: Yale University Press, 1980), pp. 3–19. De Man's analysis of figural language applies the deconstructive argumentation of Jacques Derrida to literary language. A full bibliography concerning deconstruction would cover several pages, but for an introduction to the problems surrounding lan-guage and referentiality, see Derrida, *Writing and Difference*, trans. Alan Bass (Chicago: University of Chicago Press, 1978); see also Jonathan Culler, *Structuralist Poetics* (Ith-aca, N.Y.: Cornell University Press, 1978), pp. 131–36, 241–54, and Fredric Jameson, *The Prison-House of Language* (Princeton, N.J.: Princeton University Press, 1972), pp. 136–44, 174–87.

we are to infer a spiritual goal lying at the end of the material voyage, for that is precisely the union of opposites that Whitman designs in the phrase "divine ship."

After a brief hymn to the self-reliance exemplified by the earth, the poet returns to his initial paradox, the idea of nonverbal language:

> I swear I begin to see little or nothing in audible words,
> All merges toward the presentation of the unspoken meanings
>   of the earth,
> Toward him who sings the songs of the body and of the truths of
>   the earth,
> Toward him who makes the dictionaries of words that print
>   cannot touch.
>
> (98–101)

Whitman's evolutionary vision is evident in the repeated word "toward," and the paradoxical character of the vision is implied by the concept of "the dictionaries of words that print cannot touch." This line alludes to Whitman's plans for a "Real Dictionary," one which would be more than a compilation of accepted terms and their accepted definitions.[3] But if the dictionary contains no printed words, how can it be a book?

It is clear that Whitman realizes his own extravagance, for he immediately takes an opposite stance. Rather than present "unspoken meanings," he moves toward complete silence:

> I swear I see what is better than to tell the best,
> It is always to leave the best untold.
>
> When I undertake to tell the best I find I cannot,
> My tongue is ineffectual on its pivots,
> My breath will not be obedient to its organs,
> I become a dumb man.
>
> (102–107)

This apparent humility is quickly dismissed, since "the best of the earth cannot be told anyhow" (108). And although Whitman claims to leave the best untold, he goes on to come as close as he can to telling it:

3. For a discussion of the dictionary project, see Michael R. Dressman, "Walt Whitman's Plans for the Perfect Dictionary," in *Studies in the American Renaissance, 1979*, ed. Joel Myerson (Boston: Twayne, 1979), pp. 457–73.

> But the soul is also real, it too is positive and direct,
> No reasoning, no proof has establish'd it,
> Undeniable growth has establish'd it.
>
> (113–115)

The "real words" of the earth deliver, finally, the "real soul," which grows in the same way the things and words of the earth are supposed to grow. This idea is once again progressivist, for it is based upon continual development, an eternal amelioration toward an unreachable yet somehow "real" goal.

Whitman's rhetoric always places spiritual progress within a temporal frame, so that the "soul's realization," like the "Real Dictionary," is always deferred. The final section of "Song of the Rolling Earth" illustrates this point in direct addresses to the "sayers of the earth." These sayers or singers would presumably be future poets, but Whitman admonishes them to be patient, to await their realization in a yet more distant future:

> I swear to you the architects shall appear without fail,
> I swear to you they will understand you and justify you,
> The greatest among them shall be he who best knows you, and
> 　encloses all and is faithful to all,
> He and the rest shall not forget you, they shall perceive that you
> 　are not an iota less than they,
> You shall be fully glorified in them.
>
> (126–130)

The "you" in the concluding lines of the poem is by no means clearly specified. Besides the future poet, "you" could be simply the future American reader. Or it could refer to any past, present, or future American who will be "fully glorified" in the poetry of "the greatest," which appears to be a poetry of the future rather than a poetry of Whitman's present. These multiple possibilities partake of Whitman's rhetorical strategy, which defers specific meanings to an unspecified future date. That strategy is deeply entwined with the poet's view of language as a purposive organism growing through time, for his view allows him to make huge claims for the power of language— and more specifically for the power of poetry—at the same time that he claims only to "echo the tones of souls and the phrases of souls" (116). The echoes will always sound closer and closer to the "real words," but they will always leave "the best untold."

Whitman's paradoxical treatment of words and things in terms of "the dictionaries of words that print cannot touch" finds an analogue in his concept of the "Real Grammar." The "Real Dictionary" and the "Real Grammar" are directly connected in these pages from *The Primer of Words:*

> (Because it is a truth that) the words continually used among the people are, in numberless cases, not the words used in writing, or recorded in the dictionaries by authority.—~~Probably~~ There are ~~just as~~ many words in daily use, not inscribed in ~~any~~ the dictionary, and seldom or never in any print, ~~as there are words recorded~~.—Alas, the forms of grammar are ~~seldom or~~ never ~~ob~~ persistently obeyed, and cannot be.—
> The ~~Prop~~ Real Dictionary will give all words that exist in use, the bad words as well as any.—The Real Grammar will be that which declares itself a nucleus ~~on~~of the spirit of the laws, with ~~perfect~~ liberty to all to carry out the spir~~it~~ of the laws, even by violating them, if necessary.—The English Language is grandly lawless like the ~~t~~ race who use it.—Or Perhaps– or rather breaks out of the little ? laws to enter truly the higher ones It is so instinct with that which underlies laws, ~~that~~ and the purports of laws, ~~that I think~~ it ~~goes toward the destinati~~ refuses all petty interrupt~~up~~tions in its way ~~toward~~ purports.—(*DBN* III, 734–735)

The notebook entry clarifies, to a degree, the projected Dictionary, which should actually print all the words in use in America, including the "words that print cannot touch." The mystical conception of nonverbal language in "Song of the Rolling Earth" becomes, in this passage, more earthbound. The "real words" of the Dictionary would include slang, colloquialisms, expletives, and idioms not recorded in Webster or Worcester.

The *Primer* passage sharpens Whitman's notion of the "Real Dictionary" because it plays upon the distinction between spoken and written language. In Whitman's eyes, the "real words" are spoken words, and it is this ephemeral, ever-changing lexicon that forms the "Real Dictionary." The distinction would seem to apply equally well to the concept of the "Real Grammar." Echoing the Declaration of Independence, Whitman proposes to create a theoretical "nucleus of the spirit of the laws, with liberty to all to carry out the spirit of the laws, even by violating them." Instead of confining itself to the printed letter of the law, the "Real Grammar" will "go toward the destination" of pure spirit by being "grandly lawless like the race who use it."

Several points about the "Real Grammar" can now be summarized. First, it is clear that Whitman conceives of language as an organism, one which is "instinct" with the spirit of grammatical laws. As he says in "Our Language and Literature," the "Real Grammar" is the "law of the living structure of language in its largest sense" (*DBN*, III, 810). Second, the poet's conception of organic language is clearly evolutionary, for the "Real Grammar" moves instinctively "toward purports," where "purports" carries, along with the sense of "design" or "meaning," the rare sense of "object, purpose, intention," as well as the etymological sense of a "carrying forward."[4] Third, the "Real Grammar" is a law of organic linguistic change, one which should parallel and encourage the law of organic spiritual change in America.

It still remains to be seen how Whitman's theory of the "Real Grammar" can be translated into concrete terms. In other words, what form must the "Real Grammar" take if it is to encourage the perpetual development of American language and American spirits? We can begin to answer that question by returning, first of all, to the distinction between words and things, a distinction that Whitman purposely blurs in "Song of the Rolling Earth."

In the "Song" Whitman insists upon viewing things as words; conversely, in several notebook entries the poet insists upon viewing words as things. On the first page of the *Primer of Words*, for example, Whitman asserts that "a perfect user of words uses things" (*DBN*, III, 729), and he echoes that assertion later in the same notebook:

> A perfect user of words uses things . . . they exude . . . in power and beauty from him— miracles from his hands— miracles from his mouth . . . lilies, clouds, sunshine, woman, poured consciously— things, whirled like chain-shot— rocks, defiance, compulsion, houses, iron, locomotives, the oak, the pine, the keen eye, the hairy breast, the Texan ranger, the Boston truckman, the woman that arouses a man, the man that arouses a woman.—
> (*DBN*, III, 740)

Much of the rhetorical power of this entry stems from the randomness of the catalogue, where concrete nouns like "rocks" flow directly into abstract nouns like "defiance, compulsion" and back into concrete nouns like "houses, iron," and so forth. Equally important are

4. The first two definitions are taken from Noah Webster, *An American Dictionary of the English Language*, Revised and Enlarged by Chauncey A. Goodrich (Springfield, Mass.: G.&C. Merriam, 1847). The rare sense of "object, purpose, intention" is taken from the *SOED*.

the active verbal forms, such as "exude," "poured," "whirled," and "arouses." The notebook entry is as much a performance or demonstration as it is an abstract statement, where the poet figuratively treats words as "things, whirled like chain-shot."

Two other notebook entries enrich this conception of the relationship between word and thing. In "Our Language and Literature," Whitman states that "words . . . would be a stain, a smutchy . . . except for the stamina of things" (*DBN*, III, 810). In a clear echo, one which suggests that the manuscript essay antedates the *Primer* notebook, the poet writes, "The ~~whole~~ art of the ~~great~~ use of words, ~~dwindles into a~~ would be a stain, a smutch, ~~in~~ ~~before~~ but for the stamina of things" (*DBN*, III, 746). In both passages, the word "stamina" is salient, for it appears to mean more than our current sense of "the power of sustaining fatigue." Webster's *American Dictionary of the English Language* (1847) lists "stamina" as the plural of "stamen," and it gives three definitions:

> 1. In *a general sense*, usually in the plural, the fixed, firm part of a body, which supports it or gives it its strength and solidity. Thus we say, the bones are the *stamina* of animal bodies; the ligneous parts of trees are the *stamina* which constitute their strength. Hence, 2. Whatever constitutes the principal strength or support of any thing; as the *stamina* of a constitution or of life; the *stamina* of a state. 3. In *botany*, an organ of flowers for the preparation of the pollen or fecundating dust. It consists of the filament and the anther. It is considered as the male organ of fructification.[5]

All three of these definitions apply to Whitman's use of the word "stamina," combining an organic metaphor of "fructification" with the more general and abstract meanings of the term. Whitman gives ontological priority to things, as opposed to words, but the definition of "stamina" also implies that there is an organic, developmental

---

5. These definitions also appear in both the 1828 and the 1841 editions of Webster's *American Dictionary*, but it seems clear that Whitman used an issue of the 1847 edition of *Webster's*. In "America's Mightiest Inheritance" he judges that "Webster and Worcester have done well" (p. 59). This appears to refer to the 1847 edition of *Webster's* and the 1846 edition of Joseph E. Worcester's *Universal and Critical Dictionary of the English Language* (Boston: Brewer & Tileston, 1846), which were in direct competition with one another and became involved in a "War of the Dictionaries." In addition, Whitman took extensive notes on Webster's "Introductory Dissertation" (*DBN*, III, 713–18), and in one instance the poet's notation of the page number "liii (53)" (p. 713) matches the pagination of the 1847 edition and its later issues.

connection between things and words, a connection that the poet strengthens by treating words as organic things.

Perhaps the clearest statement concerning this complex relationship comes in the last pages of *Rambles Among Words*, where Whitman addresses the question of encouraging future linguistic developments in America:

> I can see but one limitation to the theory of Words—the theory of Things. Is it for us who are borne on the billowy tides of this new humanity to limit the unfolding opulence of God—to put a girdle round the widening future of our civilization and our speech? Freely, then, may the American literat proceed to quarry and build in the architecture of the English Language. Of course the conditions of this free expressive activity are high. To him who would mould our language must go many qualities—must go large knowledge of the philosophy of speech, must go rich aesthetic instincts, among the rest. (p. 290)

Although the "theory of Things" is ostensibly a limitation upon the "theory of Words," the poet in fact dissolves the "girdle." Since both things and words are characterized as possessing the same "widening future," there can be no limitation to the perpetual development of both. The only requirements Whitman sets down are the "large knowledge of the philosophy of speech" and "rich aesthetic instincts." This combination of linguistic knowledge and literary instinct would produce the perfect combination of words and things, which in turn would contribute to the "widening future of our civilization and our speech." Once again, therefore, the priority of things gives way to the necessity of words as the poet's medium of expression. Whitman's method of avoiding this conflict between two orders of priority is to treat words as things and things as words. In his progressivist vision, all things contribute to the ever-expanding spiritual vocabulary, just as all words contribute to the ever-developing material reality.

The "Real Grammar" becomes yet more concrete when we return to Maxmilian Schele de Vere's *Outlines of Comparative Philology*. Like Whitman, Schele de Vere adheres to a progressivist interpretation of linguistic change: "Language, being a spiritual manifestation of the mind, tries, like the mind itself, to rise above matter; it has a tendency, ever active and ever progressive, to strip off all forms with which thought is encumbered; it strives to free itself more and more" (*Philology*, pp. 238–39). For Schele de Vere, the process of inflectional leveling is a progressivist process of linguistic and spiritual evolution, and it has the practical result of freeing words from the constricting morphological classes of classical grammars. Schele de Vere praises that particular result in his chapter "The Increase of Languages":

> A popular method of obtaining new words in English, is the conversion of words from one part of speech to another. This is peculiarly easy in a language so entirely without inflections and characteristic terminations; the interchange can readily be made, and the convenience is so striking as to secure it almost invariable success. (*Philology,* p. 249)

Several of Whitman's linguistic writings show that the poet fully appreciated the freedom conferred upon English by inflectional leveling. First, in "The Growth of Words" Whitman considers leveling as it applies to the "French influence" on English:

> In regard of Grammar—of structural forms and inflections—the French influence was powerful, but indirect. Indirect, I say; because the French gave few or any forms of its own. And yet one can scarcely exaggerate the power of that influence in freeing the nascent English speech from those useless and cumbersome forms with which the Anglo-Saxon was overloaded. (*Rambles,* p. 273)

Here Whitman asserts that the freedom of modern English is the direct result of the history of the composite "ensemble," where even the unproven, "indirect" influence of French contributes to the ameliorative, liberating process of leveling.

Three passages from the *Words* notebook confirm Whitman's awareness of the advantages gained through inflectional leveling. In the first, he quotes from Bunsen's *Outlines of the Philosophy of Universal History:* "Do not forget that what is now fixed was once floating and movable" (*Outlines,* I, 256; *DBN,* III, 720). In the second, he takes up Bunsen's statement and interprets it: "Thus individualism is a law in modern languages, and freedom also. . . . The words are not built in, but stand loose, and ready to go this way or that" (*DBN,* III, 723). In the first passage, "what is fixed" refers simply to the characters of the modern alphabet, but in the second passage Whitman applies the idea of "floating and movable" letters to the *words* of modern languages. In the third notebook passage, Whitman displays his acquaintance with inflectional leveling, noting the "marked difference in the way by which modern languages as different from ancient languages, express the application, modification, variation, connection

... of the main ideas of a sentence." Whereas "ancient Greek and Latin" connect the ideas by "inflexions," modern English uses "conjunctions, prepositions, articles &c." to connect ideas "any way we please" (*DBN*, III, 723). In this last phrase, Whitman joins the floating freedom and mobility of words with the process of leveling.

Two ways in which Whitman's conception of the "Real Grammar" marks the style of the 1855–56 poems are the use of foreign borrowings and the formation of new words. The use of foreign borrowings is hinted at in the poet's account of the indirect "French influence" on Anglo-Saxon grammar. And this aspect of Whitman's poetic diction becomes even clearer in the closing pages of *Rambles Among Words:*

> The sources of future enrichings of the Anglican speech are the same old fountains. In our native roots, in the plastic forms of the antique, in the noble modern idioms are the magazines of word-wealth. How much has the French language been to the English! How much has it yet to give! Nation of sublime destinies, noble, naive, rich with humanity, bearers of freedom, upholding on her shoulders the history of Europe for a thousand years! The Italian gifts, too, direct and indirect, are not nothing to America. Spain is not nothing. How much they have to contribute—Italy with her rich and rosy nature, her grand style of music and consummate intuitions of art; Spain, so noble, so proud, so much to manners, to behavior! I would not underrate the German and Scandinavian influences—mighty race, spiritual, aspiring, individual, melancholy, prudent. (*Rambles*, pp. 290–91)[6]

The second stylistic marker is more complicated than the first because there are three main processes of word formation in English. The first, *affixation*, includes *prefixation*, or adding a prefix to a base, and *suffixation*, or adding a suffix to a base. For example, through suffixation the noun *silence* can form the noun *silencer.* The second process, *conversion*, is the mirror image of suffixation because it involves no change of verbal form but a necessary change of word class. For instance, the verb *drive* can form the noun *drive.* The third pro-

6. In this passage Whitman may owe an unstated intellectual debt to Richard Chevenix Trench, *English Past and Present*, a series of lectures delivered in the spring of 1854 and first published in early 1855. The second lecture, "Gains of the English Language," treats English as "appropriating and assimilating to itself what it anywhere finds congenial to its own life, multiplying its resources, increasing its wealth" (*Everyman's Library*, no. 788 [London: J.M. Dent, n.d.], p. 30).

cess, *compounding*, features the combination of two or more bases. For example, the combination of *steam* and *boat* can produce *steamboat*.[7] Whitman uses all three processes of word formation, as well as a salient number of foreign borrowings and coinages based upon foreign words. And the general effect of all his verbal turnings is to dislodge words from any fixed grammatical categories in order to emphasize the "floating and movable" possibilities of American English.

The linguistically productive quality of Whitman's poetic diction is evident in the range of words borrowed from foreign languages. Whitman employs many place names and terms that are determined by the subject matter he treats, but he also employs both words borrowed directly from foreign sources and words coined from foreign ores. These three types of borrowings combine to create the "floating and movable" foreign word capital of the 1855–56 *Leaves of Grass*.

Subject-bound diction can be seen in the 1856 "Poem of Salutation," renamed "Salut au Monde" in 1860. The poem is Whitman's first attempt at the "international theme," which becomes more important and programmatic in the poems and revisions of 1871–81. Among the many catalogues of sights and sounds gathered from over the globe, we find the following:

> I see the steppes of Asia,
> I see the tumuli of Mongolia, I see the tents of Kalmucks and
>   Baskirs,
> I see the nomadic tribes with herds of oxen and cows,
> I see the table-lands notch'd with ravines, I see the jungles and
>   deserts,
> I see the camel, the wild steed, the bustard, the fat-tail'd sheep,
>   the antelope, and the burrowing wolf.
>
> I see the highlands of Abyssinia,
> I see flocks of goats feeding, and see the fig-tree, tamarind, date,
> And see fields of teff-wheat and places of verdure and gold.
>
> I see the Brazilian vaquero,
> I see the Bolivian ascending mount Sorata,
> I see the Wacho crossing the plains, I see the incomparable
>   rider of horses with his lasso on his arm,
> I see over the pampas the pursuit of wild cattle for their hides.
>   (112–23)

7. *Grammar*, Appendix I.24. References are keyed to chapter and section numbers.

Foreign terms include *steppes, tumuli, bustard, tamarind, teff-wheat, vaquero, Wacho, lasso,* and *pampas.* All of these words were established in the English lexicon by the time Whitman wrote, and the poet's dictional choices are determined, to a great degree, by his choice of subject. So, for instance, the rush of terms taken from the South American cattle industry represents a choice on Whitman's part, but the terms themselves do not. Whitman is not forced to use the terms taken from Spanish America, but if he did not do so, the avoidance would in itself be striking. The word *pampas,* for example, refers to the plains found south of the Amazon River; the plains north of the Amazon are called *llanos.* Thus Whitman's choice of that particular word is determined, to a great degree, by his decision to represent the "Brazilian vaquero." Indeed, only two words from the passage display any genuine poetic choice—*teff-wheat* and *Wacho.* The first of these is a pleonasm, since teff is the "principal cereal of Abyssinia" (*SOED*). But the redundancy clarifies the meaning of an obscure term, making of it an Anglicized compound. The second term, *Wacho,* is in fact a revision of the 1856 word *Guacho,* which is an erroneous but common spelling of *gaucho.* Once again, Whitman seems to wish to "domesticate" the foreign term by following the pattern of such Romance-English cognates as "Guillermo" and "William." The diction of the passage as a whole exemplifies the poet's "theory of Things," which should limit the "theory of Words." For the foreign borrowings follow necessarily from the foreign scenes Whitman recounts.

If Whitman's use of foreign words were limited to subject-bound vocabulary, there might be little to say about the stylistic effect of the borrowings on *Leaves of Grass*—exotic subjects entail exotic terminology. But this is not the case. Whitman uses foreign borrowings for expressive effect, to mark a poetic difference in the subject he treats. In the 1855 version of "Song of Myself," for example, the poet employs the following foreign words: *omnibus, promenaders, experient, savans, embouchures, vivas, venerealee, amies, foofoos, en masse, cartouches, kosmos, recitative, chef-d'oeuvre, amie, sierras, savannas, ambulanza, eleves, naivete, admirant, promulges, rendezvous, accoucheur,* and *debouch.* Several of these words are lexically established and subject-bound; *recitative* and *savannas,* for instance, appear in the 1847 *Webster's,* and each term designates a specific thing. The first is "a species of singing approaching toward ordinary speaking; language delivered in musical tones, i.e. in the sounds of the musical scale." The second is "an extensive open plain or meadow, or a plain destitute of trees, and covered with grass." Other terms in the list appear in the 1847 *Webster's,* but they are noted as being rarely used: *Promulges* and *rendezvous* are examples. The 1855 and 1856 editions of *Leaves of Grass* feature a host of such foreign borrowings, some well established, some rare, and some coined. And this practice accords with Whitman's listing of several French words that are "needed" by American English, both in "America's Mightiest Inheritance" and in "The Growth of Words."[8]

Another type of word in the list proves more interesting from a stylistic point of view. This is the word that Whitman uses for expressive effect, as is the case for *amies*. The word *amie* appears twice in the 1855 version of "Song of Myself": "Extoller of amies and those that sleep in each other's arms" (460); "Picking out here one that shall be my amie, / Choosing to go with him on brotherly terms" (700–701). The strange point about the poet's use of the word is that he employs the feminine form of the ending but applies it to male friends. Moreover, Whitman certainly was aware of this misapplication, for in "America's Mightiest Inheritance" he defines the word as follows: "Ami (ah'-me, masculine)—Amie (ah-me, feminine)—Dear friend."[9] It would seem, then, that Whitman deliberately blurs the boundaries of grammatical gender and physical sexuality. And this means that the word "amie" assumes a highly specific role in his vocabulary, for it designates a "dear friend" who is on "brotherly terms" with the poet, even to the point that the two will "sleep in each other's arms" (460). The term is sexually ambivalent, and it would seem that "amie" is an early version of the "Calamus" theme of the "need of comrades" ("In Paths Untrodden," 18). Whitman borrows the French word to designate a relationship for which the English vocabulary has no term. And the borrowing is from the French because the indirect "French influence" is to spiritualize the language and its users. As Whitman puts it in "The Growth of Words," French terms historically entered the language because they were "indicative of the new political and social relations—of war, of law—of the arts and elegancies of society, which, having had no existence in Saxon life, found no utterance in the Saxon language" (*Rambles*, p. 273). So the word "amie" is supposed to project a new social relation between men, and the poet's use of the word is supposed to help bring about the new social relation.

This same type of spiritualized relationship is behind many of the poet's French borrowings. Webster defines the word *eleve*, for instance, as "one brought up or protected by another," but the poet uses

8. "America's Mightiest Inheritance," pp. 61–64; *Rambles*, pp. 282–85. Whitman's strategy of domestication is clear in the list of words from "Song of Myself," since none is accented in the 1855 *Leaves*.

9. "America's Mightiest Inheritance," p. 62.

the term to designate the "average unending procession" of readers and writers:

> Eleves I salute you,
> I see the approach of your numberless gangs. . . . I see you
>   understand yourselves and me,
> And know that they who have eyes are divine, and the blind and
>   lame are equally divine,
> And that my steps drag behind yours yet go before them,
> And are aware how I am with you no more than I am with
>   everybody.
>
> (974–974[4])

Here the poet figures himself as a kind of spiritual master or teacher for future generations of readers. Although his "steps drag behind" because they are part of the past, they "yet go before" because they lead on the inevitable progress, the spiritual development that Whitman sees taking place within time. Thus we are always the spiritual pupils, the "eleves," of the speaking poet. We must always progress toward him, even though the poem situates him eternally beyond our reach.

Other French terms add to this vocabulary of spiritual progress. In the 1855 Preface, the poet asserts that "there will soon be no more priests. Their work is done. They may wait awhile . . . perhaps a generation or two . . . dropping off by degrees. A superior breed shall take their place . . . the gangs of kosmos and prophets en masse shall take their place" (PW, II, 456). The word "kosmos" is, of course, Greek and Emersonian, but the use of "en masse"—defined by Webster's (1847) simply as "in the mass or whole body"—is peculiar to Whitman. He repeats the word in "Song of Myself": "Endless unfolding of words of ages! / And mine a word of the modern, the word En-Masse" (477–78). In both passages, the word functions in much the same way as amies and eleves. That is, it designates a new, incipient social relation or fact, or it at least points toward such a possibility. In this case the social relation would seem to be a kind of spiritual democracy, a mass movement of progressive social spirits toward perfect linguistic and political liberty.

The final term in my short vocabulary list is, not surprisingly, ensemble. Whitman uses the word in the 1855 Preface, saying that "sanity and ensemble characterize the great master" (PW, II, 448). He defines the term in "America's Mightiest Inheritance" as "Wholeness; the whole so considered that each part has reference to the aggregate. (This expressive and long-needed word is now almost at home in English.)"[10] *Rambles Among Words* follows this definition: "The totality as distinguished from the details. A noble word with immense vista" (p. 283). When Whitman calls English the "language of ensemble" ("By Blue Ontario's Shore," 159[4]), he designates the English language as an embodiment of linguistic and spiritual wholeness. And this ideal of wholeness must also "characterize the great master," the poet. Through the wholeness of the poet's vision and language, then, the vocabulary of *amies, eleves, en masse,* and *ensemble* will become part of the "Real Dictionary" and "Real Grammar" of America.

The third category of Whitman's foreign borrowings is by far the most innovative, and it represents the third stage of the poet's use of loan words. These words are based upon foreign borrowings, but often Whitman either alters the foreign base to create an original word or employs foreign endings to create an original combination with a lexically established English word. Here is a list of salient examples from the 1855–56 editions: *venerealee* ("Song of Myself," 375), *compend* ("Song of Myself," 658), *savan* ("Song of Myself," 363; "Song for Occupations," 68; "Miracles," 14[2]), *promulge* ("Song of Myself," 1180–81; "Poem of Remembrances," [Chants Democratic. 6.] 4), *debouch* ("Song of Myself," 1298), *exurge* ("Song for Occupations," 87), *ennuyee* ("Sleepers," 8 and 151), *diminute* ("Salut au Monde," 44), *habitan* ("Salut," 132; "Poem of Remembrances," 10), *philosoph* ("Salut," 158), *embouchure* (verb) ("Blue Ontario's Shore," 75), and *literat* ("Blue Ontario's Shore," 153, 199; "Song of Prudence," 19).

The first thing to note about several of the words in this list is that Whitman tends to prefer the "leveled" or Anglicized form. Whitman uses words like "compend" instead of the Latin form "compendium." Similar examples are "promulge" instead of "promulgate," "diminute" instead of "diminutive," and "literat" instead of "literatus." Several of these terms appear in the 1847 *Webster's*, though they are often less commonly used than the Latin original. In all of them, the poet prefers the "leveled" form of the borrowed term, rendering it less Latin in its basic form and speeding up the historical process of inflectional leveling by enacting the process on Latin loan words. The impetus behind this dictional choice is surely evolutionary; by appropriating the Latin loan words and making them seem a part of the English ensemble, Whitman shows himself as the "greatest original practical example" of linguistic hospitality and of the "spirit of the modern." This is also the rationale behind such forms as "habi-

10. Ibid., p. 63. *Webster's* (1841) defines "ensemble" as a noun meaning "one with another; on an average." By 1847, however, the word is defined as "the whole; all the parts taken together. In *the fine arts*, this term denotes the masses and details considered with relation to each other."

tan," "philosoph," and "savan." By leveling the last letter of each word in French ("habitant," "philosophe," "savant"), Whitman lays claim to the foreign vocabulary, altering it as the representative of the spirit of American English.

The second method Whitman uses to create new English words from foreign borrowings is to add foreign endings to lexically established English words. Examples from the foregoing list would include *venerealee* and *ennuyee*. These two words are based upon the analogy of such lexically established forms as *warrantee* ("Occupations," 177) and *nominee* ("Sleepers," 153). The word "warrantee," which dates from the Middle English period, fits within the first definition of the *-ee* suffix given in the *SOED:* "used chiefly in technical terms of English law, denoting usually the indirect object of the verbs from which they are derived." "Nominee," which dates from the seventeenth century, seems to fit within the same legal and grammatical parameters. Moreover, Whitman's use of the *-ee* suffix also fits within the second definition given by the *SOED:* "*-ee* also appears in the English spelling of certain substantives adopted from modern French participial substantives in *-e,* as *debauchee, refugee.*" This would explain the form *ennuyee*, in any case, since the word "ennuyé" dates from the eighteenth century. This is, however, the adjectival form, and the dictionary notes that the word is only a "quasi-substantive." Whitman does not coin the word himself, but his use of it is decidedly innovative, since he anglicizes the French participle to make it more like lexically established English nouns. The word *venerealee* is even more original, since this is a Whitman coinage. The base, *venereal*, dates from the late Middle English period, and it was used as an elliptical substantive for "venereal disease" in 1843. Whitman adds to this lexically established noun/adjective the *-ee* suffix, and in doing so he creates a term for "one afflicted with venereal disease." Both *venerealee* and *ennuyee* represent, then, the passive state of the sufferer, and this representation is due both to the suffix and to the nominal or adjectival base that Whitman chooses. In both words, the poet mixes the lexically foreign and established, the borrowed and the original, to add to the lexicon of the "Real Dictionary" and to create new possibilities for the "Real Grammar." Thus Whitman's use of foreign borrowings ultimately blends with his innovative use of English word formations.

If Whitman's foreign borrowings emphasize the "floating and movable" qualities of English words, his word formations complicate and enrich the emphasis. The grammatical distinction between the "stative" and "dynamic" uses of words provides a frame for the analysis of these formations.[11] The basic distinction is straightforward: Stative words tend to signify stable, permanent concepts, whereas dynamic words tend to signify changing, temporary concepts. In general, nouns and adjectives are stative, while verbs and adverbs are dynamic, but the "floating and movable" quality of English word classes is, as Whitman correctly observed, a main principle of language (*Grammar*, 2.16). Both the general characteristics and the flexibility of movement are summed up in this diagram:

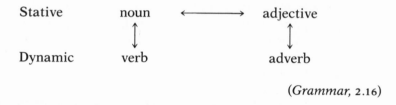

(*Grammar*, 2.16)

The two horizontal lines in the diagram indicate the general tendencies of nouns and adjectives to be stative and verbs and adverbs to be dynamic. But the arrows in the diagram complicate this generalization. First, they indicate the ability of words to shift from one word-class to another. So, for example, the adjective *fast* could denote a permanent quality, as in "He is a *fast* runner," while the adverb *fast* could denote a temporary action, as in "He may be running *fast* now, but he'll get tired soon." Similarly, nouns could be used as verbs, verbs and adjectives as nouns. Second, this does not mean that all verbs are dynamic until they form nouns, or that all nouns are stative until they form verbs. If a verb denotes static, stable concepts, it tends toward the grammatically stative use that is "natural" to nouns; conversely, a noun that denotes dynamic, changing concepts would tend toward the grammatically dynamic use that is "natural" to verbs. So the diagram shows that the "floating and movable" quality of English word classes is registered by the stative/dynamic distinction.

11. The stative/dynamic distinction is discussed in *Grammar*, 2.16. The most useful test to determine whether a verb is stative or dynamic is to see if it will form the present progressive tense. If it can, it is dynamic; if it cannot, it is stative. This is because the progressive signifies "an action in progress instead of the occurrence of an action or the existence of a state" (*Grammar*, 3.39). A verb of inert perception or cognition, for example, cannot take the progressive: "Do you see what I mean" cannot form "Are you seeing what I mean." See Marie Borroff's clear discussion of the distinction in *Language and the Poet* (Chicago: University of Chicago Press, 1979), pp. 96–97; see also *Grammar*, 3.39–41.

One of the most striking types of word formations in the 1855–56 poems is the noun formed by the suffix -er. The -er suffix is usually added to dynamic verbs to form personal nouns, and the resulting noun usually has an agentive or instrumental meaning (*Grammar*, I.24, 7.15). Two types of nouns are formed by the suffix, animate and inanimate. The animate noun denotes the occasional or habitual performer of an action: the worker, driver, baker writer, and so forth. When the action is performed habitually enough, and the word is used to designate the performer habitually enough, the -er form reaches the level of lexical independence, so that the agential noun becomes a "permanent," or "institutionalized," form. And when this lexical institutionalization takes place, the agential noun tends to become stative.[12]

The personal, or animate, -er noun is common in the 1855–56 poems, but, as in the case of foreign borrowings, Whitman frequently goes beyond institutionalized vocabulary, and his agential nouns tend to emphasize the verbal, temporal aspects of personal identity. In "Song of Myself," for example, the poet refers to himself as "less the *reminder* of property or qualities, and more the *reminder* of life" (493). "Reminder" ordinarily functions as an inanimate, instrumental noun meaning "something which reminds one; mention made for the purpose of reminding."[13] Indeed, in the 1867 revision of the poem, Whitman himself changes the line to use that more ordinary definition: "Less the reminders of properties my words, / And more the reminders they of life untold, and of freedom and extrication" (493–94). In the original version, however, Whitman uses the dynamic verb to form a personal noun meaning "one who performs the act of reminding." The dynamic aspect of personal identity is apparent both in the process of word formation and in the semantic content of the line. "Life," for the poet, is more than stable "property or qualities," for the "reminder" maintains his identity by remaining as changing and temporal as the process of life itself.

It would of course be stretching the point to say that Whitman excludes the more permanent, stable element from his -er nouns. Often they denote an institutionalized, time-honored occupation or profession. In "Song of Myself," we encounter such forms as *hunter, trapper, plougher, mower, swimmer,* and *diver,* while in "A Song for Oc-

---

12. *Grammar*, I.21, note *b*. For a discussion of inanimate and animate nouns formed by the -er suffix, see Hans Marchand, *The Categories and Types of Present-Day English Word-Formations: A Synchronic-Diachronic Approach,* 2d ed. (Munich: Beck'-sche, 1969), 4.30.1.

13. The definition is taken from *SOED.* "Reminder" does not appear in the 1828, 1841, or 1847 editions of *Webster's.*

cupations" Whitman uses *sawyer, rigger, grappler, glazier, confectioner, carver,* and *baker.* Because these forms denote permanent nominal categories, they tend not to produce the "verbal" effect of grammatically dynamic words. Perhaps the best collection of such stative *-er* nouns comes in the 1855 version of "I Sing the Body Electric," where Whitman uses the following forms: *swimmer, framer, rower, housekeeper, laborer, sleighdriver, wrestler, farmer, gunner, fisher, shipjoiner, bidder,* and *bearer.* Some of these words are more or less familiar than others, but all were established elements of the English lexicon in 1855.

Although Whitman uses established forms and meanings, he also uses a large number of temporary, ad hoc word formations. One type is the synthetic compound, as in this line from "Song of Myself": "Coon-seekers go through the regions of the Red river or through those drain'd by the Tennessee, or through those of the Arkansas" (320). In most compounds, two lexically established substantives combine to form a new word. And in "primary" compounds, such as the word *deer hunter,* the second member of the compound has a clearly established sense when seen out of context. In the synthetic compound, on the other hand, the second member does not usually have a clearly established, institutionalized sense when seen out of context. The result is that the compound forms a syntactic relation of *verb–direct object,* where the first member is the direct object of the verbal second member.[14] Hence in the line from "Song of Myself," *coon-seeker* denotes "one who is performing the act of seeking coons" rather than "a professional 'seeker' of coons." The distinction may seem overly fine, but the awkwardness of the second definition suggests its inappropriateness. Whitman's line evokes the image of men engaged in a temporary activity rather than in a permanent occupation. Other examples from the 1855–56 *Leaves* include *duck-shooter, pikefisher, faultfinder, fishtearer, sailmaker, blockmaker, good-doer, moneymaker, boat-sculler, raft-tender, seal-seeker, slave-maker, sparmaker,* and *anchor-lifter.* In the meanings of all these synthetic compounds, the salient element is that of action, creating several "verbal," or dynamic, effects. First, the base of the underlying syntactic relation is verbal rather than nominal; hence the compounds are all "deverbal" nouns.[15] Second, the temporary, ad hoc status of the sec-

14. See Marchand, 2.1.6.0–2.1.7.2.

15. Simply defined, a "deverbal" noun or substantive is any noun formed from a verbal base. Within the process of suffixation, any one of several suffixes can be added to a verbal base to form any one of several deverbal nouns. For instance, the suffix *-er* can be added to the verb base *work* to form the deverbal noun *worker.* The possibilities for forming this type of deverbal noun in English are legion (*Grammar,* I.24). I have

ond, deverbal element emphasizes the creative act of naming, an act that results in a "floating and movable" addition to the lexicon of American English. Third, this means that the new words are denoting new occupations and activities: Words and things are parallel in their dynamic, changing, temporal natures.

In addition to "deverbal compounds," the 1855–56 poems also contain a large number of -*er* nouns that are, like "reminder," formed from the simple suffixation of dynamic verbs. An -*er* noun formed from a dynamic verb will, in general, be grammatically dynamic. Some of the most innovative forms in "Song of Myself" are *thruster, howler, scooper, partaker, extoller, stander, provoker, reacher, hummer, buzzer, vexer, winder, moper, enfolder,* and *latherer.* Despite the fact that several of these words are listed in the 1828 *Webster's,* all of them retain their inherently active, verbal quality, especially in such words as *howler* and *buzzer,* which are formed from a sound-symbolic verb.

Because Whitman does not separate the howler from the act of howling, personal identity becomes, as in the case of the synthetic compound, a function of activity. An instance of this identity/activity equivalence occurs in a section of eighteen lines in the 1856 version of "Song of the Broad-Axe," where Whitman gives an extended account of the poet's identity:

> His shape arises!
> Arrogant, masculine, naive, rowdyish,
> *Laugher, weeper, worker, idler,* citizen, country-man,
> *Saunterer* of woods, *stander* upon hills, summer *swimmer* in
>   rivers or by the sea,
> Of perfect American breed, of reckless health, his body perfect,
>   free from taint from top to toe, free forever from headache
>   and dyspepsia, clean-breathed,
> Ample-limbed, a good *feeder,* weight a hundred and eighty
>   pounds, full-bodied, six feet high, forty inches round the
>   breast and back,
> Countenance sun-burnt, bearded, calm, unrefined,
> *Reminder* of animals, *meeter* of savage and gentleman on equal
>   terms,
> Attitudes lithe and erect, costume free, neck open, of slow
>   movement on foot,
> *Passer* of his right arm round the shoulders of his friends,
>   companion of the street,

---

analyzed Whitman's use of one type of deverbal noun in "The 'Real Grammar': Deverbal Style in 'Song of Myself,'" *American Literature* 56 (1984): 1–16.

Persuader always of people to give him their sweetest touches,
and never their meanest,
A Manhattanese bred, fond of Brooklyn, fond of Broadway, fond
of the life of the wharves and the great ferries,
Enterer everywhere, welcomed everywhere, easily understood
after all,
Never offering others, always offering himself, corroborating his
phrenology,
Voluptuous, inhabitive, combative, conscientious, alimentive,
intuitive, of copious friendship, sublimity, firmness, self-
esteem, comparison, individuality, form, locality, eventuality,
Avowing by life, manners, works, to contribute illustrations of
results of The States,
Teacher of the unquenchable creed, namely, egotism,
Inviter of others continually henceforth to try their strength
against his.

$$(248[1]-[18]; \text{ my emphasis})$$

The *-er* noun is a salient feature of the passage, and Whitman calls
attention to the form by beginning eight lines with it. In the third
line, three pairs represent three gradations of the stative/dynamic
relationship. The first ("laugher, weeper") is dynamic, emphasizing
the opposed acts of laughing and weeping; the second ("worker,
idler") is stative, but the stative quality is partially undercut by the
proximity to the preceding pair; and the third ("citizen, country-
man") is overwhelmingly stative. Thus the third line moves from dynamic to stative, from temporary activities to permanent roles.

Ten of the remaining eleven agential nouns occur as heads of
noun phrases.[16] Of the ten, only *teacher* designates a permanent occupation or state. Even though *swimmer* and *feeder* are also established members of the lexicon, they evoke a sense of activity rather
than a sense of being. By using *teacher* in the same way as the other
eight nouns, Whitman blurs the distinction between stative and dynamic, established and improvised forms. In the fourth line, for example, the first two noun phrases denote "one who is sauntering the
woods and standing upon hills," and the two agential nouns, *saun-*

16. The noun phrase—"that element which typically functions as subject, object,
and complement" (*Grammar*, 4.1)—can be extremely short (*"The girl* is my sister.") or
indefinitely long (*"The pretty girl standing on the corner with two cigarettes in her mouth*
is my sister."). In both examples, the word "girl" is the *head* of the noun phrase, for it
is the component "around which the other components cluster and which dictates
concord and (for the most part) other kinds of congruence with the rest of the sentence
outside the noun phrase" (*Grammar*, 13.2).

terer and *stander*, though they appear in the 1847 *Webster's*, denote dynamic qualities. As in the third line, the dynamic quality of the *-er* form tends to rub off on the following agential nouns. Hence the "summer *swimmer* in rivers or by the sea" assumes the dynamic quality of the two noun phrases preceding it.

Whitman creates a similar effect with *teacher*, which would seem to be as institutionalized as an agential noun could be. The five *-er* nouns preceding the line are all dynamic forms: *reminder, meeter, passer, persuader,* and *enterer.* Of these five nouns, *meeter, passer, persuader,* and *enterer* appear in the 1847 *Webster's*, but Whitman does not use *passer* in Webster's sense of "a passenger," nor does he use *enterer* in the sense of "one who is making a beginning." Instead, Whitman's nouns denote concrete, dynamic, usually physical actions. Moreover, the five nouns alternate between temporary, dynamic forms (*reminder, passer, enterer*) and more permanent, stative forms (*meeter, persuader*). After the noun phrase with *teacher* as head, another dynamic, though lexically established, agential noun follows: "*Inviter* of others." Because of the mixture of dynamic agential nouns, even *teacher* tends to mean, in Whitman's "Real Grammar," a person who is engaged in the activity of teaching.

By mingling the more dynamic, temporary agential nouns with the more stative, permanent agential nouns, Whitman blurs the distinction between flowing activity and stable identity. The direct result of the innovative ways in which he exploits the products and possibilities of English word formation, Whitman's dynamic deverbal style becomes a formal equivalent of his theory of linguistic and spiritual evolution, the "Real Grammar." Although the poet continually nominalizes a verbal base, the "naturally" stative character of the noun tends to assume the dynamic character of the verb. In the "Real Grammar" of concepts, this means that personal identity tends to assume the temporal, flowing character normally associated with actions and activities.

Whitman's representation of human identity as essentially dynamic and temporal relates directly to his evolutionary theory of language. Even in the 1855 poem "There Was a Child Went Forth," which does not employ the kinds of foreign borrowings and word formations I have been discussing, Whitman shows how basic the theory is to his vision of the individual's identity in an ever-shifting world of time and space:

There was a child went forth every day,
And the first object he looked upon and received with wonder or
  pity or love or dread, that object he became,

> And that object became a part of him for the day or a certain
>   part of the day . . . or for many years or stretching cycles of
>   years.
>
> (1–3)

In this first stanza the child's identity is a function of his power to identify with the world of things, and the act of identifying gives both child and things a life beyond the present, a life of "stretching cycles of years."

The following stanzas demonstrate the child's ability to become "all the changes of city and country wherever he went" (18). As diverse concrete images of human activities succeed one another, the poet intimates that the child's becoming is an act of gathering experiences. This process reaches a climax in the child's first thought:

> Affection that will not be gainsay'd, the sense of what is real,
>   the thought if after all it should prove unreal,
> The doubts of day-time and the doubts of night-time, the
>   curious whether and how,
> Whether that which appears so is so, or is it all flashes and
>   specks?
> Men and women crowding fast in the streets, if they are not
>   flashes and specks what are they?
>
> (27–30)

It is significant that the process of identification is halted by a thought that revolves around the problem of definition. Are things as they appear, or are they entirely different from their appearance? More crucial for the budding poet, if there is doubt as to the reality of things, then there must be equal doubt as to the ability of language to represent that reality. Hence the turning point of the poem hinges upon the relationship of things to words.

Whitman's answer to this moment of crisis is to move directly into a short, nine-line catalogue of concrete objects, as if the flow of the words in the catalogue will serve to substantiate the things they represent:

> The streets themselves and the facades of houses, and goods in
>   the windows,
> Vehicles, teams, the heavy-plank'd wharves, the huge crossing
>   at the ferries,
> The village on the highland seen from afar at sunset, the river
>   between,

Shadows, aureola and mist, the light falling on roofs and gables
of white or brown two miles off,
The schooner near by sleepily dropping down the tide, the little
boat slack-tow'd astern,
The hurrying tumbling waves, quick-broken crests, slapping,
The strata of color'd clouds, the long bar of maroon-tint away
solitary by itself, the spread of purity it lies motionless in,
The horizon's edge, the flying sea-crow, the fragrance of salt
marsh and shore mud,
These became part of that child who went forth every day, and
who now goes, and will always go forth every day.

(31–39)

This passage catalogues the scenes of New York and Brooklyn, scenes
that will become central to later poems like "Crossing Brooklyn
Ferry," "Out of the Cradle Endlessly Rocking," and "As I Ebb'd with
the Ocean of Life." The passage illustrates Whitman's technique of
mixing stative and dynamic forms, for there is as much emphasis on
the "streets themselves," the "heavy-plank'd wharves," and the "fragrance of salt marsh and shore mud" as there is on the movement of
the schooner "sleepily dropping down the tide," the "hurrying tumbling waves," the "slapping," and the "flying sea-crow." The tumble of
present participles toward the end of the passage does create an effect of motion and change, but it is balanced by the imagery of stable
objects. Finally, the last line of the poem places all of the changing
objects within a temporal frame of past, present, and future. Whitman's answer to the terrible doubt of appearances, then, relies upon
the image of orderly, progressive temporal movement. By projecting
the child's act of daily identification into the eternal future of "will
always," Whitman implicitly avows his faith in the "stamina of
things" and in the ability of words to represent things. That faith is
based both upon the constant factor of the child's identity, which is
the activity of identification, and upon the constant deferral of meaning, which is the poet's characteristic response to the word/thing
problem. This circular, layered relationship is even more complicated in the 1855 version of the poem, which ends with the line, "And
these become of him or her that peruses them now" (39[1]). The verbs
"become" and "peruse" are dynamic, and they indicate that through
the act of reading the reader becomes part of the child's continual
change. By insisting that the reader share the child's act of identifying with the changing world of things, Whitman makes both the
reader's identity and the meaning of the poem depend upon the twin
acts of "becoming" and "perusing." But the asserted "ensemble" of

child, poet, and reader—of word and thing—depends upon Whitman's vision of a continual, deferring temporal flow into the "vista" of the future.

The final process of word formation Whitman employs in the poems of 1855–56 is conversion, and the characteristic form he creates is the deverbal noun. This is, of course, the same type of noun that we have seen in the processes of suffixation and compounding, but in this case the deverbal noun looks exactly like the verbal base from which it is formed. So, for example, the deverbal noun *laugh* looks exactly like the verbal base *laugh*. Whitman's style in the 1855–56 poems is marked by the high frequency of deverbal nouns, and this tendency runs directly counter to the English language in general, which commonly uses conversion to create "denominal verbs." Furthermore, the poet tends to employ a significant number of non-lexical, improvised deverbal nouns, and these nouns retain the dynamic, processlike quality of the verbal base from which they are formed. In addition, Whitman's deverbal nouns tend to be sound-symbolic, emphasizing the combined qualities of sound and movement.[17]

We can appreciate the stylistic effects of conversion, as well as the ways in which the various types of word formations relate to one another, by considering in detail an extended example. My text, in this case, is Section 3 of the 1856 poem "Song of the Broad-Axe." The section is lengthy, covering some sixty-nine lines (25–93), but Whitman uses the semicolon to divide it into eight subsections of irregular length. To summarize quickly: The first section (25–35) develops images of pioneers; the second (36–40) meditates upon the beauty of the pioneer "types"; the third (41–44) moves into a catalogue of occupations, focusing on lumbermen; the fourth (45–60) expands into a catalogue of house-building terms; the fifth (61–66) treats shipbuilding; the sixth (67–72) delivers the scene of a city fire; the seventh (73–76) focuses upon the craftsmen who make axes; and the eighth (77–93) concludes with an extended meditation upon the ancient users of the broadax.

The first subsection contains only one deverbal noun, *outset*, which was already lexically established in the eighteenth century (*SOED*). But the poet does use his characteristic mixture of stative

17. "Deverbal Style," pp. 1–16. In establishing the lexical status of Whitman's deverbal nouns, I have used the following: *Webster's* (1828, 1841, and 1847 editions); *A Dictionary of Americanisms on Historical Principles*, ed. Mitford M. Mathews, 2 vols. (Chicago: University of Chicago Press, 1951); *A Dictionary of American English on Historical Principles*, ed. Sir William A. Craigie and James R. Hulbert, 4 vols. (Chicago: University of Chicago Press, 1938–44); and *SOED*.

and dynamic forms, for he employs the present participle to balance precariously between nominal and verbal modes:

> The log at the wood-pile, the axe supported by it,
> The sylvan hut, the vine over the doorway, the space clear'd for
>   a garden,
> The irregular *tapping* of rain down on the leaves after the storm
>   is lull'd,
> The *wailing* and *moaning* at intervals, the thought of the sea,
> The thought of ships struck in the storm and put on their beam
>   ends, and the *cutting away* of masts,
> The sentiment of the huge timbers of old-fashion'd houses and
>   barns,
> The remember'd print or narrative, the voyage at a venture of
>   men, families, goods,
> The disembarkation, the *founding* of a new city,
> The voyage of those who sought a New England and found it,
>   the *outset* anywhere,
> The settlements of the Arkansas, Colorado, Ottawa, Willamette,
> The slow progress, the scant fare, the axe, rifle, saddle-bags;
>
> > (25–35; my emphasis)

Only one of the underlined substantives seems particularly original: *Cutting away* is striking because Whitman has created a noun from a phrasal verb, "to cut away." But the lexically established participles all function in this introductory passage as images of sound, movement, and activity. The section begins with a series of noun phrases, and the grammatically stative character of the first two lines reflects the conceptually static character of the pioneer set piece. But then the scene comes alive with sounds and movements as it is invaded by the "irregular *tapping*" of the rain and the "*wailing* and *moaning*" of the wind. These sound-symbolic participles promote the effect of action on several grounds, and they lead to the series of mental actions forming the rest of the section. From the first "thought of the sea," the poet moves to ships in a storm, to "old-fashion'd houses and barns," and then on to public memories of "the *founding* of a new city." The poet's mental movement toward the past is temporary, for he proceeds to bring himself and his readers back toward the present and on into the future, much as he did in "There Was a Child Went Forth." Here, that vistalike movement is signaled by the phrase "the slow progress." Thus the introductory movement of Section 3 is stylistically similar to the conclusion of "There Was a Child Went Forth," for in both poems the balance between stative and dynamic forms is struck by the image of "progress."

The "slow progress" of Whitman's deverbal nouns continues through the next two sections (36–44). After three parallel lines focusing on "the beauty" of American pioneers, the poet interprets the pioneers as exemplars of "the loose *drift* of character, the *inkling* through random types, the solidification" (40). The word *drift* is a deverbal noun formed by conversion of the dynamic verb "to drift," but it is a time-honored member of the English lexicon. The word appears to mean a "tendency; aim; main force," but it also retains the dynamic sense of "a driving; a force impelling or urging forward" (*Webster's*). If these two definitions are at play, they would combine to create an image of dynamic, natural change, a change that would be a further indication of "slow progress." The same can be asserted of *inkling*, which is a deverbal noun formed from the obsolete verb "to inkle." The *inkling* is "a hint or whisper; an intimation" (*Webster's*) of the "solidification" of American ideals within concrete personalities or types. The sound-symbolic quality of the frequentative base applies equally well to the deverbal noun, so that *inkling* becomes an active, dynamic form. Although the second section ends with this dynamic imagery of progress, the accumulation of deverbal nouns is slow. The third section contains only three, and they are all lexically established: "the occasional *snapping*" (42); "the sweet *taste* of supper" (44); and "the *talk*" (44). The third section does have elements of dynamic change within it, but they are more the result of the poet's random cataloguing than the product of his deverbal style.

In the fourth section, however, the poet develops fully his use of the deverbal noun. Focusing on the images of house building, Whitman combines the various types of word formations to create a vivid, dynamic portrait of progress:

> The *house-builder* at work in cities or anywhere,
> The preparatory *jointing, squaring, sawing, mortising,*
> The *hoist-up* of beams, the *push* of them in their places, *laying*
>   them regular,
> *Setting* the studs by their tenons in the mortises according as
>   they were prepared,
> The *blows* of mallets and hammers, the attitudes of the men,
>   their curv'd limbs,
> *Bending, standing,* astride the beams, *driving* in pins, *holding* on
>   by posts and braces,
> The hook'd arm over the plate, the other arm *wielding* the axe,
> The floor-men *forcing* the planks close to be nail'd,

Their postures *bringing* their weapons downward on the *bearers*,
The echoes *resounding* through the vacant building;
The huge storehouse carried up in the city well under way,
The six *framing-men*, two in the middle and two at each end,
    carefully *bearing* on their shoulders a heavy stick for a cross-
    beam,
The crowded line of masons with trowels in their right hands
    rapidly *laying* the long side-wall, two hundred feet from front
    to rear,
The flexible *rise* and *fall* of backs, the continual *click* of the
    trowels *striking* the bricks,
The bricks one after another each laid so workmanlike in its
    place, and set with a *knock* of the trowel-handle,
The piles of materials, the mortar on the mortar-boards, and
    the steady *replenishing* by the hod-men;

(45–60)

The only nonlexical form in this passage is *hoist-up*, which uses conversion of the phrasal verb in much the same way that *cutting away* did in the first section. Whitman's verbal art is in this instance not so much his invention of original word formations as it is his ability to exploit the possibilities presented by the structures of the language. So, for instance, he uses five more deverbal nouns formed by conversion: *the push, rise and fall, click,* and *knock.* All six deverbal nouns are dynamic, for all six retain the grammatically dynamic, verbal quality of the base. Further, the last two in the list are sound-symbolic; the sound /k/ at the end of a monosyllabic word of appropriate meaning expresses "quick, abrupt, short-stopping or explosive noises and/or rapid, short or short-stopping movements."[18] In addition to this inherent sound symbolism, the alliteration and assonance of the line containing three of the six nouns contribute to the stylistic effect of dynamic motion and sound: "The flexible rise and fall of backs, the continual click of the trowels striking the bricks." The repetition of the /k/ sound in "flexible," "backs," "continual," "striking," and "bricks" adds to the verbal dynamism of the line, and it causes even such lexical forms as *rise* and *fall* to take on a dynamic, active quality.

More important than the deverbal nouns formed by conversion is the present participle, which occurs nineteen times in just sixteen lines. Many of the participles function as verbal forms:

18. Marchand, 7.8.

The hook'd arm over the plate, the other arm *wielding* the axe,
The floor-men *forcing* the planks close to be nail'd,
Their postures *bringing* their weapons downward on the
    bearers,
The echoes *resounding* through the vacant building;

(51–54)

In these lines the participle functions as an abbreviated form of the present progressive tense; in each instance, there is an implicit "to be," so that we can read the lines as "the other arm [is] wielding the axe," "the floor-men [are] forcing the planks," and so on. Because the present progressive tense indicates the dynamic aspect of the verb, the present participles create the impression of dynamic, ongoing activity.

This verbal, dynamic effect is also engendered by participles used as nouns. In the line "The preparatory *jointing, squaring, sawing, mortising,*" for instance, the participles function as deverbal nouns, for they are clearly associated with the dynamic verbal bases from which they are formed. The peculiar grammatical status of the present participle—its ability to be both verb and noun, as it were—is particularly striking in this line: "*Bending, standing,* astride the beams, *driving* in pins, *holding* on by posts and braces" (50). The participles describe the actions and positions of the working men, but Whitman seems as concerned with the active, verbal quality of the words as he is with the men who engage in the actions. Thus the participles, which are ostensibly adjectives, function as moments of action. And this type of "floating and movable" use of grammatical categories allows Whitman to combine activity and identity as two sides of the same coin.

The merging of identity and activity is also evident in the two *-er* nouns, *house-builder* and *bearers.* The first is a primary compound, and the form *builder* is a long-established deverbal noun. Hence the first line of the section would seem to begin in a grammatically stative way, even though this effect may be altered by the adverbial phrase "at work" that follows the agential compound. The second is also lexically established, but Whitman's use of the word in this context is innovative: "Their postures bringing their weapons downward on the bearers" (53). "Bearers" refers to floor joists, but in context the word emphasizes the dynamic act of bearing the weight of the floorboards.

The next three sections of the catalogue employ this same mixture of stative and dynamic forms. The section on shipbuilding, for instance, uses such forms as *spar-makers, swarming, the swing, shap-*

ing, crackle, and *flying.* These are dynamic, deverbal forms, and they combine with nouns like "wharves, bridges, piers, bulk-heads, floats, stays against the sea" (66) to effect a continual motion between objects and actions. In the sixth section, the action-filled scene of the city fire, Whitman employs a preponderance of participial forms, as well as such deverbal conversions as "the *rise* and *fall*" (69) and "the *crash* and *cut away*" (71). When this scene gives way to the meditation on the makers of the broadax, however, the *-er* agential noun takes over in forms like *forger, user, maker, welder, temperer,* and *chooser.* As in the case of *bearers,* these agential nouns emphasize activity as much as occupation or position.

The seven sections I have examined display little evidence of a thematic or formal progression. The sections are connected to one another, and together they form a loose "ensemble," but there is no strict logic behind the shift from lumbermen to house builders, from house builders to ship builders, or from ship builders to firemen. The transitions between sections in the catalogue are fluid and unforced, and it seems that the "loose drift" or "slow progress" in the catalogue itself is an enactment of the "slow progress" of American types.

The last section of the catalogue supports this idea, and it also shows how Whitman reinscribes the idea of progressive change to conclude Section 3 of the poem. Having devoted seven sections to the present, Whitman turns in the eighth to the past:

> The shadowy processions of the portraits of the past *users* also,
> The primal patient mechanics, the architects and engineers,
> The far-off Assyrian edifice and Mizra edifice,
> The Roman lictors *preceding* the consuls,
> The antique European warrior with his axe in combat,
> The uplifted arm, the *clatter* of blows on the helmeted head,
> The *death-howl,* the limpsy *tumbling* body, the *rush* of friend and foe thither,
> The siege of revolted lieges determin'd for liberty,
> The summons to surrender, the *battering* at castle gates, the truce and parley,
> The sack of an old city in its time,
> The *bursting in* of mercenaries and bigots tumultuously and disorderly,
> *Roar,* flames, blood, drunkenness, madness,
> Goods freely rifled from houses and temples, *screams* of women in the *gripe* of brigands,
> Craft and thievery of *camp-followers,* men *running,* old persons *despairing,*

The hell of war, the cruelties of creeds,
The list of all executive deeds and words just or unjust,
The power of personality just or unjust.

(77–93)

The image of the "shadowy processions" recalls the earlier phrase "the slow progress." Indeed, the structure of the passage is temporal and progressivist; beginning with "primal patient mechanics," the poet proceeds chronologically through representatives of civilization: the Assyrians, the Persian-Indian empire based on Mithraism, and the Roman empire. The "European warrior" brings on a host of images pertaining to the sack of Rome and to revolts against feudal lords. Thus the passage gives a concrete image of "slow progress," for it details the ways in which the barbarian hordes broke up "the crystalline structure of the classical mould" (*Rambles*, p. 271).

It is surely no accident that Whitman's version of political history in "Song of the Broad-Axe" parallels his version of linguistic history in *Rambles Among Words*. Both histories display the "power of personality just or unjust," and both show the ever-increasing freedom of spirit and of language. In the conclusion of Section 3, the poet employs several deverbal forms to enact this dynamic movement. So, for instance, the sound-symbolic words *clatter, tumbling, rush, battering, bursting in, roar, screams,* and *gripe* contribute to the effect of dynamic action, and this dynamic action is to be seen within the context of a larger historical movement, one which Whitman always interprets as progressive and ameliorative. When the poet closes Section 3 with the last three short lines, from which all deverbal forms are conspicuously absent, he brings the dynamic catalogue to a temporary stasis.

The reader may well ask whether we have arrived at a clear assessment of the "words just or unjust, / The power of personality just or unjust" as they are displayed in this long passage. The answer is implied by the kinds of images Whitman has chosen to develop in the eight sections, but it is perhaps clearer in the phrase "the power of personality." Whether it appears just or unjust, the power of personality is constant, and the main characteristic of that power is to be able to change, to act. Whitman does not discount the "hell of war, the cruelties of creeds," but the temporal structure of the conclusion implies that all of the hell and cruelties of the past have contributed to the perfect freedom of his present.

The remaining nine sections of "Song of the Broad-Axe" continue to play upon that central contradiction, but the contradiction is never so much resolved as deferred. Thus the poem concludes with the image of an ideal Democracy, but that image is more "shape" than substance:

> The main shapes arise!
> Shapes of Democracy total, result of centuries,
> Shapes ever projecting other shapes,
> Shapes of turbulent manly cities,
> Shapes of the friends and home-givers of the whole earth,
> Shapes bracing the earth and braced with the whole earth.
>
> (249–54)

Even though this passage purports to give an image of "ensemble," of the mutual bracing and being braced of America and the rest of the "whole earth," it does not resolve the central contradiction between "ensemble" and "vista." The "main shapes" of a "total Democracy" are invoked, but at the same time the poet asserts that the shapes are "ever projecting other shapes." The participle *projecting* is, of course, dynamic and verbal, and the image of an ongoing projection of shapes contradicts the sculptural closure of the poem. This open-ended, vistalike conclusion is further suggested by the line that follows in the 1856 version of the poem: "Shapes of a hundred Free States, begetting another hundred north and south" (251[1]). The image of a hundred states clearly echoes the 1856 "Letter" to Emerson: "America is not finished, perhaps never will be; now America is a divine true sketch. There are Thirty-Two States sketched—the population thirty millions. In a few years there will be Fifty States. Again in a few years there will be A Hundred States, the population hundreds of millions, the freshest and freest of men."[19] The problem with Whitman's enthusiastic vision is that the idea of the United States as only a "divine true sketch" contradicts the idea of the country as a complete "ensemble." Even in the last line of the poem, the image of America as containing "shapes bracing the earth and braced with the whole earth" is utopian and visionary, for the poet claims to see a "divine true sketch" that most of his readers would be hard-pressed to recognize.

Whitman's "Real Grammar" is, in the final analysis, as much a part of his rhetoric of deferral as it is a program for linguistic and spiritual progress. The innovative use of foreign borrowings and word formations enacts the deferral and the progress, and both movements are tied to the central opposition between "ensemble" and "vista." These sets of oppositions are essentially irresolvable, but

19. *CRE*, p. 736.

the irresolvability produces a host of formal and thematic insights on the part of both poet and reader. I have developed one particular insight in this chapter—the irreconcilable conflict between stative and dynamic forms, indicating the irresolvable conflict between identity and activity, permanence and change. But the "Real Grammar" allows for other perspectives and other insights. In chapter 3, I move to the grammatical level of syntax in order to explore some of those possibilities.

3

The "Real Grammar": Syntactic Parallelism in *Leaves of Grass*, 1855–1856

The Real Grammar will be that which declares itself a nucleus of the spirit of the laws, with liberty to all to carry out the spirit of the laws, even by violating them.

—The Primer of Words

Whitman's concept of the "Real Grammar" confers, as we have seen, a great deal of freedom on both the poet and poetic diction. The "liberty" of the spirit affords creative space for the importation of foreign loan words, for the application of those words to special situations, and for the formation of new words to enrich the vocabulary of American English. The poetic effect of that liberty, furthermore, is to establish an essentially irresolvable conflict between the conceptual and grammatical poles of action and being. When Whitman's "Real Grammar" moves to the level of syntactic structures, similar conflicts arise from the "liberty" the Grammar "declares" for itself.

The most obvious of these conflicts concerns the distinction between meter and rhythm. Whitman's "Real Grammar" is based upon the "passage from synthesis to analysis" in the history of the English language, a history that the poet reads as "breaking up the crystalline structure of the classic mould, freeing the grammatical forms from their absorption in the terminations of nouns and verbs" (*Rambles*, p. 271). In poetics, the "crystalline structure of the classic mould" corresponds to the isolating frame created by the metrical form of the poem, while the "freeing" of forms corresponds to the emphasis on rhythm as the particular verse instances within a metrical scheme.[1]

Whitman's most famous statement on metric form appears in the 1855 Preface, where he claims that "the rhyme and uniformity of perfect poems show the free growth of metrical laws, and bud from them as unerringly and loosely as lilacs and roses on a bush, and take shapes as compact as the shapes of chestnuts and oranges, and melons and pears, and shed the perfume impalpable to form" (*PW,* II, 439–40). The phrase "metrical laws" recalls immediately the "spirit of the laws" that is the "Real Grammar." And in both linguistic and literary form, the key is the "free growth" of the laws, which will obey only the "nucleus of the spirit" and violate the laws themselves if necessary. This means that Whitman's prosody will be based not upon the tradition of the metrical "crystalline structure," but rather upon the organic rhythm of the "Real Grammar."

One point to make at once, however, is that Whitman's concept of organic rhythm is an enabling fiction. The passage from the 1855 Preface itself establishes a relatively uniform rhythm, but it certainly does not do so by some mystically "organic" means. Whitman's twin conception of organic language and organic form is militantly blind to the actual workings of poetic language. In this passage, the sentence establishes a pattern of coordinate syntax and parallel phrasing:

The rhyme and uniformity of perfect poems

    show the free growth of metrical laws,   *and*
    bud from them

        as unerringly and loosely
        as lilacs and roses on a bush,

                and

   take shapes

      as compact as the shapes of
             chestnuts *and* oranges,

1. For a lucid discussion of the distinction, see John Hollander, *Vision and Resonance: Two Senses of Poetic Form* (New York: Oxford University Press, 1975), pp. 135–64 and 187–211.

and

melons and pears,

and

shed the perfume impalpable to form.

This admittedly crude schematization points out several instances of syntactic parallelism. First, the series of active, dynamic verbs moves from the palpable to the impalpable, from visible form to invisible perfume, by way of the budding and taking shape of the organic metaphor. Second, the parallel images of flowers and fruits enact the loose rhythm of syntactic structure; the random quality of the three noun pairs counterpoints the progressive structure of the dynamic verbs. Finally, the parallel phrasing of comparison ("as X as Y") establishes two relationships between dynamic and stative forms. Alliteration joins "unerringly and loosely" to "lilacs and roses" in a subtle rhetorical chiasmus; moreover, the adverbs parallel the simple adjective "compact." Here the liberty of the dynamic adverbs counterpoints the form of the stative nouns and adjective.

The sentence from the 1855 Preface raises several points, then, about Whitman's "Real Grammar" of poetic form. It demonstrates, first of all, that the poet wishes to substitute rhythm for meter in order to escape the "crystalline structure" of traditional verse forms. Second, it shows that the organic metaphor serves as a mask for a formally revolutionary move, disguising the deliberate patterning of language with the language of liberation. In addition, it indicates that syntactic parallelism is the rhythmic principle of Whitman's language. In order to understand the "Real Grammar" of Whitman's syntactic prosody, therefore, we must construct a prosodic grammar that will account both for the "rhythmical frame" of the poems and for the ways in which Whitman's language escapes the frame it sets.

Gay Wilson Allen's attempt at providing such a rhythmical frame has been the most influential of the last fifty years. Using the work of Bishop Robert Lowth and Samuel R. Driver, Allen posited four types of syntactic parallelism as the basic structural units of Whitman's free-verse rhythm, and those four types placed *Leaves of Grass* in the tradition of the poetical and prophetical books of the Bible.[2] Recently

2. Allen's argument is set forth in the following: "Biblical Analogies for Walt Whitman's Prosody," *Revue anglo-americaine* 10 (1933): 490–507; *American Prosody* (New York: American Book, 1935), pp. 217–43; and *The New Walt Whitman Handbook*, pp. 207–48. Allen's account has become so generally accepted that it is repeated in the article "Parallelism," *Princeton Encyclopedia of Poetry and Poetics*, ed. Alex Preminger (Princeton, N.J.: Princeton University Press, 1974). Allen's four types of syntactic parallelism

I have shown in some detail that the four types of syntactic parallelism do not provide an adequate account of Whitman's rhythmical frame. I have also suggested that the rhythmical frame in Whitman's poetry is a sequence of coordinate clauses, from two to four lines long, which features some form of syntactic parallelism between lines. Finally, I have suggested a new taxonomy of Whitman's catalogues, his escapes from the rhythmical frame. This taxonomy is based upon the syntactic groups of the *phrasal* catalogue, the *clausal* catalogue, and the *mixed*, or phrasal/clausal, catalogue.[3]

The opposition between phrase and clause is the basis for the taxonomy, and it turns upon the grammatical distinction between the stative and dynamic aspects of nouns and verbs. The traditional definition of a phrase is a sequence of words that functions syntactically as a noun, adjective, or adverb, and that therefore contains no finite verb element. A clause, on the other hand, does contain the finite verb element, and it therefore functions syntactically as both subject and predicate. In terms of the stative/dynamic opposition, we might expect the phrase to be naturally stative, since it has no verbal element, whereas the clause would be naturally dynamic, since it does contain a verbal element. This hypothesis accords with the frequency of finite verb elements: A relatively low frequency of finite verb elements tends to produce a stative effect, removing the content of a given statement from the temporal realm of tense inflections.[4] As we have seen in chapter 2, however, the grammatical distinction does not designate a hard and fast rule, but rather a general tendency. And the example from the 1855 Preface indicates that Whitman's practice is to mix stative and dynamic forms in a complex play of counterpoint.[5]

---

are based upon the work of Robert Lowth, who posited three types of parallelism in *Isaiah, A New Translation; with a Preliminary Dissertation, and Notes Critical, Philological, and Explanatory,* 5th ed. (Edinburgh: George Caw, 1807), and in the nineteenth lecture of *De sacra poesie Hebraeorum,* first published in 1753. For an English translation of the latter work, see *Lectures on the Sacred Poetry of the Hebrews,* ed. Calvin E. Stowe (Boston: Crocker and Brewster, 1829), pp. 154–66. A second source for Allen's taxonomy is Samuel R. Driver, *An Introduction to the Literature of the Old Testament* (New York: Scribner's, 1920).

3. " 'The Free Growth of Metrical Laws': Syntactic Parallelism in 'Song of Myself,' " *Style* 18 (1984): 27–42.

4. See Borroff, pp. 93–95, and *Grammar,* 2.11, 3.10–15.

5. Modern grammarians define traditional infinitive, present participial, and past participial phrases as "non-finite verb clauses" (*Grammar,* 2.11, 11.3). Non-finite verb clauses can show either a stative or a dynamic aspect (*Grammar,* 3.23, 3.36). Thus the traditional phrase reveals a wealth of possibilities for the mixture of stative and dynamic forms.

The vistalike, temporally dynamic aspects of Whitman's poetics become clear in the poet's use of catalogues in the 1855 poem "The Sleepers," where the catalogue is a key element both in the poem's structure and in Whitman's self-representation. Howard J. Waskow has pointed out that "The Sleepers" is a companion piece to "Song of Myself," for in both poems the speaker is involved in performing an action.[6] The twin relationship between the poems is apparent in the first line of "The Sleepers": "I wander all night in my vision" echoes Section 33 of "Song of Myself," where the poet asserts, "I am afoot with my vision" (716). Because of this initial echo, we might expect "The Sleepers" to use the same catalogue techniques for the same effects created in "Song of Myself."[7] But the speaker of "The Sleepers" is not simply energizing himself through the rhetorical act of speaking, an act that constitutes a poetic self. In the first lines of "Song of Myself," the speaker is a "loafer"; in the beginning of "The Sleepers," he is already moving:

> I wander all night in my vision,
> Stepping with light feet, swiftly and noiselessly stepping and
>   stopping,
> Bending with open eyes over the shut eyes of sleepers,
> Wandering and confused, lost to myself, ill-assorted,
>   contradictory,
> Pausing, gazing, bending, and stopping.
>
>   (1–5)

The first stanza of the poem establishes a rhythmical frame based upon coordination and syntactic parallelism. The clause "I wander all night in my vision" sets the frame for the series of phrasal parallels. These participial phrases form a paratactic sequence mod-

---

6. *Whitman: Explorations in Form* (Chicago: University of Chicago Press, 1966), p. 157. Waskow distinguishes between monodrama and dramatic monologue, using the former as a "convenient rubric for poems in which the focus is an action and the mask that of an 'actor,' a speaker involved at the present time in an action, not describing an action and giving us guides into it, like a narrator, but actually *going through* the action" (p. 139).

7. See " 'Free Growth' " for an account of how the three types of catalogues relate to the creation and actifying of the poetic self in "Song of Myself." For the prevailing interpretation of the poem as the process of creation of a poetic self, see Ivan Marki, *The Trial of the Poet: An Interpretation of the First Edition of "Leaves of Grass"* (New York: Columbia University Press, 1976), pp. 195–205, John B. Mason, "Walt Whitman's Catalogues: Rhetorical Means for Two Journeys in 'Song of Myself,' " *American Literature* 45 (1973): 34–49, and Thomas J. Rountree, "Whitman's Indirect Expression and Its Application to 'Song of Myself,' " *PMLA* 73 (1958): 549–55.

ifying both the speaker and the speaker's action, and the framing effect of the initial clause is strengthened by the anaphora of the modifying participles: "Stepping," "Bending," "Wandering," and "Pausing" function as the primary repetends, and "Wandering" is particularly important because it repeats the verb of the clausal frame.

This description of the syntactic rhythm of the first stanza emphasizes the order of Whitman's free verse. But it is equally important to stress the effects of disorder created by the rhythm of syntactic parallelism. On the most basic semantic level, the words themselves emphasize movement and action, but they also denote movement without direction. A major concern for the poet in this lyric of crisis is to find a personal center for the "wandering" self. But the parallelisms that frame his concern also provide the possibility of escape from the frame. Thus, for instance, the last two lines of the stanza shift from the repetition of dynamic verbal forms to a seemingly chaotic whirl of stative forms. The repetition of the image of "wandering" gives way to "confused, lost to myself, ill-assorted, contradictory" (4). By shifting from present participial forms to past participial forms, Whitman moves from the representation of an active self to the representation of a passive self. The passage becomes quite literally "contradictory," in the sense that it seems to speak against itself. But this "ill-assorted" use of parallelism accords perfectly with the performative quality of Whitman's poetics, for the syntax mimes the representation of an "ill-assorted" self.

The last line of the stanza brings us back to the present participle and to action, but the actions represented are hesitant. There is no celebration in the acts of "pausing, gazing, bending, and stopping." Indeed, the tentative quality of the actions undermines the poet's return to the dynamic verbal form. This is especially true of the last term in the series. The terminal repetition of "stopping" (2, 5) contradicts the anaphoric repetition of dynamic present participles. Unlike the final line of "Song of Myself," which it clearly echoes, the act of "stopping" threatens to block the performing of the speech act. At the threshold of "The Sleepers," then, Whitman halts, and the effect of this pause is to raise doubts about the poet's ability to "loose the stop from your throat" ("Song of Myself," 84).

Whitman solves the problem he sets himself in the first stanza by constructing a transcendental self out of the act of "wandering." That is, he forges a poetic identity by going through the action of identifying with the sleepers in the poem. The answer to the problem of poetic identity thus revolves about the relationship of the many to the one, the world of persons and objects to the poet.

This problematic premise for the poem is evident in a prose

manuscript notebook that is the basis for "The Sleepers."[8] On the first leaf of the notebook, Whitman considers the future realization of the soul, and he does so in terms that recall his pronouncements upon the "Real Grammar":

> No doubt the efflux of the soul comes through beautiful gates of laws that at some future period perhaps a few score millions of years, we may understand better.—At present, its tide is what folks call capricious, and cannot well be traced. Why as I look in the railroad car at some half turned face, do I love that woman? Though she is neither young nor fair complexioned?—She remains in my memory afterward for a year, and I calm myself to sleep at night by thinking of her. (*DBN*, III, 764)[9]

This passage begins with a meditation on the "vista" of spiritual evolution, but it quickly moves to the mysterious affection Whitman feels for an unknown woman and, from there, to his memory of the woman and its calming influence: "I calm myself to sleep at night by thinking of her." The "efflux of the soul" remains a mystery, a divine tendency reminiscent of Emerson's meditation in "Experience," but it is somehow connected to the poet's unspoken love for other persons.[10]

A second manuscript passage clarifies this vague connection. On

8. The notebook is part of Container 38 in the Charles E. Feinberg Collection, housed in the Library of Congress Manuscript Division. It is a small, paper-covered notebook containing eleven full leaves and one half-leaf of ruled paper and ruled margins. A similar notebook is the source for much of "Starting from Paumanok," and yet another twelve-leaf notebook contains a few trial lines for "The Sleepers." The "Sleepers" notebook is edited by White in *DBN*, III, 764–70. My quotations from the notebook are taken from this edition, but I have silently omitted the various strike-outs and false starts to present a coherent transcription of the given passage.

9. *DBN*, III, 764. The phrase "efflux of the soul," as well as much of the imagery of attraction to strangers, appears in Section 7 of "Song of the Open Road," published in the 1856 edition. It would appear that the first four leaves of the "Sleepers" notebook form trial lines later used in the 1856 poem.

10. Writing about the concept of "Succession" as one of the seven "Lords of Life," for example, Emerson strikes the same tone of mystery: "The secret of the illusoriness is in the necessity of a succession of moods or objects. Gladly we would anchor, but the anchorage is quicksand. This onward trick of nature is too strong for us: *Pero si muove.* When at night I look at the moon and stars, I seem stationary, and they to hurry. Our love of the real draws us to permanence, but health of body consists in circulation, and sanity of mind in variety or facility of association. We need change of objects. Dedication to one thought is quickly odious." *The Complete Works of Ralph Waldo Emerson*, ed. Edward Waldo Emerson (Boston: Houghton Mifflin, 1903), III, 5. We might be tempted to infer from this passage that Whitman's "love of the real" was more focused upon the human than was Emerson's abstract lyricism.

the fifth leaf of the "Sleepers" notebook, Whitman returns to the relationship of the many to the one:

> While the curtain is down at the opera, while I swim in the bath, while I wait for my friend at the corner, while I behold and am beheld by people; I speak little or nothing; I make no gifts to them: I do not turn as much as my neck or pat my instep . . . we never met before—never heard or shall hear names nor dates nor employments.—With all this, some god walks in noiseless and resistless, and takes their hearts out of their breasts, and gives them to me for ever.—Often I catch the sign; and oftener, no doubt, it flies by me as unknown as my neighbor's dreams. (*DBN*, III, 765–66)

"Some god walks in noiseless and resistless." The "god" figures the transcendental or poetic self, and the figure mediates between the poet and the numberless other, between the one and the many. But the presence of the god may fly by the poet, as "unknown as my neighbor's dreams." So the poem "The Sleepers" would seem to be Whitman's attempt to "catch the sign" of the "god," both in himself and in other sleepers.

Whitman's strategy for catching the sign involves, first and foremost, the act of identifying with the other sleepers. Thus the next five stanzas of the poem move away from the "ill-assorted" speaker to the vision of the many. And this movement coordinates with the further development of the rhythmical frame. The five stanzas are comprised of two, three, and four lines, and the number of lines creates a dream-like, tentative effect, in much the same way that the three-line and two-line stanzas of Section 11 of "Song of Myself" mark the transition from the rowdy, good-natured "loafer" to the hesitant observer of the "twenty-eight young men."

The first of the five stanzas is the shortest: "How solemn they look there, stretch'd and still, / How quiet they breathe, the little children in their cradles" (6–7). The rhythmical frame is set by the paired clauses and the anaphoric repetition of "How." The stanza creates a tone of hushed exclamation because the frame is not developed any further. The tone is signally appropriate to the situation presented in the first stanza of the poem, and it has its origins in the following passage from the "Sleepers" notebook:

> Has what I have said . . . seized upon you[r] soul and set its sign there   If not then I know there is no elementary vigor in my word: If not, then I throw my words among the other parings an

crusts of the swill tub, and go home and bathe myself, and listen
to music, and touch my lips to the flesh of sleeping children,
an[d] come and try again. (*DBN*, III, 769)

The manuscript passage recounts the same drama of doubt that in-
forms the first stanza of the poem, and the drama is resolved in both
cases—at least temporarily—by the image of sleeping children. As
in *Rambles* and "Song of the Rolling Earth," the "stamina of words"
is supported by the "theory of things."

The poet's search for the "elementary vigor in . . . words" continues in the next four stanzas of "The Sleepers." The clausal frame set
by the second stanza of the poem gives way to a mixed stanza:

> The wretched features of ennuyés, the white features of corpses,
>   the livid faces of drunkards, the sick-gray faces of onanists,
> The gash'd bodies on battle-fields, the insane in their strong-
>   door'd rooms, the sacred idiots, the new-born emerging from
>   gates, and the dying emerging from gates,
> The night pervades them and infolds them.
>
> (8–10)

The first two lines of the stanza represent the poet's initial attempt
to expand into a catalogue, and the nine phrases progress from the
"wretched" and "livid" faces to the "sacred idiots" and the "emerging
from gates" of both the newly born and the newly dead. The image
of "gates" recalls the first sheet of the "Sleepers" notebook, where
Whitman asserts that "the efflux of the soul comes through beautiful
gates of laws" (*DBN*, III, 764). Moreover, the phrasal catalogue enacts
that spiritual efflux, for the progression in the catalogue remains
half-hidden and "cannot well be traced" (*DBN*, III, 764). The movement from the phrasal catalogue to the clause controlling the phrases
parallels the movement from the many to the one, from disunity to
unity. Whitman seals both the effect and the stanza with the closing
line: "The night pervades them and infolds them."

The next three stanzas maintain the steady tone of affirmation
through the regularity of form and rhythm. All three contain four
lines, and all three employ the repetition of the "*X* sleeps" syntactic
formula. The twelve lines could form an effective clausal catalogue
of the type Whitman creates in Section 15 of "Song of Myself," but in
"The Sleepers" the poet emphasizes the separate character of the
sleepers by grouping them in separate stanzas.[11] Thus the first of the

11. I describe the clausal catalogue of Section 15 in " 'Free Growth of Metrical

three stanzas presents images of family, the second images of loss and evil, and the third images of frustrated desires. The movement in the three stanzas returns to the confusion and chaos of the earlier phrasal catalogue, but this apparent regression masks the "efflux of the soul," which, Whitman notes, "folks call capricious" (*DBN*, III, 764).

The process of identification again becomes important in the rest of Section 1 of the poem. The poet returns to himself as a figure of the separate observer:

> I stand in the dark with drooping eyes by the worst-suffering
> and the most restless,
> I pass my hands soothingly to and fro a few inches from them,
> The restless sink in their beds, they fitfully sleep.
>
> (23–25)

Even though the observer passes his hands a few inches from the sleepers, he remains separate from any physical contact with them. As in the passage from the "Sleepers" notebook, "some god" must "walk in noiseless and resistless" to close the gap between the many and the one.

Whitman's need for a transcendental self to mediate between the many and the one clearly emerges in the next two stanzas:

> Now I pierce the darkness, new beings appear,
> The earth recedes from me into the night,
> I saw that it was beautiful, and I see that what is not the earth
> is beautiful.
>
> I go from bedside to bedside, I sleep close with the other
> sleepers each in turn,
> I dream in my dream all the dreams of the other dreamers,
> And I become the other dreamers.
>
> (26–31)

The first line in this passage is an addition made in the 1860 edition of *Leaves of Grass*, and it adumbrates the poet's movement away from

---

Laws,' " pp. 34–36. My reading of the section emphasizes the mixture of verbs in the simple present tense and verbs in the present progressive tense, a mixture which represents the poetic self and the objective world of occupations as dynamic and temporally performative. Significantly, Section 15 does not divide any of the actions it represents into stanzas; rather, the succession of dynamic lines form one gigantic "stanza," though this is to make the formal term assume proportions nearly monstrous.

the physical beings of the earth. In receding, the earth becomes a part of the past ("I *saw* that it *was* beautiful"), and the poet can now perceive "new beings" in "what is not the earth." This allows him to return to the sleepers in order to place himself in a new relation with them. He dreams the one dream that includes the many dreams of the dreamers, and in so doing he asserts that he "become[s] the other dreamers." The act of observation gives way to the act of identification.

By enacting the identification of the poetic self with the sleepers, Whitman gains verbal power over the problem he addresses in the poem. It is hardly surprising, then, that the ensuing stanzas celebrate the active role of the poet in perceiving the beautiful "efflux of the soul" where it is least apparent.

> I am a dance—play up there! the fit is whirling me fast!
>
> I am the ever-laughing—it is new moon and twilight,
> I see the hiding of douceurs, I see nimble ghosts whichever way
>   I look,
> Cache and cache again deep in the ground and sea, and where it
>   is neither ground nor sea.
>
> Well do they do their jobs those journeymen divine,
> Only from me can they hide nothing, and would not if they
>   could,
> I reckon I am their boss and they make me a pet besides,
> And surround me and lead me and run ahead when I walk,
> To lift their cunning covers to signify me with stretch'd arms,
>   and resume the way;
> Onward we move, a gay gang of blackguards! with mirth-
>   shouting music and wild-flapping pennants of joy!
>
> (32–41)

Whitman's manuscript notebook for "The Sleepers" reveals that he worked on several versions of these lines. The second leaf of the notebook contains the phrase "pennants of joy" (*DBN*, III, 765), but in that passage the phallic image conveys a sense of frustration or impotence, where the "pennants . . . sink flat and lank in the deadest calm."[12] On the seventh and eighth leaves, Whitman changes the tone to commendation and power. The passage is headed "The Poet," and

---

12. The phrase "pennants of joy sink flat and lank" appears in "Song of the Open Road," 1.98. The occurrence of the image of "pennants of joy" indicates the close relationship of "Song of the Open Road" to "The Sleepers," for in both poems Whitman is concerned with working through his sexual and spiritual attraction to the many, and in both poems the means of doing so is the dynamic syntax of the catalogue.

Whitman celebrates the penetrating sight that can perceive beauty where "ten million supple-fingered gods are perpetually employed hiding beauty in the world—burying it everywhere in everything—and most of all spots that men and women do not think of, and never look—as in death" (*DBN*, III, 766). The final leaf of the notebook presents the most thorough development of the passage, and most of the wording of the two stanzas is worked out completely (*DBN*, III, 770).

The salient point in the manuscript trials is the image of the "supple-fingered gods" who hide beauty in "Death and Poverty and Wickedness" (770). In the poem, these gods become "nimble ghosts" (34), and in both the manuscript and the poem they are referred to as the "journeymen divine." The poem assumes the same power as the "nimble ghosts" by hiding the theme it develops. Whitman excludes all mention of hidden beauty, and the previous stanzas of the poem allow him to omit the blatant reference to death, poverty, and wickedness. But because we now know that the "Sleepers" notebook contains Whitman's meditations on the "god [who] walks in noiseless and resistless," we can understand that the poet becomes the "boss" and "pet" of the seemingly capricious "efflux of the soul." In this context, moreover, the play on the word "journeymen" becomes clear, for it mingles the image of democratic workingmen with the image of a spiritual journey.

The image of spiritual evolution continues in the final movement of the first section. And the "Sleepers" notebook once again renders valuable service. The extended seduction scene that closes Section 1 creates the same dreamlike tone that characterizes Section 11 of "Song of Myself." In both sections, the poet assumes the role of a female, and in both the physical act of sex is displaced by the metaphysical act of identification. In "The Sleepers," the connection between the seduction scene and the foregoing account of the "journeymen divine" is far from clear. But in the manuscript notebook, Whitman makes the connection for us:

> I reckon he is Boss of those gods; and the work they do is done for him, and all that they have concealed for his sake—Him they attend outdoors or indoors. . . . They run ahead when he walks, and lift their cunning covers, and signify him with pointed stretched arms.—(They undress and bring her naked to his bed, that they may sleep together; and she shall come again whenever he will, and the taste shall be sweeter and sweeter always)[13]

13. *DBN*, III, 766. The "Sleepers" notebook presents several interesting problems in paleography and interpretation. White transcribes the notebook from recto to verso,

The figure of the naked female is clearly the gift of the gods to their "Boss," the poet. Whitman complicates the figure in the poem by assuming the role of the female and by enacting a seduction of the female by the darkness instead of by a lover. These alterations of the figure obscure its function, but it is nonetheless certain that the figure of the naked female parallels the "journeymen divine," who "lift their cunning covers" for the poet. The double displacement also becomes apparent, for the seduction is spiritual instead of physical.

Whitman develops the spiritual nature of the scene and the connection with the "supple-fingered gods" in the last two stanzas of the section:

> My hands are spread forth, I pass them in all directions,
> I would sound up the shadowy shore to which you are
> journeying.
>
> Be careful darkness! already what was it touch'd me?

---

but the grammar of the quoted passage demands that manuscript leaf [6] follow manuscript leaf [8]. Leaf [6] begins "and bring her naked to his bed," while leaf [8] ends "(They undress." Furthermore, leaf [6] closes the parenthesis begun on sheet [8]. It is tempting to reverse the order of the third and fourth pages of the notebook, in which case the order of the text would run as follows: [7] (recto), [8] (verso), [5] (recto), [6] (verso). This requires some mental gymnastics on the reader's part. Leaf [7] is a self-contained text, while leaf [8] follows the subject and grammar of leaf [7]. Leaf [5], however, does not follow the grammar of "They undress" which ends leaf [8]; instead, the passage on leaf [5] appears self-contained. Leaf [6] begins *in medias res*, but the dull pencil stroke matches exactly that of leaf [8], and neither recto bears this type of pencil stroke. We must conclude, then, that regardless of the order of the two pages, Whitman wrote *verso to verso*, from leaf [8] to leaf [6], even though this is not the practice in the rest of the notebook.

Professor Ed Folsom has pointed out to me that leaf [24] of the notebook (*DBN*, III, 770) corroborates the ordering of leaves [7], [8], and [6]. The passage on leaf [24] begins with the image of "ten million supple-wristed gods," which is a revision of leaf [7]; it then develops the image of the poet as "Boss of those gods," a revision of leaf [8]; and it concludes with the image of the poet at the head of the divine "procession," a revision of leaf [6].

Other leaves in the "Sleepers" notebook indicate that Whitman did not always write recto to verso. For instance, the top halves of leaves [14] and [15] bear the same pencil strokes, but the bottom half of [14] is not continuous with the text of the top half. Similarly, leaves [20] and [21] run across the bottom half, from verso to recto. Finally, leaves [21] and [23] seem to be an example of the poet writing from recto to recto.

The jumbled sequence is hardly surprising, and it may explain why the notebook has only recently been identified as connected to "The Sleepers." See R. S. Mishra, " 'The Sleepers" and Some Whitman Notes," *WWQR* 1 (1983): 30–36. I would suggest that the connection is even stronger than Mishra argues; the notebook in fact forms the beginnings of the poem.

I thought my lover had gone, else darkness and he are one,
I hear the heart-beat, I follow, I fade away.

(55–59)

The image of darkness as "journeying" recalls, of course, the "journeymen divine," and the "shadowy shore" surely signifies death. The
last stanza partially undercuts these images of spiritual evolution,
for it represents the physical lover and the darkness as a unity. Whitman closes the section with the sound of the heartbeat and the fading
of the dream, which is also the fading of the poet's voice and the
fading of the female's identity. This is to say that the instant of spiritual oneness, the joining of the many and the one, is only momentary,
for it only takes place in the poet's act of identification. And that act,
however spiritual, remains bound to the world of time and change.

The temporal aspect of Whitman's concern with the "efflux of the
soul" figures prominently in the setting of the rhythmical frame. The
first section of the poem features short stanzas and coordinate
clauses, and these formal elements combine to represent an active,
searching poetic self, a transcendental spirit that forms itself through
the act of identifying with the many sleepers it encounters on its
journey through the night. Moreover, this paradoxical crossing between the many and the one can never be completed. The perpetual
action of the god who "walks in noiseless and resistless" must be repeated again and again, for the action both removes the poet from
the world of time and returns him to that world.

In sections 2 through 6 of the poem, Whitman develops both the
rhythmical frame and the paradoxical relationship of the poetic self
to the world of time. The poet maintains his active search for the
dreams of the many sleepers, and he enacts identification as a means
toward identity. The dreams Whitman presents in these sections of
the poem feature loss, physical danger, and death, and these themes
accord well with the overarching concern with the "efflux of the soul."
So, for example, in Section 2 the poet becomes the old grandmother
(62–63), the sleepless widow (64–65), and the shroud (66–67).

In Section 3 Whitman turns to the nightmarish vision of the
"beautiful gigantic swimmer" (70–80). The swimmer recalls the poet's
own pleasure in bathing, as well as the "twenty-ninth bather" of
"Song of Myself." The passage in the poem also supports this identification between the poet and the swimmer, for Whitman notes that
the "courageous giant" is "in the prime of his middle age" (75). This
recalls the image of the poet presented in the final version of "Song
of Myself": "I, now thirty-seven years old in perfect health begin, /
Hoping to cease not till death" (8–9). Whitman added these lines to

the 1881 edition of the poem, a clear idealization of his earlier physical and poetic health.[14]

Despite this measure of identification, the representation of the poetic self in Section 3 emphasizes a certain degree of separation. In Section 2, the poet becomes the various people or objects he sees, but here he remains caught in the act of seeing. This degree of separation leads to the crisis of Section 4, a crisis that echoes the opening stanza of the poem. Separation from the many leads to a meditation on the poet's one self, and this meditation echoes the helplessness of the drowning swimmer of Section 3:

> I turn but do not extricate myself,
> Confused, a past-reading, another, but with darkness yet.
>
> The beach is cut by the razory ice-wind, the wreck-guns sound,
> The tempest lulls, the moon comes floundering through the drifts.
>
> I look where the ship helplessly heads end on, I hear the burst as she strikes, I hear the howls of dismay, they grow fainter and fainter.
>
> I cannot aid with my wringing fingers,
> I can but rush to the surf and let it drench me and freeze upon me.
>
> I search with the crowd, not one of the company is wash'd to us alive,
> In the morning I help pick up the dead and lay them in rows in a barn.
>
> (81–89)

The first stanza here clearly echoes the opening lines of the poem. The poet returns to his original "confused" state, a situation from which he is unable to extricate himself. The compound "past-reading" parallels the idea Whitman hits upon in the "Sleepers" notebook: "She remains in my memory afterward for a year" (*DBN*, III, 764). Further, it recalls the receding earth in Section 1 of "The Sleepers," an image that allowed the poet to extricate himself from the confused relationship of the many and the one. Here, however, the act of "past-reading" does not appear to have freed the poet; instead,

14. The lines added to the 1881 version of "Song of Myself" originally appeared in "Starting from Paumanok," the introductory poem to the 1860 edition of *Leaves of Grass*. See *Variorum*, II, 275.

the "new moon" of Section 1 (33) becomes "the moon . . . floundering through the drifts" (84). The immediacy of both Section 3 and Section 4 appears to work against the poet, as if the act of identifying with the imaginings of the many dreamers threatened to destroy the barely created poetic self.

In Section 5 and 6, Whitman extricates himself from the confusion of dark dreams by pushing them into the past and by creating a temporal frame for his transformations of identity. The initial word of Section 5, "Now," signals a series of "past-readings" that the poet presents in the form of memories. Section 5 delivers two scenes with General Washington, where defeat and farewell disguise the founding of the new republic. Section 6 begins with the repetition of the "Now" that signals both a present performance and a pushing of the performing act into the past: "Now what my mother told me one day as we sat at dinner together" (100). The phrase "one day," which is a revision of 1881, replaces the more immediate phrase "today," and the revision places the performance of telling the story of the "red squaw" at a further remove from the present.

In the first five editions of *Leaves of Grass*, Whitman moves from his mother's dinnertime memory of the red squaw to the evocation of a black slave:

> Now Lucifer was not dead. . . . or if he was I am his sorrowful
>   terrible heir;
> I have been wronged. . . . I am oppressed. . . . I hate him that
>   oppresses me,
> I will either destroy him, or he shall release me.
>
> Damn him! how he does defile me,
> How he informs against my brother and sister and takes pay for
>   their blood,
> How he laughs when I look down the bend after the steamboat
>   that carries away my woman.
>
> Now the vast dusk bulk that is the whale's bulk. . . . it seems
>   mine,
> Warily, sportsman! though I lie so sleepy and sluggish, my tap is
>   death.
>
> (116[1]–[8])[15]

15. The passage was dropped in the 1881 edition of *Leaves*, when Whitman arranged and revised the poems for the final time. Early draft lines of the passage appear in the twelve-leaf notebook mentioned above. See *DBN*, III, 763. The Barrett Collection at the University of Virginia also contains manuscript drafts of the section, though they

The repetend "Now" once again signals the play between the past and the present, as does the mixture of past and present tenses in the first line of the passage. The figure of the slave who has lost his woman parallels the figures of isolation and loss in the previous "past-readings." Still, the 1881 deletion of these lines has its rationale. The two "past-readings" of Section 5 and Section 6 play upon the distinction between public and private loss, and the figure of "Lucifer's sorrowful terrible heir" seems historical and topical. Moreover, the figures in the two sections are not only figures of loss, for in both the public and the private scenes joy mingles with sorrow. This mixture is undercut by the figure of the slave, so Whitman's revision adds coherence to the movement of the poem, which carries us toward the "efflux of the soul" the poet seeks.

The efflux comes, finally, in Section 7 and Section 8 of "The Sleepers," and it is figured by the poet's use of catalogues. Through the first six sections of the poem, Whitman rarely extends a series of syntactic parallelisms beyond three lines, and when he does (11–22) he breaks the catalogue into stanzas of no more than four lines. This formal feature, we have seen, parallels the poet's dreamlike, hesitant performance of identification. The movement between the many and the one corresponds to the flow between the past and the present, but these twin movements must be repeated in a never-ending dialectic from which the poet cannot disentangle himself. In the last two sections of the poem, Whitman brings together his many transformations, and he does so by framing the many acts within temporal catalogues. The catalogues represent the final expansion by the poet, the ultimate "efflux of the soul."

Section 7 effectively announces this final expansion by shifting the imagery from darkness to "a show of the summer softness—a contact of something unseen—an amour of the light and air" (117). The "something unseen" recalls the "hiding of douceurs" and the work of the "journeymen divine" developed in Section 1. In the next stanza of Section 7, Whitman joins the new imagery of light and love with both himself and the many sleepers: "O love and summer, you are in the dreams and in me" (120). The imagery of changing seasons and plentiful harvests further develops the poet's tone of affirmation and provides the transition to the first of four catalogues.

The first catalogue is exclusively clausal, and it presents the dynamic return of the many, who are no longer confined to the role of sleepers:

---

have been mistakenly bound in a volume containing the manuscript drafts of "Song of Myself."

Elements merge in the night, ships make tacks in the dreams,
The sailor sails, the exile returns home,
The fugitive returns unharm'd, the immigrant is back beyond
    months and years,
The poor Irishman lives in the simple house of his childhood
    with the well-known neighbors and faces,
They warmly welcome him, he is barefoot again, he forgets he
    is well off,
The Dutchman voyages home, and the Scotchman and
    Welshman voyage home, and the native of the Mediterranean
    voyages home,
To every port of England, France, Spain, enter well-fill'd ships,
The Swiss foots it toward his hills, the Prussian goes his way,
    the Hungarian his way, and the Pole his way,
The Swede returns, and the Dane and Norwegian return.

                                        (123–31)

The image of the "well-fill'd ships" echoes the "barns . . . well-fill'd"
in the previous stanza, and it effectively reverses the nightmarish vision of the shipwreck in Section 4. The catalogue concentrates upon
the return of the many to their respective homelands, and that return
is represented as an ongoing activity through the use of dynamic
verbs. The clausal character of the passage insists upon this dynamic
image, and Whitman further emphasizes the progressivist quality of
the return by stating that "the immigrant is back beyond months and
years" (125). This is a curious turn of phrase, for we expect to read
"*after* months and years." The word "beyond" suggests, then, that the
return is taking place at some infinitely distant time in the future,
even though Whitman's catalogue enacts the arrival in the present.
In this sense of future deferral, the phrase recalls the image of the
poet and "journeymen divine" in Section 1: "Onward we move, a gay
gang of blackguards" (41). The assertion of arrival or return results
in the incantatory performance of the act of arriving or returning.
    The dynamic nature of the first clausal catalogue gives way im-
mediately to a catalogue based on phrases:

The homeward bound and the outward bound,
The beautiful lost swimmer, the ennuyé the onanist, the
    female that loves unrequited, the money-maker,
The actor and actress, those through with their parts and those
    waiting to commence,
The affectionate boy, the husband and wife, the voter, the
    nominee that is chosen and the nominee that has fail'd,

> The great already known and the great any time after to-day,
> The stammerer, the sick, the perfect-form'd, the homely,
> The criminal that stood in the box, the judge that sat and
>   sentenced him, the fluent lawyers, the jury, the audience,
> The laugher and weeper, the dancer, the midnight widow, the
>   red squaw,
> The consumptive, the erysipalite, the idiot, he that is wrong'd,
> The antipodes, and every one between this and them in the
>   dark,
> I swear they are averaged now—one is no better than the other,
> The night and sleep have liken'd them and restored them.
>
> (132–43)

The phrases at first appear to summarize the earlier images of the sleepers, but it is clear that the poet both develops certain images more fully than before and adds new images. For instance, the earlier images of the murderer and prisoner (16–17) are given full play (138), while the image of "the homely" recalls most closely the unused passage from the "Sleepers" notebook: "She is neither young nor fair complexioned" (*DBN*, III, 764).

The phrases in the catalogue tend to create a stative effect, even though the random ordering of the phrases and the addition of new images cause the language of the passage to act in more dynamic ways than we might expect from a simple summary. Whitman furthers this tentative effect by reducing the welter of images to "the antipodes." He then provides a temporal frame for the many by ending the catalogue with three clauses: "I swear they are averaged now—one is no better than the other, / The night and sleep have liken'd them and restored them" (142–43). The key word "now" parallels the poet's earlier uses of the word in Section 5 and Section 6. It asserts, moreover, that the many are being "averaged" at this present moment, in the act of the poet's saying or writing. In summarizing his "past-readings," therefore, Whitman transforms the act of "past-reading" into the act of "present-saying." Moreover, he enables himself to affirm a positive vision of the relationship between apparent evil and eventual good, and this affirmation, in the simple "I swear," is the first real assertion of the poet's belief in the "elementary vigor in [his] words" (*DBN*, III, 769).

The poet enacts the "elementary vigor" in the four stanzas that close Section 7. The hidden themes of beauty and the soul become explicit here, and this adumbration of the themes shows just how central to the poem the "Sleepers" notebook must be:

I swear they are all beautiful,
Every one that sleeps is beautiful, every thing in the dim light is
   beautiful,
The wildest and bloodiest is over, and all is peace.

Peace is always beautiful,
The myth of heaven indicates peace and night.

The myth of heaven indicates the soul,
The soul is always beautiful, it appears more or it appears less,
   it comes or it lags behind,
It comes from its embower'd garden and looks pleasantly on
   itself and encloses the world,
Perfect and clean the genitals previously jetting, and perfect
   and clean the womb cohering,
The head well-grown proportion'd and plumb, and the bowels
   and joints proportion'd and plumb.

$$(144-53)$$

The first two stanzas create a stative effect through the use of the
stative verb "to be." And this grammatical effect accords with the
poet's act of swearing that "peace and night" are now the result of all
the dynamic scenes of suffering and loss he has presented as his own.
The stative quality of the lines continues in the first part of the third
stanza. "The myth of heaven indicates the soul, / The soul is always
beautiful" (149–50) forms a rhetorical chiasmus with the previous
stanza ("Peace is always beautiful, / The myth of heaven indicates
peace and night."), and the chiasmus establishes a complex homology
of equivalences through syntactic parallelism. The homology breaks
down to this basic idea: The soul is peace (and night), and the myth
of heaven points toward these equivalent terms.

The rest of the third stanza does not remain stative in its grammar or in its effects. After the poet asserts that "the soul is always
beautiful," he moves into a presentation of the soul's activities. The
soul "appears," "comes," "lags behind," "comes," "looks," and "encloses." These dynamic verbs create the effect of activity and process,
so that the image of the stable, permanently beautiful soul gives way
to the image of the dynamic, perpetually active soul. Once again,
however, Whitman mixes stative and dynamic forms, creating a balance between them: The dynamic clauses frame the last two lines of
the stanza, where phrases conclude with the mixture of dynamic syntax ("jetting" and "cohering") and stative syntax ("The head well-

grown proportion'd and plumb, and the bowels and joints proportion'd and plumb").

The three stanzas move toward the slight expansion of the five-
line third stanza, but they function as a transition for the third of
Whitman's four catalogues, seven lines that close the section. The
counterpointing of stative and dynamic syntax enacts the dialectic of
past and present, identity and activity.

> The soul is always beautiful,
> The universe is duly in order, every thing is in its place,
> What has arrived is in its place and what waits shall be in its
>   place,
> The twisted skull waits, the watery or rotten blood waits,
> The child of the glutton or venerealee waits long, and the child
>   of the drunkard waits long, and the drunkard himself waits
>   long,
> The sleepers that lived and died wait, the far advanced are to
>   go on in their turns, and the far behind are to come on in
>   their turns,
> The diverse shall be no less diverse, but they shall flow and
>   unite—they unite now.
>
> (154–60)

The catalogue begins with three stative lines featuring the verb "to
be" and simple predication. But the lines do not remain simply "in
. . . place." In order to give a true idea of the "efflux of the soul," the
poet must emphasize that the realization of the soul may take place
"at some future period perhaps a few score millions of years" (DBN,
III, 764). Thus the syntactic repetend becomes "waits," then "waits
long."

The movement from "past-reading" to "present-saying" appears
in the last two lines of the catalogue: The poet attempts to balance
the "far-advanced" and the "far behind" by presenting the "efflux of
the soul" as it "comes through beautiful gates of laws" (DBN, III, 764).
So the paired verb phrases combine the stative and the dynamic:
"are to go on in their turns" and "are to come on in their turns"
present future possibility as present law. The act of asserting leads
the poet to his most extravagant performance of "present-saying":
"The diverse shall be no less diverse, but they shall flow and unite—
they unite now." Again the future "efflux of the soul" is figured as
taking place in the present of the poem, in the act of saying or writing. Whitman's assertion "they unite now" climaxes the series of temporal transformations, the "past-readings," he has performed. Most

important, the poet manages the assertion by placing his many iden-
tifications and the identities of the many sleepers within the temporally flowing frame of spiritual progress. Only by deferring the "efflux
of the soul" to an infinitely distant future can he earn the possibility
of asserting that the flowing outward is taking place in the present.

This paradoxical relationship between two orders of time and
two aspects of Whitman's poetics is one reason why the poem does
not end with the simple assertion of unity within variety. The final
lines of Section 7 mix stative and dynamic forms, future realization
and present action, the one and the many, but the mixture is never a
perfect one. Thus the poet must continue his expansions beyond the
temporal and rhythmical frames he sets himself, for the "efflux of the
soul" remains a vistalike process, a perpetually deferred ideal that
provides the poet with the power of the god who "walks in noiseless
and resistless."

Whitman's poetic power becomes strongest in the last section. It
is apparent, first of all, in the longest catalogue of the poem, a
sixteen-line series of clauses that enacts the transfiguration of ugli-
ness into beauty, sickness into health, evil into good. The catalogue
begins with the repetition of the idea of beauty as a permanent characteristic, and the characteristic is presented in the stative line "The
sleepers are very beautiful as they lie unclothed" (161). The image
echoes the closing movement of Section 1, where the naked female
represents the spiritual union of the many and the one. The poet
elaborates upon this theme in the next thirteen lines, and the syntactic parallelism of the catalogue once again mixes the stative and dynamic aspects of the sleepers. For instance, the second line of the
catalogue is dynamic, for the static sleepers now begin to "flow hand
in hand over the whole earth from east to west as they lie unclothed"
(162), but then the dynamic syntax gives way to two lines featuring
the "are hand in hand" repetend, which reestablishes the stative aspect of the catalogue. This in turn is transformed into several lines of
dynamic syntax, where verbs like "cross," "press," "hold," "shine," "go,"
"kiss," "salute," "step," "become," "stop," "move," and "open" stress the
active, dynamic characteristics of the transfiguration. Of course,
these dynamic verbs are counterpointed by several instances of the
stative verb "to be": "friend is inarm'd by friend" (168), "the wrong'd
is made right" (169), "the call of the slave is one with the master's
call" (170), "the suffering of sick persons is reliev'd" (171), and "the
poor distress'd head is free" (172). Four of the five stative clauses occur at the end of lines, and the effect of this formal feature is to sta-
bilize the dynamic action enacted in the first part of the lines.

The perpetually productive character of the oppositions must find some terminus, of course, else the processes of writing and reading would never end. Whitman's strategy for closing the catalogue is to play upon the image of the sleepers:

> The swell'd and convuls'd and congested awake to themselves
>   in condition,
> They pass the invigoration of the night and the chemistry of the
>   night, and awake.
>
> (175–76)

Since there is no formal element to effect the necessary closure, Whitman uses the image of the awaking sleepers, as if the catalogue somehow traversed the span of one night. This technique is similar to the strategy employed in his longest clausal catalogue, Section 15 of "Song of Myself." In that catalogue, the poet effects closure by developing imagery of sleep, whereas here the imagery is the reverse. But in both cases a temporal transition marks the boundary for the potentially endless series of clauses.[16]

A second point about these last two lines of the catalogue is that the poet once again echoes the "Sleepers" notebook. The "invigoration of the night" recalls Whitman's concern for the "elementary vigor in . . . words" (*DBN*, III, 769). The poet transforms his concern with language into a supposedly objective fact of nature. But this is clearly a rhetorical strategy, closely akin to the statement that "I can see but one limitation to the theory of Words—the theory of Things" (*Rambles*, p. 290). Whitman in fact shows that the "vigor" or "chemistry" exists not in the night but in his words, even though he gestures toward the night as the repository of power.

The final stanzas of "The Sleepers" support this contention, for in them the poet returns to a meditation upon himself. The catalogues develop the image of the many and the dynamic transformations of the many through language. Now Whitman turns to the one, the "I" that began the poem in complete—though active—confusion:

> I too pass from the night,
> I stay a while away O night, but I return to you again and love
>   you.
>
> Why should I be afraid to trust myself to you?
> I am not afraid, I have been well brought forward by you,

---

16. For an account of this method of closure, see Barbara Herrnstein Smith, *Poetic Closure: A Study of How Poems End (Chicago: University of Chicago Press, 1968), pp. 172–82.*

I love the rich running day, but I do not desert her in whom I
   lay so long,
I know not how I came of you and I know not where I go with
   you, but I know I came well and shall go well.

I will stop only a time with the night, and rise betimes,
I will duly pass the day O my mother, and duly return to you.
                                                   (177–84)

The "I" in this passage is still active, but it now acts coherently, with
direction. The poet asserts that he has been "well brought forward"
by the night, a phrase clearly adumbrating the theme of spiritual
evolution, the "efflux of the soul." The dynamic poetic self is reflected
in the dynamic syntax, and it is especially clear in the closing cou-
plet, where the poet echoes the opening stanza of the poem in order
to deny the "stopping" that threatened the "elementary vigor" of his
words. Here, he enacts a return from the night to the day, and his
action thus parallels the awakening of the many sleepers. But that
action gives rise to the second return, a return to the night, the
mother, the soul. The poem closes in much the same manner as does
Section 15 of "Song of Myself," by effecting a figurative return to
sleep. But in "The Sleepers" Whitman figures the return as a movement that must inevitably give rise to the countermovement, the
passing of the night into day. This figure of the natural cycle of day
and night becomes the image of perpetual progress, the infinite process of the "efflux of the soul." Whitman's catalogues do effect a transformation in the speaker of the poem, to be sure, just as they transfig-
ure the many sleepers, restoring them through the "elementary
vigor" of syntactic parallelism. But the transformations take place
within the temporal frame of perpetual progress, so the ultimate "efflux of the soul" remains both present in the act of the poet's saying
and deferred to an always approaching future.

In "The Sleepers," the catalogue functions as an ultimate expansion
beyond the rhythmical frame, where the expansion paradoxically effects the closure of the poem. But one of the principal difficulties of
"The Sleepers" arises from the fact that there is no obvious structural
relationship between the meanderings of the rhythmical frame in the
first six sections of the poem and the expansions of the catalogues in
the last two sections. We reduce the difficulty by applying the logic
of analogical or mimetic form: The meandering form of the poem
mimes the meandering quality of dreams and the capricious quality
of the "efflux of the soul." But this type of reduction is not always

necessary, for in a poem like "Crossing Brooklyn Ferry" the catalogue and rhythmical frame function together in a clear formal structure.[17]

Whitman's strategy in "Crossing Brooklyn Ferry" is to create a series of three orderly expansions. The nine sections of the poem divide neatly into three movements, where each movement begins with a short section, expands to a somewhat longer section, and culminates in a catalogue. Thus the poem provides two axes for interpretation: We can approach each movement as such, analyzing the formal relationships of the three sections to one another, after which we can establish the logic of the entire sequence of three expansions; or we can discuss the three classes of sections by grouping sections 1, 4, and 7, sections 2, 5, and 8, and sections 3, 6, and 9. These two approaches correspond to the syntagmatic and paradigmatic poles of language.[18] If I wished to inscribe my argument within the tradition of "high" structuralism, the structuralism of Jakobson and of the early Barthes, I would use the syntagmatic, sequential aspect of the poem only in order to establish the paradigmatic, systematic aspect. But this approach, besides being arbitrarily rigid, runs counter both to the notion of formal movements and to the temporal nature of representation. Most important, it denies the temporal, dynamic qualities of the reading process. For all these reasons, I prefer to move in the opposite direction, from paradigmatic to syntagmatic.

The short introductory sections resemble one another formally, for each section establishes some version of the Whitmanian rhythmical frame. Section 1, for instance, is five lines long, and it is formed by a two-line and a three-line stanza. The syntactic parallelism of all five lines is clausal, where the repetend "I see you face to face" forms the first stanza and the repetend "how curious you are to me" subtly modulates to form the second. Section 4 is also five lines long, though in this case the section makes up a five-line stanza. The stanza is, in a sense, anomalous, because it features no obvious syntactic parallelism. Repetitions of such key words as "same," "loved well," and "others" lend coherence to the stanza, which presents the poet's characteristic meditation on the many and the one, but the lack of par-

17. In a recent essay, Tenney Nathanson presents an account of Whitman's concern with the relationship between language and representation, concentrating on the imagery of presence or voice in "Crossing Brooklyn Ferry." See "Whitman's Tropes of Light and Flood: Language and Representation in the Early Editions of *Leaves of Grass*," *ESQ* 31 (1985): 116–34. Although Nathanson's focus differs sharply from my own, his argument centers, like mine, upon the performative nature of Whitman's rhetoric, an aspect discussed by Hollis in *Language and Style*, pp. 65–123.

18. For a clear account of the two axes of language, see Roland Barthes, *Elements of Semiology*, trans. Annette Lavers and Colin Smith (New York: Hill and Wang, 1967), pp. 58–88.

allelism appears to be a deliberate strategy for changing the rhythm of the poem. Finally, Section 7 combines the techniques of sections 1 and 4. It is six lines long, made up of two three-line stanzas. The first stanza features no syntactic parallelism, though the key word "you" occurs five times in just three lines. The second stanza, on the other hand, is structured by syntactic parallelism and anaphora, and the parallelism is once again clausal: "Who was to know" in the initial line becomes "Who knows . . . but I am" in the second and third lines.

The formal connections among the three sections are important when we consider the thematic links among them. Section 1 presents the ferry scene of 1856 in present tense, but the last line of the section moves into an address to future ferry riders through the use of the future tense. Section 4 can only be understood fully when we consider the effects of sections 2 and 3, but for now it suffices to say that the poet develops the tension between the present and the future by representing himself in the past. The first line of the section, "These and all else were to me the same as they are to you" (49), figures the poet as already absent and the reader as already present, but it does so in order to claim that the poet's power will affect readers in such a way as to destroy the distinctions of past, present, and future: "Others the same—others who look back on me because I look'd forward to them, / (The time will come, though I stop here to-day and to-night.)" (52–53). The close relationship between the poet and the reader, between past and present or present and future, goes a step further in Section 7, where Whitman approaches the reader so closely that both appear to exist in an eternal present tense: "Who knows but I am enjoying this? / Who knows, for all the distance, but I am as good as looking at you now, for all you cannot see me?" (90–91). Thus the three sections present three stages in a dramatic progression, a progression in which the poet projects himself from the 1856 scene into our future—and beyond.

The second paradigm class alters this scheme of progression. In Section 2, the first stanza, which is based upon the repetition of phrases, focuses upon the poet's relationship to "the simple, compact, well-join'd scheme" (7), and the scheme leads to a consideration of "the others that are to follow me, the ties between me and them" (11). The second stanza develops the theme of the future "others" in a series of clauses in the future tense. Section 5 returns to the theme of the many and the one in terms of the future and the present, and Whitman dramatizes his own "pastness" by creating a nine-line stanza based on the simple past tense (56–64). Finally, in Section 8 the poet uses two stanzas to evoke, first, the 1856 ferry scene (92–97) and, second, the present-tense community of the poet and the reader

(98–100). The three sections do not exhibit any real progression, temporal or otherwise; rather, each section presents an attempt to balance between the poet's present and the reader's present.

The third paradigm class, that of the catalogue expansions, is similar to the second in that there is little evidence of a formal or thematic progression. The catalogue sections run 29 lines, 21 lines, and 32 lines, respectively; if we discount the 7-line stanza that introduces Section 3 and the 7-line stanza that concludes Section 9, each section contains a catalogue of a little more than 20 lines (22, 21, and 25, respectively). Sections 3 and 6 are formally similar, for both employ a mixture of clauses and phrases and both represent the poet in the simple past tense. Section 3 concentrates upon the 1856 ferry scene, whereas Section 6 presents the poet's meditation upon "the old knot of contrariety." Section 9 summarizes the two earlier catalogues, so that the opposition between the joy of Section 3 and the despair of Section 6 is resolved by the poet's insistent rhetoric of imperatives. This description of the three catalogues, then, would make it seem that Whitman creates a rough dialectic, one that results in the synthesis of the final catalogue.

This description of the three paradigm classes in "Crossing Brooklyn Ferry" adumbrates a central problem in interpreting the poem. Like "Song of Myself" and "The Sleepers," the 1856 poem exhibits elements of progression at the same time that it exhibits elements of nonprogression. As readers, our attempts to find a thematic progression to tally with the progressive formal surface are repeatedly frustrated. But Whitman deliberately gestures in both directions at the same time, in much the same way that his syntax gestures both toward the stasis of phrases and toward the dynamism of clauses. By reconstructing the sequential movement of the poem, we can avoid the indeterminacy created by the analysis of the paradigmatic axis of the poem.

The first movement of the poem comprises, of course, the first three sections. Section 1 establishes the 1856 ferry scene as the temporal present, even though that present is precariously capable of change, since the sun is only a "half an hour high" (2). The last line of the section moves from the present to the future tense, from the 1856 "crowds of men and women" (3) to "you that shall cross from shore to shore years hence" (5). In the expansion of Section 2, the poet repeats this movement from present to future. The first stanza is a seven-line catalogue of phrases (6–12), and the effect of the phrases is to hold the potentially dynamic quality of the sundown in check. Only in a relative clause near the end of the catalogue does the poet inject a finite verb into the relatively static meditation, and the verb balances between present and future: "The others that are to follow me, the ties between me and them" (11). Whitman's concern for "the others" becomes the driving force behind the second stanza of the section, where the repetition of "others will" signals the movement toward future ferry riders. At this point in the poem, these "others" are not figured as readers; rather, the poet maintains his focus upon the ferry scene by projecting an image of those who will "cross from shore to shore" (13). The repetition of the phrase from Section 1 solidifies the parallel movement of the first two sections.

The final expansion in the first movement—the catalogue of Section 3—is set up by the poet's first projection of himself beyond the temporal confines of the 1856 scene. In the first stanza of the section, which effectively introduces the catalogue, Whitman figures the time of the 1856 scene as already past, though the scene itself now exists in a new present, the present of "the others that are to follow."

It avails not, time nor place—distance avails not,
I am with you, you men and women of a generation, or ever so
    many generations hence,
Just as you feel when you look on the river and sky, so I felt,
Just as any of you is one of a living crowd, I was one of a crowd,
Just as you are refresh'd by the gladness of the river and the
    bright flow, I was refresh'd,
Just as you stand and lean on the rail, yet hurry with the swift
    current, I stood yet was hurried,
Just as you look on the numberless masts of ships and the thick-
    stemm'd pipes of steamboats, I look'd.

(20–26)

In this introductory stanza, the terms "present" and "past" become relative. The poet claims to be present to the "men and women of a generation, or ever so many generations hence" (21), but at the same time he asserts that he "felt," "was refresh'd," and so forth. The key to Whitman's double assertion is the figure of the ferry itself, for it presents the rider with the paradoxical situation of being both static and dynamic, both motionless and moving: "Just as you stand and lean on the rail, yet hurry with the swift current, I stood yet was hurried" (25).

This paradox develops further in the mixed catalogue of looking and seeing (27–48). The first twelve lines establish a clausal frame, where the poet "watched," "saw," and "look'd" at the seagulls, the changing light, and the arriving vessels. After the first line of the catalogue the poetic "I" drops out, leaving only the dynamic verbs of perception. This rhetorical strategy enacts the poet's assertion in Section 2 that he is "myself disintegrated" (7), for the "I" effectively disintegrates into the various dynamic actions of seeing. Thus the first half of the catalogue performs the Emersonian act of becoming nothing and seeing all.

This self-disintegration goes a step further in the second half of the catalogue. The dynamic verbs of perception disappear, giving way to ten lines of phrases:

> The sailors at work in the rigging or out astride the spars,
> The round masts, the swinging motion of the hulls, the slender
>   serpentine pennants,
> The large and small steamers in motion, the pilots in their
>   pilot-houses,
> The white wake left by the passage, the quick tremulous whirl
>   of the wheels,
> The flags of all nations, the falling of them at sunset,
> The scallop-edged waves in the twilight, the ladled cups, the
>   frolicsome crests and glistening,
> The stretch afar growing dimmer and dimmer, the gray walls of
>   the granite storehouses by the docks,
> On the river the shadowy group, the big steam-tug closely
>   flank'd on each side by the barges, the hay-boat, the belated
>   lighter,
> On the neighboring shore the fires from the foundry chimneys
>   burning high and glaringly into the night,
> Casting their flicker of black contrasted with wild red and
>   yellow light over the tops of houses, and down into the clefts
>   of streets.
>
> (39–48)

The mediating presence of the poet becomes nearly transparent here, for the scene takes on a life of its own. Even though the phrases might create an effect of timelessness, as if the scene were present for all time, they do not create an effect of motionlessness. Present participles and deverbal nouns combine to create a scene of ever-changing action, one that presents "swinging motion," "the quick tremulous whirl of the wheels," "the falling," "glistening," "the stretch afar growing dimmer and dimmer," "burning high and glaringly," "casting their flicker." All of these deverbal nouns and participles point up the sounds and motions of the 1856 ferry scene, and they do so to emphasize, in turn, the continuous, temporally infinite quality that the poet perceives in the scene.

The paradox of the first movement is that the three sections assert a temporal progression from Whitman's present to the "others' " present, but at the same time they focus upon the inherently dynamic qualities of the 1856 scene itself. In the initial movement of the poem, the expansion of Section 3 returns the poet to the 1856 scene, and the catalogue presents the spatial movement from one shore to the other and the temporal movement from a half hour before sundown to the gathering darkness: "On the neighboring shore the fires from the foundry chimneys burning high and glaringly into the night, / Casting their flicker of black contrasted with wild red and yellow light over the tops of houses, and down into the clefts of streets" (47–48). As in the catalogues of "Song of Myself" and "The Sleepers," then, Whitman employs the imagery of closure to effect the closure of the catalogue. In "Crossing Brooklyn Ferry," moreover, he uses the imagery to conclude the first movement of the poem.

The second movement begins with the anomalous Section 4, which breaks the rhythm of syntactic parallelism set by Section 3. The change in rhythm punctuates the two major themes of the poem: the relationship of the many to the one, and the relationship of the future to the present. Despite these changes, there is a strong element of continuity to the section, for the poet once again represents himself as already in the past:

> These and all else were to me the same as they are to you,
> I loved well those cities, loved well the stately and rapid river,
> The men and women I saw were all near to me,
> Others the same—others who look back on me because I look'd
>   forward to them,
> (The time will come, though I stop here to-day and to-night.)
>
> (49–53).

The section gathers several of the key words used in the first movement of the poem. For instance, the phrase "these and all else" recalls "all things at all hours of the day" in the first line of Section 2. The phrase "men and women I saw" recalls the "crowds of men and women" in Section 1. And, most important, the phrase "others" recalls the "others that are to follow me" in Section 2.

The image of "others" changes significantly in Section 4, however, for now the "others" are no longer simply ferry riders. Instead, the riders now become readers, since they are able to "look back on me because I look'd forward to them." This metamorphosis is clear in the 1856 version of the poem, where Whitman adumbrates the drama of temporal projection: "I project myself a moment to tell you—also I return" (49[1]). The paradoxically "simultaneous" temporal position of the poet, in which he figures himself as present both in his time and in ours, accounts for the mixture of past and present tenses in the first four lines of the section. It also helps to explain the temporal shift in the last line of the section. The poet parenthetically remarks that "the time will come, though I stop here to-day and to-night." The use of the future tense and the present tense signals the complete return of the poet to the 1856 ferry scene. And the image of "stopping" recalls the first section of "The Sleepers" and the final section of "Song of Myself." In all three poems, the image represents the limits or boundaries of "looking forward." In Section 4, the poet pairs the image of limitation with the assertion of certain expansion ("the time will come"), but the image of limitation closes the section. Section 4 presents, then, the return of the poet both to his solitary oneness and to his limited present.

The tone of limitation becomes stronger in the next two sections of the movement. Section 5 opens with these seemingly assertive lines:

> What is it then between us?
> What is the count of the scores or hundreds of years between us?
>
> Whatever it is, it avails not—distance avails not, and place avails not.
>
> (54–56)

The assertions are supposed to answer the difficult questions that open the section, but do they? The section returns to the image of the poet as already past, and it effects an expansion of sorts through the use of syntactic parallelism:

> I too lived, Brooklyn of ample hills was mine,
> I too walk'd the streets of Manhattan island, and bathed in the waters around it,
> I too felt the curious abrupt questionings stir within me,
> In the day among crowds of people sometimes they came upon me,
> In my walks home late at night or as I lay in my bed they came upon me,
> I too had been struck from the float forever held in solution,
> I too had receiv'd identity by my body,
> That I was I knew was of my body, and what I should be I knew I should be of my body.
>
> (57–64)

Even though these lines are assertive, they are far from affirmative in tone. The questions that open the section are not answered; instead, they reappear as the "curious abrupt questionings" that "come upon" the poet, as if they were thrust upon him from the outside. The figure of identity is limited by the confines of the body and by the simple past tense. The figure of the reader is implied by the anaphoric repetition of "I too," but the figure is as limited as that of the poet.

The modulating tone of doubt and limitation develops yet more strongly in the climactic section of the movement. Whitman asserts an identity between himself and his future readers, but the communion becomes the means for a confession:

> It is not upon you alone the dark patches fall,
> The dark threw its patches down upon me also,
> The best I had done seem'd to me blank and suspicious,
> My great thoughts as I supposed them, were they not in reality
>   meagre?
> Nor is it you alone who know what it is to be evil,
> I am he who knew what it was to be evil,
> I too knitted the old knot of contrariety,
> Blabb'd, blush'd, resented, lied, stole, grudg'd,
> Had guile, anger, lust, hot wishes I dared not speak,
> Was wayward, vain, greedy, shallow, sly, cowardly, malignant,
> The wolf, the snake, the hog, not wanting in me,
> The cheating look, the frivolous word, the adulterous wish, not
>   wanting,
> Refusals, hates, postponements, meanness, laziness, none of
>   these wanting,
> Was one with the rest, the days and haps of the rest,
> Was call'd by my nighest name by clear loud voices of young
>   men as they saw me approaching or passing,
> Felt their arms on my neck as I stood, or the negligent leaning
>   of their flesh against me as I sat,
> Saw many I loved in the street or ferry-boat or public assembly,
>   yet never told them a word,
> Lived the same life with the rest, the same old laughing,
>   gnawing, sleeping,
> Play'd the part that still looks back on the actor or actress,
> The same old role, the role that is what we make it, as great as
>   we like,
> Or as small as we like, or both great and small.
>   (65–85)

The limitation of this catalogue appears, first of all, in the relatively short lines and in the relatively short section itself. It is as if the expansion must figure itself as limited, for it figures the potential evil in both the poet and his readers. The limiting power of evil and doubt is apparent in the image of the "dark patches," which fall or are thrown down upon us. It continues in the poet's "abrupt questioning" of his own poetic power and his previous poetic performances. And it climaxes in the list of evils, which moves from figurative terms to the specific question of homosexuality. The catalogue is mixed, but the clausal line predominates, and the repeated finite verbs relentlessly figure repeated evil actions. Only in the last five lines of the catalogue does this harsh tone of self-recrimination modulate into a slightly more affirmative one. When the poet accuses himself of loving the many but never telling them a word (81), he moves from doubts about his words to the virtue of using language to join the many and the one. In many ways this movement is reminiscent of "The Sleepers," with its litany of doubt and evil and loss. And like "The Sleepers," the catalogue moves from the negative litany of limitation to a positive view of the "efflux of the soul." In the last four lines of the section, then, Whitman abandons self-recrimination in favor of the similitudes joining the many and the one. The "same life" and the "same old laughing, gnawing, sleeping" (82) present neutral images of our similitudes, and the "same old role" becomes an image of gathering power. That role is "what we make it, as great as we like, / Or as small as we like, or both great and small" (84–85). It is no accident that the catalogue ends in the present tense, with the repeated subject "we." The poet escapes his past-tense oneness in these lines, performing the act of expansion in an admittedly limited fashion. The "efflux of the soul" is far from joyous and confident at this point in the poem, but its "time will come."

The third movement of the poem represents the resolution of the thematic opposition between expansion and limitation. Section 7 returns to the dialectic between Whitman and his future readers, mixing past and present tenses to figure the temporal projection of the poet:

> Closer yet I approach you,
> What thought you have of me now, I had as much of you—
>   I laid in my stores in advance,
> I consider'd long and seriously of you before you were born.
>
> Who was to know what should come home to me?
> Who knows but I am enjoying this?

> Who knows, for all the distance, but I am as good as looking at
>   you now, for all you cannot see me?
>
> (86–91)

The questions in the second stanza recall the opening questions and the "curious abrupt questionings" of Section 5, but they alter the tone of the previous section. Here, the lack of certainty becomes the basis for the poet's affirmations. In lines deleted after the 1856 edition, Whitman clarifies the reason for his optimism:

> It is not you alone, nor I alone,
> Not a few races, not a few generations, not a few centuries,
> It is that each came, or comes, or shall come, from its due
>   emission without fail, either now, or then, or henceforth.
>
> (91[1]–[3])

The first line echoes the first line of Section 6, but it governs three lines devoted to the theory of spiritual evolution. Whitman's belief in a "due emission" parallels the idea of the "efflux of the soul" in "The Sleepers," and both phrases figure the eventual perfection of humankind by deferring that perfection to the "due emission" of the future.

The first stanza of Section 8 returns to the 1856 ferry scene and to the present tense. The phrasing echoes the affirmative catalogue of Section 3: "scallop-edg'd waves of flood-tide" (93), "the sea-gulls oscillating their bodies, the hay-boat in the twilight, and the belated lighter" (94). It also echoes the negative questioning of Section 6: "What gods can exceed these that clasp me by the hand, and with voices I love call me promptly and loudly by my nighest name as I approach" (95). Thus the stanza brings the positive first movement and the negative second movement to bear upon one another, but the fundamental effect of the juxtaposition is to reconceive the negative as positive. The questions of the first stanza are overwhelmingly positive in tone, and even the threatening image of the poet being called by his "nighest name" is transformed into an image of communion.

The positive echoes of previous catalogue sections set up a series of addresses to the reader:

> What is more subtle than this which ties me to the woman or
>   man that looks in my face?
> Which fuses me into you now, and pours my meaning into you?
>
> We understand then do we not?
> What I promis'd without mentioning it, have you not accepted?

What the study could not teach—what the preaching could not
accomplish is accomplish'd, is it not?

                                                            (96–100)

These lines recall the magical, incantatory style of Section 7 of "The
Sleepers," where the poet asserts that "the diverse shall be no less
diverse, but they shall flow and unite—they unite now" (160). And in
"Crossing Brooklyn Ferry" the effect is also to create an instance of
"present-saying," phrased as rhetorical questions. Here the "efflux of
the soul" is figured as the fusion of the poet and reader and as the
pouring of meaning into the reader. This displaced sexuality figures
a future spiritual communion, but it is important to remember that
Whitman cannot specify his meaning, for his meaning is grounded in
the paradoxical rhetoric of deferral. As in "The Sleepers," the poet's
assertiveness is based upon the idea of a "due emission," but here
Whitman is at his most extravagant, for he claims that the "due emission" has already been accomplished through the language of the
poem itself, which becomes the field of spiritual evolution.

    The final expansion of "Crossing Brooklyn Ferry" returns to the
1856 scene, but it does so with a renewed sense of poetic power. The
twenty-five-line catalogue is the longest of the three expansions, and
it is also the most dynamic. The structure of the catalogue is based
upon the repetition of dynamic verbs in the imperative mood: "Flow,"
"Frolic," "drench," "Cross," "Stand," "Throb," "Suspend," "Gaze,"
"Sound," "Live," "Play," "Consider," "haste," "Fly," "Receive," "Diverge,"
"Come," "Flaunt," and "Burn" govern the first nineteen lines, and in
all but two instances the imperative occurs at the head of the line.
The effect of this rush of imperative verbs is double: It returns the
poet to the 1856 ferry scene, summarizing the imagery of sections 3,
5, and 6, and it enacts the poet's belief in the communion both of the
one and the many and of the present and the future. In both aspects
of the verbal effect, the poet urges on the dynamic, temporal qualities
of the ferry scene, for the rhetoric of deferral allows him to envision
the "due emission" of the ferry scene in his imagined future.

    The last six lines of the catalogue continue the rush of imperative
verbs, though more of these forms are buried within the line:

Appearances, now or henceforth, indicate what you are,
You necessary film, continue to envelop the soul,
About my body for me, and your body for you, be hung our
    divinest aromas,
Thrive, cities—bring your freight, bring your shows, ample and
    sufficient rivers,

Expand, being than which none else is perhaps more spiritual,
Keep your places, objects than which none else is more lasting.
                                                            (120–25)

The first three lines emphasize the "appearances," "necessary film,"
and "body," respectively, and the repetition of stative nouns slows
down the flow of dynamic verbal forms. But then the last three lines
of the catalogue return to the anaphoric repetition of imperative
verbs, emphasizing temporal change. This mixture of stative and dynamic lines insists upon the mixed nature of the scene itself. The poet
revels in appearances and surfaces, but at the same time he projects
their potential spirituality and depth. Similarly, he revels in the present scene, but he does so only because he envisions the movement
of the scene toward a spiritualized future.

The final stanza of the poem functions, as I have said, as a coda.
After 125 lines of concrete imagery, Whitman turns to a more abstract
summary of his theme of "due emission":

You have waited, you always wait, you dumb, beautiful
    ministers,
We receive you with free sense at last, and are insatiate
    henceforward,
Not you any more shall be able to foil us, or withhold
    yourselves from us,
We use you, and do not cast you aside—we plant you
    permanently within us,
We fathom you not—we love you—there is perfection in you
    also,
You furnish your parts toward eternity,
Great or small, you furnish your parts toward the soul.
                                                            (126–32)

The phrase "dumb, beautiful ministers" refers to the silent persons
and objects of the ferry scene, which we can subsume under the term
"the many." In his final affirmation of the communion of the many
and the one, Whitman alters the subject from "I" to "We," for his
means toward achieving the "free sense" of communion has been to
forge a sense of communion between himself and his future readers.
But this double sense depends, finally, upon the future itself. The poet
finds "perfection" in all aspects of the scene, but he does so because
they "furnish . . . parts toward eternity." The word "toward" is a key
to the rhetoric of deferral, and Whitman emphasizes that rhetoric by
repeating the word in the final line of the poem. The many "minis-

ters," whether "great or small," "furnish . . . parts toward the soul."
The two lines present, then, the eternal soul as the final goal of the
temporally dynamic, ever-changing flux of appearances. But this "efflux of the soul" is never completely realized or enacted in the poem,
nor can it be. Whitman thus plays the "same old role, the role that is
what we make it, as great as we like, / Or as small as we like, or both
great and small" (84–85). That role is, in all its complexity, the role of
the poetic self, which joins expansion and limitation, eternity and
time, the many and the one, in the rhetorical performance of the
poem.

PART 2

PART 2

4

The "Thought of the Ensemble": Whitman's Theory of Language, 1856–1892

Whitman's notebooks and published essays indicate that the "thought of the ensemble" continued to occupy the poet's attention for the remainder of his career. The *Words* notebook, for instance, shows that the "thought" is an abiding one, for Whitman collected newspaper and journal clippings relating to language throughout the nearly four decades following the publication of the second edition of *Leaves of Grass*. In addition, he continued to meditate upon the various ramifications of his organic language theory, and the theory continued to exercise an important influence upon his poetic practice.[1]

---

1. Although it is difficult to trace the clippings in the *Words* notebook container, at least one clipping can be dated from each of the decades of the 1850s, 1860s, 1870s, and 1880s; see *DBN*, III, 703–9, 724–27. In addition, the Thomas Harned Collection in the Library of Congress contains a host of clippings, dating from 1869 to 1884, relating to names, Americanisms, and philological studies. Most of this material is catalogued under the title "Notes on the American Idiom" (LC #73), which also contains draft material and proof sheets of "Slang in America." For transcriptions of Whitman's late meditations on language, see *NUPM*, V, 1663–1709.

Besides the manuscript musings of *Words,* two essays published during the four decades display both the coherence and the depth of Whitman's theory of language. "Slang in America," published in 1885, contains the clearest formulation of the theory outside the last two chapters of *Rambles Among Words.*[2] And *Democratic Vistas,* which is in fact the product of notes made during the 1850s, 1860s, and early 1870s, shows how the theory relates to Whitman's overarching concern for the future of language and literature in America.[3] In both essays, moreover, the "thought of the ensemble" fuses inextricably with the "vista" of linguistic and spiritual evolution.

Although Whitman denigrated "Slang in America," the essay is really a crystallization of his theorizings about language, theorizings that began more than thirty years before the essay appeared in the *North American Review.* In the second paragraph, for example, Whitman asserts that "the United States inherit by far their most precious possession—the language they talk and write—from the Old World" (*PW,* II, 572). The sentence clearly echoes the opening of "America's Mightiest Inheritance," published in 1856. In addition, when Whitman calls slang the "lawless germinal element, below all words and sentences, and behind all poetry" (p. 572), he echoes another of his early linguistic texts. The idea of lawlessness recalls the idea of the "Real Grammar" announced in the *Primer* notes: "The Real Grammar will be that which declares itself a nucleus of the spirit of the laws, with liberty to all to carry out the spirit of the laws, even by violating them, if necessary.—The English Language is grandly lawless like the race who use it" (*DNB,* III, 735).

This vision of linguistic lawlessness relates directly to the idea of slang formulated in *Rambles:* "Thousands of words, too, make their debut as slang—gipseys and outlaws that are afterwards reclaimed by civilized society. And it is curious to observe how many of our

---

2. "Slang in America" was first published in *The North American Review* 141 (November 1885), 431–35. It was reprinted in *November Boughs* (Philadelphia: David McKay, 1888). The text cited here appears in *PW,* II, 572–77.

3. The publication history of *Democratic Vistas* is discussed by Floyd Stovall in *PW,* II, 361–62, and in Allen, *New Walt Whitman Handbook,* pp. 128–32. The text cited appears in *PW,* II, 361–426. I should note here two significant earlier interpretations of *Democratic Vistas:* Kenneth Burke, "Policy Made Personal: Whitman's Verse and Prose—Salient Traits," in *"Leaves of Grass": One Hundred Years After,* ed. Milton Hindus (Stanford, Calif.: Stanford University Press, 1955), pp. 74–108, and Richard Chase, "The Theory of America," in *Walt Whitman Reconsidered* (New York: William Sloane, 1955), pp. 153–65. For two important recent essays, see Robert J. Scholnick, "Toward a 'Wider Democratizing of Institutions': Whitman's *Democratic Vistas,*" *ATQ* 52 (1983): 287–302, and Robert L. Pincus, "A Mediated Vision, a Measured Voice: Culture and Criticism in Whitman's Prose," *WWQR* 2:1 (1984): 22–31.

stateliest terms rest on some free popular idiom, some bandied catch-word—spontaneous creation of the hour" (pp. 280–81). The figure of "gipseys and outlaws" in *Rambles* becomes, in "Slang in America," a "personage like one of Shakspere's clowns," who enters the "majestic audience-hall of the monarch" of the Old World to "play a part even in the stateliest ceremonies" (p. 573). The figure of the clown emphasizes the special position of slang as a "free popular idiom," one that can poke fun at—and thereby correct—the pretensions and errors of "civilized society." Moreover, the clown represents a nascent democracy, for the liberty of the clown allows him to move "under and out of . . . feudal institutes" (p. 572). Thus Whitman's view of slang emphasizes the political evolution from monarchy to democracy, and this evolution parallels the linguistic and spiritual evolution springing organically from the "lawless germinal element."

A second idea crystallized in "Slang in America" is that of language as an unconscious inheritance. Whitman states that "Language, be it remember'd, is not an abstract construction of the learn'd, or of dictionary-makers, but is something arising out of the work, needs, ties, joys, affections, tastes, of long generations of humanity, and has its bases broad and low, close to the ground" (p. 573). The sentence recalls Whitman's earlier project for a "Real Dictionary," and it insists that language is the organic, unconscious product of "people nearest the concrete" (p. 573).

Third, the notion of language as an unconscious inheritance of the common people is joined to Whitman's ideas about the sources of poetic expression. He says that slang is "indirection, an attempt of common humanity to escape from bald literalism, and express itself illimitably, which in highest walks produces poets and poems" (p. 573). Slang is thus equivalent to figuration itself, to "the propensity to approach a meaning not directly and squarely, but by circuitous styles of expression" (p. 574). The idea of poetry as essentially indirect harks back to the 1855 Preface, where Whitman states, "The expression of the American poet is to be transcendent and new. It is to be indirect, and not direct or descriptive or epic" (*PW*, II, 437). It also recalls his manuscript notes on the "Real Grammar," which emphasize the "elliptical and idiomatic" qualities of American English (*DBN*, III, 666–67, 809–10). It would seem, therefore, that the concept of slang is Whitman's reformulation of the earlier concepts of "indirection" and "Real Grammar," and all three ideas pertain to the essentially new, democratic, and poetic "inner life-principle" of American English.

A fourth conceptual connection between the early linguistic work and "Slang in America" relates to the idea of English as a composite language. Indeed, Whitman introduces the 1885 essay with the thought:

> View'd freely, the English language is the accretion and growth of every dialect, race, and range of time, and is both the free and compacted composition of all. From this point of view, it stands for Language in the largest sense, and is really the greatest of studies. It involves so much; is indeed a sort of universal absorber, combiner, and conqueror. The scope of its etymologies is the scope not only of man and civilization, but the history of Nature in all departments, and of the organic Universe, brought up to date; for all are comprehended in words, and their backgrounds. This is when words become vitaliz'd, and stand for things, as they unerringly and soon come to do, in the mind that enters on their study with fitting spirit, grasp, and appreciation. (p. 572)

This paragraph summarizes many of the ideas formulated in "The Growth of Words" and "English in America." Whitman shows his characteristically evolutionary view of language in the phrase "accretion and growth." Moreover, this evolutionary view places American English at the pinnacle of the "ensemble" of languages, for English is the "free and compacted composition of all." As Whitman puts it in *Rambles Among Words*, "an appreciation of the organic laws of the English Language in its historic unfolding is inseparable from considerations that embrace the ensemble of Languages" (p. 268). As in *Rambles*, then, Whitman insists upon joining the concepts of "ensemble" and "vista," for English is the "universal absorber, combiner, and conqueror" of all past languages.

The most important point is that Whitman joins his conception of American English to his vision of poetic language in general. Words, in his view, must "become vitaliz'd, and stand for things." The phrase shows the influence of Emerson's essay "The Poet," and it recalls Whitman's statements in the *Primer* notes and in *Rambles* on the necessary connection between words and things (*DBN*, III, 729, 740, 746; *Rambles*, p. 290). As we have seen, the connection insists upon the fundamentally figurative quality of all words. But it also stresses the linguistic and spiritual evolution that should result from the "fitting spirit, grasp, and appreciation" of the poet. This appreciation is most fully shown in the following paragraph from "English in America":

The future expansions of the English Language in America are already marked in the great lines of development this idiom shows. It is for us freely to follow the divine indications. And here a spinal fact is the composite character of our language: to what new realizations is it lifted in America! The immense diversity of race, temperament, character—the copious streams of humanity constantly flowing hither—must reappear in free, rich growths of speech. From no one ethnic source is America sprung: the electric reciprocations of many stocks conspired and conspire. This opulence of race-elements is in the theory of America. Land of the Ensemble, to her the consenting currents flow, and the ethnology of the States draws the grand outline of that hospitality and reception that must mark the new politics, sociology, literature and religion. (p. 288)

The parallels between the early and late formulations of Whitman's theory reveal a substantial coherence and continuity in the poet's "thought of the ensemble." And that coherence depends, furthermore, on his characteristic strategy of deferral. Whitman reveals his strategy in the concluding paragraph of "Slang in America," where he asserts that "the science of language has large and close analogies in geological science, with its ceaseless evolution, its fossils, and its numberless submerged layers and hidden strata, the infinite go-before of the present. Or, perhaps Language is more like some vast living body, or perennial body of bodies. And slang not only brings the first feeders of it, but is afterward the start of fancy, imagination and humor, breathing into its nostrils the breath of life" (p. 577). The paragraph reveals Whitman's rhetorical strategy in the imagery of "ceaseless evolution," which moves from the "infinite go-before" of the past to the "present," and from the "present" to "afterward the start of fancy, imagination and humor." In Whitman's organic metaphor, language is figured as a living organism, a body that absorbs all other bodies. And slang, a synonym for poetry, causes the body of language to live beyond the present, into an infinite future of "ceaseless evolution." By meditating upon the "lawless germinal element" of American English, then, Whitman projects American English as the idiom of all future poetic expressions.

The final paragraph of "Slang in America" suggests that the "science of language has large and close analogies in geological science, with its ceaseless evolution, its fossils, and its numberless submerged layers and hidden strata." The sentence can also stand as a double metaphor for Whitman's important essay *Democratic Vistas*. The poet notes in the beginning of the piece that "the passages of it have been written at widely different times" and that "it is, in fact, a collection of memoranda, perhaps for future designers, comprehenders" (*PW*, II, 362). Here Whitman places the burden of coherence and comprehension upon his future reader, a strategy of deferral that is by now familiar. More important, he suggests that the essay is a summation of the "ceaseless evolution" of his thought, an example of the biologist's dictum that ontogeny recapitulates phylogeny.

An examination of the three sources of *Democratic Vistas* substantiates Whitman's suggestion, and it shows that the essay is the culmination of the poet's lifelong meditation upon language as the mediator between the many and the one. Two of the sources have been documented for years—the paired essays "Democracy" and "Personalism" from the 1867–68 volumes of *The Galaxy*.[4] But the third source, the projected "third essay," remains largely unknown, for it "was not then published and perhaps not finished" (*PW*, II, 361). And this "third essay" shows most clearly the continuity and the "ceaseless evolution" of Whitman's "thought of the ensemble."

The original of the third essay is now part of the Feinberg Collection in the Library of Congress. Whitman titled it "Rough MS. of 'Democratic Vistas,' " and the "Rough MS." is precisely the "collection of memoranda" written "at widely different times" during the poet's career. The manuscript is a fascinating document, for it is written upon sheets that date from as early as the middle 1850s, perhaps prior to the first edition of *Leaves of Grass*. Furthermore, many of the sheets correspond to the types of paper Whitman used in his linguistic notebooks, *Words* and *The Primer of Words*. Several sheets are made of the same yellow paper Whitman used in the *Primer* notes, paper that was used to bind the first edition of *Leaves*. Even more of the sheets are made of the salmon-colored paper and the Williamsburgh tax forms that Whitman used in *Words*. As I have shown elsewhere, all three of these types of paper can be dated prior to 1856, and there is good reason to believe that they date from earlier years.[5] A fourth type of paper is the white sheet taken from the attorney general's office, which must date from sometime after 1 July 1865.[6] So the "Rough MS." is the result of many of Whitman's notes, made over a period of at least ten years.

The paleography of the "Rough MS." is important because it re-

4. "Democracy" appeared in *Galaxy* 4 (December 1867): 919–33; "Personalism" appeared in *Galaxy* 5 (May 1868): 540–47.

5. See "Dating Whitman's Language Studies," *WWQR* 1:2 (1983), 1–7.

6. This is the date Whitman was hired by the attorney general's office. See Gay Wilson Allen, *Solitary Singer* (New York: Macmillan, 1955), pp. 344–46.

turns us to the "long foreground" of Whitman's poetic career, a foreground that features most prominently the poet's study of language. This connection becomes especially salient when we consider the function of the "third essay" in the published version of *Democratic Vistas*. The two published sources of *Democratic Vistas* cover the two central sections of the essay (11. 368–1275). The "Rough MS." covers the fourth section, where Whitman speaks most directly about the language and literature of America.

Before considering this section in detail, we must attend to the brief introduction of the essay, which covers 367 lines. Whitman asserts that "democracy can never prove itself beyond cavil, until it founds and luxuriantly grows its own forms of art, poems, schools, theology, displacing all that exists, or that has been produced anywhere in the past, under opposite influences" (p. 365). The image of art as a natural growth of democracy recalls the last two sentences of *Rambles Among Words:* "Over the transformations of a Language the genius of a nation unconsciously presides—the issues of Words represent issues in the national thought. And in the vernal seasons of a nation's life the formative energy puts forth verbal growths opulent as flowers in spring" (p. 291).

The idea of linguistic growth becomes the basis for one of Whitman's most extravagant claims concerning the importance of literature:

> To the ostent of the senses and eyes, I know, the influences which stamp the world's history are wars, uprisings or downfalls of dynasties, changeful movements of trade, important inventions, navigation, military or civil governments, advent of powerful personalities, conquerors, &c. These of course play their part; yet, it may be, a single new thought, imagination, abstract principle, even literary style, fit for the time, put in shape by some great literatus, and projected among mankind, may duly cause changes, growths, removals, greater than the longest and bloodiest war, or the most stupendous merely political, dynastic, or commercial overturn. (p. 366)

Several rhetorical moves distance Whitman from his central claim. The conditional "it may be" tempers the tone of the passage, as does the word "even" in the phrase "even literary style." As in *Rambles Among Words*, moreover, Whitman does not name himself as the "great literatus" who will effect the verbal and spiritual "growths" of America. But these distancing devices, despite their apparent modesty, allow Whitman to assert that a "literary style" is more important than political and social events in the history of a nation. And that assertion immediately recalls the similar claim, made in "America's Mightiest Inheritance," in *Rambles Among Words*, and in "Slang in America," that the English language is the grandest and most powerful heritage America receives from the past. Whitman's "thought of the ensemble," then, lies behind this passage as the "single new thought, imagination, abstract principle, even literary style," for it is in fact all four of these rolled into one.

The idea of growth is important for yet another reason, for it is the basis of the temporal structure of *Democratic Vistas*. This organization is apparent in the penultimate paragraph of the introductory section:

> First, let us see what we can make out of a brief, general, sentimental consideration of political democracy, and whence it has arisen, with regard to some of its current features, as an aggregate, and as the basic structure of our future literature and authorship. We shall, it is true, quickly and continually find the origin-idea of the singleness of man, individualism, asserting itself, and cropping forth, even from the opposite ideas. But the mass, or lump character, for imperative reasons, is to be ever carefully weigh'd, borne in mind, and provided for. Only from it, and from its proper regulation and potency, comes the other, comes the chance of individualism. The two are contradictory, but our task is to reconcile them. (p. 373)

The central contradiction is between the two published sources of *Democratic Vistas*, "Democracy" and "Personalism." And that contradiction is synonymous with the opposition between the many and the one, an opposition with which Whitman is concerned from the beginning of his poetic career. In *Democratic Vistas*, moreover, the poet's strategy for reconciling the contradictory pair is to appeal to the idea of spiritual and linguistic evolution. The paragraph reveals this in the ordering of the two concepts. Democracy, the realm of the many, is the "basic structure," and from this structure springs "individualism," the sphere of the one. In a note to this paragraph, furthermore, Whitman suggests that "the two will merge, and will mutually profit and brace each other, and that from them a greater product, a third, will arise" (p. 373). Although he does not name the third product, Whitman's mention of "our future literature and authorship" as arising from the basic structure of political democracy indicates that these will be the means of resolving the conflict between the many and the one. Thus literature would seem to be the "greater product" of the conflict, and it is characteristic of Whitman's rhetoric to place the "greater product" in the future, for only there will the conflict actually be resolved.

The temporal structure of the paragraph provides an insight into the plan of *Democratic Vistas* as a whole. Just as the basis for all future "growth" is "political democracy," so the basis for the essay is the section derived from the *Galaxy* essay "Democracy." Just as "individualism" succeeds democracy, so the essay "Personalism" succeeds the essay "Democracy." Finally, just as literature becomes the third, "greater product," so the section devoted to language and literature follows "Personalism." The "literary style" of Whitman's magisterial piece enacts, then, the "abstract principle" of linguistic and spiritual evolution, for it presents literature as the organic product of the temporal "growth" of the many and the one in the American "land of the Ensemble."[7]

The two central sections of the essay repeatedly hint at the principle of evolution as the means to resolve the conflict between the many and the one. For instance, in the "Democracy" section, the poet asserts that "law is the unshakable order of the universe forever; and the law over all, and law of laws, is the law of successions; that of the superior law, in time, gradually supplanting and overwhelming the inferior one" (p. 381). The evolutionary principle is clear in Whitman's vision of "succession" as the "law of laws," and it places democracy on a higher level than previous forms of government. But democracy is not "of exhaustive account, in itself." Rather, it is "the best, perhaps only, fit and full means, formulater, general callerforth, trainer, for the million, not for grand material personalities only, but for immortal souls" (p. 380). Self-government becomes, in Whitman's vistalike scheme, the basis for the evolution of "grand material personalities," which in turn provide the basis for the evolution of "immortal souls."

Whitman returns to the idea of evolution in the "Personalism" section:

The problem, as it seems to me, presented to the New World, is, under permanent law and order, and after preserving cohesion (ensemble-Individuality,) at all hazards, to vitalize man's free play of special Personalism, recognizing in it something that

7. This three-part temporal and evolutionary structure is hinted at in the earliest stages of Whitman's plans for the essay. A December 1867 note on the three-part plan appears in *NUPM*, II, 859; for the "organic" imagery of literature as the spiritual result of democracy, see *NUPM*, II, 866–67.

calls ever more to be consider'd, fed, and adopted as the substra-
tum for the best that belongs to us, (government indeed is for it,)
including the new esthetics of the future. (p. 396)

The compound word "ensemble-Individuality" represents the poet's
attempt to reconcile the many and the one under the aegis of "permanent law and order." But the law that actually frames the recon-
ciliation is, once again, the law of successions. Whitman's evolutionary, progressivist principle is apparent in phrases like "after," "ever
more," and "the future." And the evolutionary frame repeats the
movement announced in the introductory section of *Democratic Vistas*, for the "permanent law and order" of democracy gives way to
"man's free play of Personalism," which in turn gives way to "the new
esthetics of the future." Thus the paradoxical idea of "ensemble-
Individuality" can be reconciled and realized only within the context
of the future, the "vista" of democratic literature in America.

The role of the "abstract principle" of evolution becomes yet
more pronounced in the fourth section of the essay. In a crucial passage (which I have mentioned in chapter 1), Whitman adumbrates
his temporal, progressivist version of the Hegelian dialectic:

I say we can only attain harmony and stability by consulting
ensemble and the ethic purports, and faithfully building upon
them. For the New World, indeed, after two grand stages of
preparation-strata, I perceive that now a third stage, being ready
for, (and without which the other two were useless,) with unmis-
takable signs appears. The First stage was the planning and put-
ting on record the political foundation rights of immense masses
of people—indeed all people—in the organization of republican
National, State, and municipal governments, all constructed
with reference to each, and each to all. This is the American programme, not for classes, but for universal man, and is embodied
in the compacts of the Declaration of Independence, and, as it
began and has now grown, with its amendments, the Federal
Constitution—and in the State governments, with all their inte-
riors, and with general suffrage; those having the sense not only
of what is in themselves, but that their certain several things
started, planted, hundreds of others in the same direction duly
arise and follow. The Second stage relates to material prosperity,
wealth, produce, labor-saving machines, iron, cotton, local,
State and continental railways, intercommunication and trade
with all lands, steamships, mining, general employment, organization of great cities, cheap appliances for comfort, number-

less technical schools, books, newspapers, a currency for money circulation, &c. The Third stage, rising out of the previous ones, to make them and all illustrious, I, now, for one, promulge, announcing a native expression-spirit, getting into form, adult, and through mentality, for these States, self-contain'd, different from others, more expansive, more rich and free, to be evidenced by original authors and poets to come, by American personalities, plenty of them, male and female, traversing the States, none excepted—and by native superber tableaux and growths of language, songs, operas, orations, lectures, architecture—and by a sublime and serious Religious Democracy sternly taking command, dissolving the old, sloughing off surfaces, and from its own interior and vital principles, reconstructing, democratizing society. (pp. 409–10)

The first point to make about the passage is that it expands upon the original version in the "Rough MS." The particular expansions need not be enumerated, but it is important to realize that the original is written on three salmon-colored sheets of the type Whitman used in the *Words* notebook. It would appear, then, that the printed version is a simple expansion of an early memorandum, so that the passage reveals a fundamental continuity in Whitman's "thought of the ensemble."

Second, the three stages clarify the somewhat vague reference, in the introductory section of *Democratic Vistas*, to the "greater product" resulting from the conflict between democracy and individualism, the many and the one. True, the present passage alters the terms of the dialectic: Most notably, the "Second stage" does not present evidence of "Personalism"; instead, it develops detailed images of "material prosperity." The evidence of individuality is now centered in the "Third stage," where the poet announces "American personalities, plenty of them, male and female, traversing the States." But Whitman's alteration of the Hegelian scheme is clearly part of a rhetorical strategy. By providing evidence of "Personalism" within the "Third stage," he effectively spiritualizes the "American personalities" he has presented in the third section of the essay. And this spiritual transformation resolves the conflict between the many and the one by appealing to the idea of a "Religious Democracy" that will result from the "native expression-spirit" and "growths of language" he projects. Whitman's transformation of the three-part scheme thus enacts the very transformation he "promulges" throughout *Democratic Vistas*.

The third and most important point raised in the passage relates to the connection between the spiritualization of America and the "growths of language." Whitman makes this connection more explicit in the following passage:

> The individuality of one nation must then, as always, lead the world. Can there be any doubt who the leader ought to be? Bear in mind, though, that nothing less than the mightiest original non-subordinated SOUL has ever really, gloriously led, or ever can lead. (This Soul—its other name, in these Vistas, is LITER-ATURE.) (p. 413)

In addition to the obvious parallel drawn between the "SOUL" and "LITERATURE," the passage reveals several links to other texts. The first sentence recalls the lines from "By Blue Ontario's Shore": "Any period one nation must lead, / One land must be the promise and reliance of the future" (58–59). More important, the idea of a nation as the leader of all other nations recalls the linguistic ethnocentrism of Bunsen and Schele de Vere, an attitude best summed up in the *Outlines of Comparative Philology:* "Language becomes, to a certain extent, a standard by which to measure the intellectual power of races, and often marks out a nation for the accomplishment of great deeds. By its intimate connection with all branches of intellectual effort, it is read by the observant student as a promise of future eminence; for he views it as an evidence of the vigor of the national mind, and as a powerful instrument of progress" (p. 89). Finally, the adjective "mightiest" echoes the 1856 essay, "America's Mightiest Inheritance," and in the passage from *Democratic Vistas* the adjective modifies both the "SOUL" and "LITERATURE." Whitman insists, therefore, on the transcendental, spiritual quality of language and literature, and he views America as the "leader" of all future progress, both linguistic and spiritual.

Implicit in the popularized versions of Hegelian dialectic is the influence of Wilhelm von Humboldt, and Whitman reveals that influence most clearly when he considers the "inner life-principle" of American English. Whitman's phrase for the principle is "the infant genius of American poetic expression," which he locates, not in the "sentimental and butterfly flights" of tradition-bound, imitative literature, but in the western states, which he calls in "Slang in America" the "special areas of slang" (p. 575). In *Democratic Vistas*, the "infant genius . . . lies sleeping, aside, unrecking itself, in some western idiom" (p. 412). Through a catalogue of American types of speech, Whitman arrives at the premise that "only from such beginnings and stocks, indigenous here, may haply arrive, be grafted, and sprout, in time, flowers of genuine American aroma, and fruits truly and fully our own" (p. 413). This last assertion employs the imagery of horticulture, dating from as early as the 1855 Preface and *Rambles Among Words*, and it explicitly echoes the final sentence of *Rambles*, the call for "verbal growths opulent as flowers in spring." The "inner life-principle," then, is the "genius of a nation," which "unconsciously presides" over its language and thought (*Rambles*, p. 291). Whitman's image of that principle as an "infant genius" reiterates the view of America as poised on the threshold of maturity, in the "vernal seasons" of its linguistic and spiritual life.

A final point concerning *Democratic Vistas* is that Whitman employs his characteristic rhetoric of deferral. Although he goes far toward outlining the task awaiting American "poets to come," he can never specify the form that American literature will take. It will be democratic, based upon the spoken, figurative indirections of slang; it will be an expression of the individual and collective "SOUL"; and it will found a "Religious Democracy" that will be, in time, the spiritualized tally to the material progress of the nation. But Whitman clearly sees that he cannot specify the form any further. As he remarks in an earlier paragraph from the fourth section, "what, then, do we mean by real literature? especially the democratic literature of the future? Hard questions to meet. The clues are inferential, and turn us to the past. At best, we can only offer suggestions, comparisons, circuits" (p. 405). The idea of "real literature" represents a significant transformation of the poet's earlier calls for a "Real Grammar" and a "Real Dictionary." Only through writing literature itself will the "real" language of the future take form. And this means that, as in the poetry of 1855–56, only the rhetorical performance of the poem can offer "suggestions, comparisons, circuits," and it can offer these figural deferments only to a perpetually deferred reader of the future. In its own circuitous style of expression, *Democratic Vistas* becomes as much a performance of "real literature" as a delineation of it.

Whitman's transformation of the "Real Grammar" into the "real literature" returns us to the rhetorical performances of *Leaves of Grass*. Several poems from the 1860 edition employ the rhetoric of deferral, and many of them do so when the poet meditates upon his "thought of the ensemble." In Section 12 of "Starting From Paumanok," for example, Whitman uses the temporal frame of linguistic and spiritual evolution to explore the relationships among democracy, the individual, and language. He begins Section 12 by directly addressing democracy:

Democracy! near at hand to you a throat is now inflating itself
and joyfully singing.

Ma femme! for the brood beyond us and of us,
For those who belong here and those to come,
I exultant to be ready for them will now shake out carols
stronger and haughtier than have ever yet been heard upon
earth.

I will make the songs of passion to give them their way,
And your songs outlaw'd offenders, for I scan you with kindred
eyes, and carry you with me the same as any.

(156–61)

The one-line opening dramatizes the act of writing poetry as the act
of singing. Then the second stanza concentrates upon the future audience of the democratic songs, "the brood beyond us and of us." Finally, the third stanza places the democratic songs in a metaphysical
light, for the democracy of literature will include the songs of "outlaw'd offenders." The first movement of Section 12 thus employs the
poet's vision of the future as a frame for the resolution of the conflict
between good and evil, and in this rhetorical strategy it is reminiscent of both "The Sleepers" and "Crossing Brooklyn Ferry."
    The second movement of Section 12 turns from democracy to the
individual, from the many to the one:

I will make the true poem of riches,
To earn for the body and the mind whatever adheres and goes
    forward and is not dropt by death;
I will effuse egotism and show it underlying all, and I will be
    the bard of personality,
And I will show of male and female that either is but the equal
    of the other,
And sexual organs and acts! do you concentrate in me, for I am
    determin'd to tell you with courageous clear voice to prove
    you illustrious,
And I will show that there is no imperfection in the present,
    and can be none in the future,
And I will show that whatever happens to anybody it may be
    turn'd to beautiful results,
And I will show that nothing can happen more beautiful than
    death,

And I will thread a thread through my poems that time and
    events are compact,
And that all the things of the universe are perfect miracles, each
    as profound as any.

(162–71)

From the generality of democracy, the poet moves to the specific
character of "personality," detailing in the clausal catalogue the
"riches" of sexuality. When he turns to the idea of the future, moreover, the theme of personality is transfigured into the theme of death,
the most perfect of all the "perfect miracles."

The final movement of Section 12 develops the theme of poetry
as the proper means toward spiritualizing democracy:

I will not make poems with reference to parts,
But I will make poems, songs, thoughts, with reference to
    ensemble,
And I will not sing with reference to a day, but with reference to
    all days,
And I will not make a poem nor the least part of a poem but has
    reference to the soul,
Because having look'd at the objects of the universe, I find there
    is no one nor any particle of one but has reference to the soul.

(172–76)

This is one of Whitman's clearest expressions of the theory of linguistic and spiritual evolution. He first announces the theme of "ensemble," and then he quickly joins that theme to its twin, the "vista"
of "all days." The double reference further leads to the goal of the
evolving ensemble, "the soul." Each of these three themes depends,
finally, upon the promise made by the poet himself, that the themes
will appear in his poems. So poetry stands as the locus of linguistic
and spiritual progress. Moreover, the organization of Section 12 indicates that Whitman's vision of the crucial role to be played by poetry is coherent with the theory of language and literature developed
in *Democratic Vistas*. For the three themes—democracy, the individual, and poetry—anticipate both the themes and their ordering in
the 1871 essay.

An important group of poems contained in the 1860 edition
shows the degree to which Whitman's linguistic concerns provide the
basis for his poetry. The first, "Vocalism," appeared in the 1860 edition
as two separate poems, "Chants Democratic," 12, and "Leaves of

Grass," 21. The second, "Laws for Creations," appeared as "Chants Democratic," 13; the third, "Poets to Come," as "Chants Democratic," 14; and the fourth, "Mediums," as "Chants Democratic," 16. If we ignore for the moment the poem "Excelsior" ("Chants Democratic," 15), the four poems of 1860 form a coherent group of meditations upon linguistic and spiritual evolution.

"Vocalism" is certainly the most developed of the four poetic meditations. The first section, in a direct address to "oratists" (1[1]), details the necessary prerequisites for future poets to come "duly to the divine power to speak words" (4). Significantly, the first stanza of the 1860 version is structured by the repetition of the temporal adverb "after," which signals the temporal, progressivist nature of Whitman's vision:

> For only at last after many years, after chastity, friendship,
>   procreation, prudence, and nakedness,
> After treading ground and breasting river and lake,
> After a loosen'd throat, after absorbing eras, temperaments,
>   races, after knowledge, freedom, crimes,
> After complete faith, after clarifyings, elevations, and removing
>   obstructions,
> After these and more, it is just possible there comes to a man, a
>   woman, the divine power to speak words.
>
>   (5–9)

The poet figures "the divine power to speak words" as the conclusion of a complex temporal catalogue that characteristically mixes stative and dynamic forms. The result is rendered concretely in the last three lines of the stanza, which figure "armies, ships, antiquities, libraries, paintings, machines, cities, hate, despair, amity, pain, theft, murder, aspiration" (11) as troops forming "in close ranks" behind the oratist. The figure recalls Section 1 of "The Sleepers," where the poet leads "a gay gang of blackguards! with mirth-shouting music and wild-flapping pennants of joy" (41), but here the "blackguards" or "journeymen divine" (36) appear as words themselves, rather than as objects, for the troops will eventually "debouch as they are wanted to march obediently through the mouth of that man or that woman" (12).

A stanza omitted from the final version of "Vocalism" reveals a close relationship between the poem and the essays "Slang in America" and *Democratic Vistas*. In the stanza, Whitman hits upon the question of the many and the one:

O now I see arise orators fit for inland America,
And I see it is as slow to become an orator as to become a man,
And I see that power is folded in a great vocalism.

$$(12[1]-[3])$$

The theme of "inland America" recalls Whitman's concern in both essays to find "the special areas of slang" (p. 575), where the "infant genius of American poetic expression . . . lies sleeping, aside, unrecking itself" (p. 412). But these "orators" exist, ultimately, only in Whitman's rhetorical act of "seeing" them arise. The second line of the stanza moves away from this rhetorical mixture of the single speaker and the many orators, for it returns to the "slow," gradual development of the "divine power to speak words," equating that development with the growth of a single individual. In the third line, Whitman figures the "divine power" as lying "folded in a great vocalism," but it must be unfolded—etymologically, evolved—by the progressing literary spirit of the American nation. Once again, the three lines employ the triad Whitman uses in *Democratic Vistas* and "Starting from Paumanok": The first line concentrates upon the democratic many; the second line focuses upon the personal development of the individual; and the third line presents "a great vocalism" as the resolution of the contradiction between the many and the one.

Whereas Section 1 of "Vocalism," titled "To Oratists" in the 1871 edition of *Leaves of Grass*, depends upon the direct address of the poet to future orators, Section 2, titled "Voices" in the 1871 edition, presents the poet's meditations upon spoken language itself. The 1860 version of the section opens with the following line: "Now I make a leaf of Voices—for I have found nothing mightier than they are" (13[1]). The word "mightier" immediately recalls "America's Mightiest Inheritance," as well as the other echoes of the phrase in *Rambles Among Words* and "Slang in America." Moreover, the ensuing lines of the section directly echo the theme of the "efflux of the soul" developed in Section 1 of "The Sleepers":

And I have found that no word spoken, but is beautiful, in its
    place,
O what is it in me that makes me tremble so at voices?

Surely whoever speaks to me in the right voice, him or her I
    shall follow,
As the water follows the moon, silently, with fluid steps,
    anywhere around the globe.

$$(13[2]-15)$$

The image of someone speaking to the poet "in the right voice" harks back to the "Sleepers" notebook, and the parallel with that early text is reinforced by the echo of Section 7: "The soul is always beautiful, it appears more or it appears less, it comes or it lags behind" (150). Even more striking is the parallel between Section 7 of "The Sleepers" and the next stanza of "Vocalism":

> All waits for the right voices;
> Where is the practis'd and perfect organ? where is the
>   develop'd soul?
> For I see every word utter'd thence has deeper, sweeter, new
>   sounds, impossible on less terms.
>
> (16–18)

The verb "waits" echoes the principal repetend of the closing stanza of Section 7, where the poet first asserts that the "universe is duly in order, every thing is in its place" (155) but then shifts into his more characteristic rhetoric of deferral: "The twisted skull waits, the watery or rotten blood waits, / The child of the glutton or venerealee waits long, and the child of the drunkard waits long, and the drunkard himself waits long" (157–58). The triple echo of "The Sleepers"— "beautiful," "in its place," and "waits"—reinforces the twin themes of the "develop'd soul" and language, and it treats the themes in exactly the same manner as does the 1855 poem.

Whitman's characteristic treatment emphasizes the always deferring process of linguistic and spiritual evolution, a process that becomes the basis for the poet's most extravagant attempts at resolving the contradictions between the many and the one. In the final stanza of "Vocalism," these same strategies are at work:

> I see brains and lips closed, tympans and temples unstruck,
> Until that comes which has the quality to strike and to unclose,
> Until that comes which has the quality to bring forth what lies
>   slumbering forever ready in all words.
>
> (19–21)

In the first line, the rhetorical chiasmus between the quasi-mental ("brains" and "temples") and the sensory ("lips" and "tympans") envelops the two aspects of voices in silence. In the second line, however, a second rhetorical chiasmus "strikes" and "uncloses" the "closed" and "unstruck" silence. The last line joins two unspecified sources of poetic power: The first appears to reside in the "develop'd soul" of the poet, while the second "lies slumbering forever ready in all words." This last phrase clearly forecasts the "infant genius" passage of *Democratic Vistas*, presenting the image of a democracy of words. Whitman's rhetoric joins the individual power of the poet to the democratic power of "what lies slumbering forever ready in all words" through the mediating power of linguistic and spiritual evolution. For the resolution of the paradox of the one and the many depends upon the deferring rhetoric of the repeated word "until," which postpones the resolution to an ever-receding future. As in "The Sleepers," then, Whitman's act of "present-saying" springs from his vision of the always developing soul, a soul that finds its voice in an always developing language.

The next poem in the group gives Whitman's "Laws for Creations," which center upon future creators. The poet announces the laws "for fresh broods of teachers and perfect literats for America, / For noble savans and coming musicians" (2–3). The word "coming" anticipates the following poem, "Poets to Come," and it frames the pronouncement of Whitman's laws within the rhetoric of deferral. Significantly, those laws feature three of Whitman's characteristic themes:

> All must have reference to the ensemble of the world, and the
>   compact truth of the world,
> There shall be no subject too pronounced—all works shall
>   illustrate the divine law of indirections.
>
> What do you suppose creation is?
> What do you suppose will satisfy the soul, except to walk free
>   and own no superior?
> What do you suppose I would intimate to you in a hundred
>   ways, but that man or woman is as good as God?
> And that there is no God any more divine than Yourself?
> And that that is what the oldest and newest myths finally
>   mean?
> And that you or any one must approach creations through such
>   laws?
>
> (4–11)

The first theme is "the ensemble," although here Whitman applies the concept to the world rather than to language. That displacement reveals the poet's tendency to view the word and the thing as ontologically equivalent and interchangeable. The second theme is "the divine law of indirections," a concept that immediately recalls Whitman's concern for the figurative quality of language. That concern, as we have seen, is the focus of "Slang in America," and it is already evident in the 1855 Preface. The third theme is "the soul," which the poet treats here in terms of "personalism." Thus the third theme recalls the final movement of *Democratic Vistas*.

The arrangement of the three themes reveals Whitman's inevitable mixture of "ensemble" and "vista." The first theme concerns the composite character of the "world," a word that includes both America and American English as significant instances of the law of "ensemble." But Whitman's focus on "ensemble" gives rise to "the divine law of indirections," which implies a temporal, evolutionary goal for all figurative transformations. That goal becomes specified in the third theme, "the soul" or "Yourself." The divine self is the goal of the ensemble, and the means to that goal is "indirection," or poetic language. In these terms, then, "Laws for Creations" strongly echoes "The Sleepers," for in both poems language implicitly brings about the spiritual transformation of all language users.

In "Poets to Come" and "Mediums," Whitman turns even more explicitly to future creators, to those who will obey the laws for creation that he has announced. The first of the poems employs the rhetoric of direct address, and in doing so it marks its continuity with the final stanza of "Laws for Creations." In addressing the "new brood" (3) of poets, Whitman calls for them to "justify" him, for he frankly admits that "of to-day I know I am momentary, untouched— I am the bard of the future" (4[7]). The rhetoric of deferral functions here to create a tone of unusual humility: "I myself but write one or two indicative words for the future, / I but advance a moment only to wheel and hurry back in the darkness" (5–6). The second line recalls both "The Sleepers" and "Crossing Brooklyn Ferry." In both of those earlier poems, the poet presents himself as involved in complementary movements of projection and return, and in both poems language functions to protect the poet from his inevitable return to the "darkness" of death. These echoes contribute to the restrained power of "Poets to Come," for they indicate a limited version of two of Whitman's most dramatic poetic performances. The echoes multiply even further in the last stanza of the poem:

> I am a man who, sauntering along without fully stopping, turns
>   a casual look upon you and then averts his face,
> Leaving it to you to prove and define it,
> Expecting the main things from you.

$$(7–9)$$

The image of the poet as "sauntering along without fully stopping" recalls the casual loafer of "Song of Myself," but the previous echo of "The Sleepers" tempers the apparent casualness of the image. This becomes clearer when we remember the opening stanza of "The Sleepers," where Whitman portrays himself as "pausing, gazing, bending, and stopping" (5). In "Poets to Come," Whitman both declares his faith in the future and recognizes his limitations in the present, and this combination creates one of his most effective short lyrics.

In "Mediums" the poet no longer "averts his face." Instead, he turns it fully to the future:

> They shall arise in the States,
> They shall report Nature, laws, physiology, and happiness,
> They shall illustrate Democracy and the kosmos,
> They shall be alimentive, amative, perceptive,
> They shall be complete women and men, their pose brawny and
>   supple, their drink water, their blood clean and clear,
> They shall fully enjoy materialism and the sight of products,
>   they shall enjoy the sight of the beef, lumber, bread-stuffs, of
>   Chicago the great city,
> They shall train themselves to go in public to become orators
>   and oratresses,
> Strong and sweet shall their tongues be, poems and materials of
>   poems shall come from their lives, they shall be makers and
>   finders,
> Of them and of their works shall emerge divine conveyers, to
>   convey gospels,
> Characters, events, retrospections, shall be convey'd in gospels,
>   trees, animals, waters, shall be convey'd,
> Death, the future, the invisible faith, shall all be convey'd.
>
> (1–11)

The entire poem is a future-tense clausal catalogue, and the catalogue rhetoric indicates the expansive, affirmative tone of the poem. After having announced the "Laws for Creations" and addressed the "Poets to Come," Whitman now confidently lists the qualities of the future "Mediums." The catalogue reveals the same evolutionary vision that structures both "Vocalism" and *Democratic Vistas*. From the foundation of "Democracy" (3) and "materialism" (6) spring the individual "makers and finders" (8), and these poets in turn grow into "divine conveyors, to convey gospels" (9). Thus the spiritual inevitably grows out of the material, and its means for doing so is, as always, language. In addition, the active character of the "conveying" moves toward Whitman's ever-present goal: "Death, the future, the invisible faith" (11). So Whitman's catalogue of the many, the "ensemble," finds its ultimate unity in the "vista" of the future linguistic and spiritual "Mediums."

The poet's vistalike "thought of the ensemble" resurfaces in an important later poem, "Thou Mother with Thy Equal Brood." Like "Vocalism," the poem is a composite of two separate texts. Section 1 of "Thou Mother" is a revision of "One Song, America, Before I Go," which appeared as a prefatory poem to the 1872 volume *As A Strong Bird on Pinions Free* (*Variorum*, III, 632–33). Sections 2–6 appeared in the same volume as the title poem (*Variorum*, III, 634). Only in the 1881 edition of *Leaves of Grass* did Whitman bring the two texts together. And as in the case of "Vocalism," the revision joins two parallel strands of thought.

Section 1 of "Thou Mother with Thy Equal Brood" begins with a direct address to America, recapitulating several of the poet's characteristic themes:

> Thou Mother with thy equal brood,
> Thou varied chain of different States, yet one identity only,
> A special song before I go I'd sing o'er all the rest,
> For thee, the future.
>
> I'd sow a seed for thee of endless Nationality,
> I'd fashion thy ensemble including body and soul,
> I'd show away ahead thy real Union, and how it may be
>   accomplish'd.
>
> The paths to the house I seek to make,
> But leave to those to come the house itself.
>
> Belief I sing, and preparation;
> As Life and Nature are not great with reference to the present
>   only,
> But greater still from what is yet to come,
> Out of that formula for thee I sing.
>
> (1–13)

The "equal brood" of the first line transforms the image of the "new brood" of poets developed in "Laws for Creations" and "Poets to Come," for here it refers to the "varied chain of different States." Still, the fundamental theme of the many and the one is present in the familial image, and Whitman relates the theme to his poetry in the following line: "A special song before I go I'd sing o'er all the rest." The "special song" is "Thou Mother with Thy Equal Brood" itself, especially as it appears in the final edition of *Leaves of Grass*. And the poet conceives of that song as the one which will stand "o'er all the rest" of his many poems. Finally, the stanza resolves the double opposition between the one and the many by appealing to "the future," and this is by now a familiar rhetorical act.

The rhetoric of deferral structures the rest of Section 1. The poet conditionally announces the future "ensemble" of America, which will include "body and soul," and this characteristic image becomes, in the following line, the "real Union." The image of the "real Union" brings to mind Whitman's earlier plans for a "Real Grammar," "real dictionary," and "real literature." And as in the use of the word "brood," the poet displaces the linguistic and literary, transfiguring them into an image of a spiritualized America of the future. In the third stanza, the poet returns to the restrained tone of "Poets to Come," for the "house" he refers to will be the language and literature of America.[8] Thus the figuration of Section 1 conceals Whitman's concern with the purely verbal, and this act of concealment attempts to render the mediating presence of literary language as transparent as possible.

Whitman's persistent emphasis on the future, the realm where the many and the one will be resolved, remains the keynote of sections 2 through 6 of "Thou Mother with Thy Equal Brood," but his treatment of the relationship between the past and the present changes as the poem progresses. In Section 2, for instance, the poet presents the opposition between past and present poetic forms:

> The conceits of the poets of other lands I'd bring thee not,
> Nor the compliments that have served their turn so long,
> Nor rhyme, nor the classics, nor perfume of foreign court or
>   indoor library;
> But an odor I'd bring as from forests of pine in Maine, or breath
>   of an Illinois prairie,
> With open airs of Virginia or Georgia or Tennessee, or from
>   Texas uplands, or Florida's glades,

8. The linguistic and literary qualities of the "house" are apparent in the following manuscript "Introduction" to *Leaves of Grass:* "I commenced Leaves of Grass in my thirty-sixth year, by my publishing their first issue. Four times have I issued them since, each time with successive increase; this being the fifth issue. I am to-day, (May 31, 1870) fifty-one years old; for I write. . . . The paths to the house are made—but where is the house itself? At most, only indicated or touched" (*NUPM*, IV, 1485–86).

> Or the Saguenay's black stream, or the wide blue spread of
>   Huron,
> With presentment of Yellowstone's scenes, or Yosemite,
> And murmuring under, pervading all, I'd bring the rustling sea-
>   sound,
> That endlessly sounds from the two Great Seas of the world.
>
> (18–26)

This opposition parallels the one set by the "infant genius" passage in *Democratic Vistas:* Instead of the "highly-refined imported and gilt-edged themes" of the Old World, the poet calls for "flowers of genuine American aroma" (*PW,* II, 412–13). In the present passage, the catalogue of American place-names parallels the similar catalogue in the "infant genius" passage, and in both the names represent the democratic many, which will now replace the aristocratic few of Old World literature.

This seemingly unresolvable opposition is reminiscent of the image of American English as the "speech of the Modern" in *Rambles Among Words,* for the poet sees American poetry as absolutely discontinuous with the antidemocratic "perfume of foreign court or indoor library." But this absolute discontinuity between past and present raises a serious problem, for how is American English to be seen as organically growing out of the past if it is absolutely other than past languages and the national spirits expressed by those languages? The contradiction is already contained in *Rambles,* of course, where the image of American English as "breaking up the crystalline structure of the classic mould" (p. 271) opposes the image of the language as "displaying successive processes of growth and development within the limits of its linguistic individuality" (p. 266).

But Whitman is not interested in resolving this contradiction. Instead, the two views of the relationship between past and present languages become two possibilities of poetic expression. The discontinuous view appears in Section 2 of "Thou Mother with Thy Equal Brood," and it seems to be the main outlook Whitman adopts in *Democratic Vistas.* It reappears in the first stanza of Section 3, where the poet addresses the "Brain of the New World" and assigns it the following task:

> To formulate the Modern—out of the peerless grandeur of the
>   modern,
> Out of thyself, comprising science, to recast poems, churches,
>   art,

(Recast, may-be discard them, end them—may-be their work is
   done, who knows?)
By vision, hand, conception, on the background of the mighty
   past, the dead,
To limn with absolute faith the mighty living present.

(35–39)

The image of "recasting" corresponds to the earlier image of "breaking up the crystalline structure of the classic mould," and the poet
even goes so far as to suggest that it might be best to discard all past
models of art and religion.

The image of the "background of the mighty past," however, hints
at the second view of the relationship between past and present,
which the second stanza of Section 3 develops in detail:

And yet thou living present brain, heir of the dead, the Old
   World brain,
Thou that lay folded like an unborn babe within its folds so
   long,
Thou carefully prepared by it so long—haply thou but
   unfoldest it, only maturest it,
It to eventuate in thee—the essence of the by-gone time
   contain'd in thee,
Its poems, churches, arts, unwitting to themselves, destined
   with reference to thee;
Thou but the apples, long, long, long a-growing,
The fruit of all the Old ripening to-day in thee.

(40–46)

The organic metaphors of birth and growth evoke Whitman's gradualist, organic view of change. They also recall the geological metaphor of linguistic "strata" with which he ends "Slang in America."
Moreover, the "living present brain" corresponds to the image of the
clown entering "the majestic audience-hall of the monarch" (p. 573).
For, like the clown, the role of American English is to bring wit to the
"unwitting" past, to express illimitably what has only been expressed
in a limited fashion in the past.

In the last three sections of "Thou Mother with Thy Equal
Brood," Whitman abandons the discontinuous view in favor of the
more conservative, gradualist conception of linguistic and spiritual
change. Thus, for instance, in Section 4 he figures America as the
"ship of Democracy" (47), and he asserts that "the antecedent nations
sink or swim with thee" (52). In Section 5, he specifically mentions

language in terms that recall the organic view of "The Growth of Words":

> Yet in beginning only, incalculable masses of composite
>   precious materials,
> By history's cycles forwarded, by every nation, language, hither
>   sent,
> Ready, collected here, a freer, vast, electric world, to be
>   constructed here,
> (The true New World, the world of orbic science, morals,
>   literatures to come.)
>
> (66–69)

Language is figured here as the medium of history's evolutionary "forwarding," and the passage implies that language will be the instrument for the construction of the future "true New World." The implication becomes explicit in the catalogue that closes Section 5, for there the poet emphasizes the crucial role to be played by "these leaves and chants" (91) in "formulating" the "soaring course" of America (90).

If Section 3 reveals the first turning point in the poem, where the opposition of past and present is transfigured to become an "ensemble," Section 5 is the second turning point, for it is here that Whitman moves from the present to the future. Significantly, this is also where the poet emphasizes the special role of literature in bringing about the linguistic and spiritual transformation of America. Section 6 continues this movement, which takes place under the "natal stars" of "Ensemble, Evolution, Freedom" (102). And the movement from past to present, from present to future, "debouches" in Whitman's double goal—the soul and the future:

> The soul, its destinies, the real real,
> (Purport of all these apparitions of the real;)
> In thee America, the soul, its destinies,
> Thou globe of globes! thou wonder nebulous!
> By many a throe of heat and cold convuls'd, (by these thyself
>   solidifying,)
> Thou mental, moral orb—thou New, indeed new, Spiritual
>   World!
> The Present holds thee not—for such vast growth as thine,
> For such unparallel'd flight as thine, such brood as thine,
> The FUTURE only holds thee and can hold thee.
>
> (123–31)

Whitman's rhetoric of deferral functions here in much the same way as in "The Sleepers," for in both poems the image of future spiritual realization grounds the poet's optimistic "present-saying." As in Section 1 of "Thou Mother with Thy Equal Brood," moreover, Whitman attempts to render language transparent, since the "Spiritual World" he announces cannot be "held" by language. But Whitman's rhetoric inevitably contradicts itself: By appealing to the "FUTURE," the poet wishes to erase the very medium of appeal. Thus "the real real" (123) replaces Whitman's earlier conceptions of the "Real Grammar" and the "real literature," but the substitution is ultimately metaphorical, and it points out the central role of language as the figural medium of "indirection."

This new emphasis on the "real real" causes Whitman to pursue the technique of figurative displacement throughout the later poems of *Leaves of Grass*, and as a result it is often difficult to find poetic meditations upon language itself. Still, because of the contradictory quality of Whitman's rhetoric, language is implied in his meditations upon the future. In "Prayer of Columbus," for example, the poet develops a dramatic monologue in which the situation of Columbus in 1503 parallels that of the aging poet in 1876, for each is a "batter'd, wreck'd old man" (1). In the note to the *Two Rivulets* version of the poem, Whitman focuses upon language as the means of presenting the parallel: "See, the figure of the great Admiral, walking the beach, as a stage, in this sublimest tragedy—for what tragedy, what poem, so piteous and majestic as the real scene?—and hear him uttering—as his mystical and religious soul surely utter'd, the ideas following—perhaps, in their equivalents, the very words" (*Variorum*, III, 661–62). The sentence plays upon the mixture of the literary and the real, as in the figures of the "stage" and "the real scene." That mixture parallels the merging of the "mystical and religious soul" and the "very words" in the second half of the sentence. And Whitman negotiates these figurative transactions by appealing to the truth of his "very words," even though he wishes to present the "real scene" as a drama of the soul.

The tension between the verbal and the nonverbal organizes much of the poem, which takes the form of a direct address to God. When Columbus asserts, for instance, that God is the source of all his ambitions, he catalogues nonverbal elements of the spirit:

O I am sure they really came from Thee,
The urge, the ardor, the unconquerable will,
The potent, felt, interior command, stronger than words,

> A message from the Heavens whispering to me even in sleep,
> These sped me on.
>
> (26–30)

The passage paradoxically lists qualities that are supposed to be "stronger than words," but it does so in terms of a "command" or "message" that is "whispered" to the speaker "from the Heavens." Similarly, in a later passage the speaker figures this divine source as having lighted his life "with ray of light, steady, ineffable, vouchsafed of Thee, / Light rare untellable, lighting the very light, / Beyond all signs, descriptions, languages" (42–44). But this vision of an inexpressible source of light, beyond the merely verbal, gives rise in the next lines to the verbal: "For that O God, be it my latest word, here on my knees, / Old, poor, and paralyzed, I thank Thee" (45–46).

The human response, or "latest word," to the divine "Light rare untellable" culminates, in the final stanza of the poem, in a mixture of sight and sound:

> And these things I see suddenly, what mean they?
> As if some miracle, some hand divine unseal'd my eyes,
> Shadowy vast shapes smile through the air and sky,
> And on the distant waves sail countless ships,
> And anthems in new tongues I hear saluting me.
>
> (62–66)

The imagery of sight parallels the earlier imagery of light, and in both cases the images represent the inexpressibility of the divine. But in this last stanza the speaker's eyes are "unseal'd," and he is allowed a vision of the "shadowy vast" future of America. When that vision is delivered, Whitman figures it in terms of sound, the "anthems in new tongues." The poem therefore portrays the resolution of the one and the many through language, for the single "prayer" of the solitary Columbus gives rise to the many "anthems in new tongues" of the future American singers. And those anthems "salute" the speaker, reassuring him that his ambitions will be realized in ways he cannot concretely imagine in the present.

The twin dialectic of present and future, verbal and nonverbal, elucidates Whitman's continuing need to put his vision of the future into words. The poet can never be satisfied with the composite "ensemble," for only the "vista" of the future provides the "real" resolution of the many into a unified, organic one. The late poem "The Unexpress'd" (1891) clearly shows this poetic need, and it does so by focusing upon the literary tradition itself:

How dare one say it?
After the cycles, poems, singers, plays,
Vaunted Ionia's, India's—Homer, Shakspere—the long, long
   times' thick dotted roads, areas,
The shining clusters and the Milky Ways of stars—Nature's
   pulses reap'd,
All retrospective passions, heroes, war, love, adoration,
All ages' plummets dropt to their utmost depths,
All human lives, throats, wishes, brains—all experiences'
   utterance;
After the countless songs, or long or short, all tongues, all lands,
Still something not yet told in poesy's voice or print—
   something lacking,
(Who knows? the best yet unexpress'd and lacking.)

The poem moves from past literary performances to Whitman's own present "retrospective" vision of his performances in *Leaves of Grass*. This movement is only implied here, but the position of "The Unexpress'd" in the *Good-Bye My Fancy* annex supports the inference, for the poem immediately follows "L. of G.'s Purport" (*Variorum*, III, 748–49). "The Unexpress'd," then, is a catalogue of summation, running through the "countless songs, or long or short, all tongues, all lands," including Whitman's own productions. But this act of summation fails to recapitulate the entire "ensemble," since Whitman characteristically turns to the future in the last two lines of the poem. The image of "something not yet told" provides Whitman the possibility of future expression, and it does so in progressivist terms: "the best yet unexpress'd and lacking." By deferring the realization of "the best" to an unspecifiable future, Whitman clears himself imaginative space for his own "countless songs, or long or short." So far as *Leaves of Grass* itself is concerned, this vistalike conception of the "ensemble" helps to explain why the poet continued to add the "annexes" to the "final" edition of the poems. For there can be no final expression if the "best" remains "unexpress'd and lacking."

   The prose and poetry of 1856 through 1892 reveal a fundamental continuity in Whitman's "thought of the ensemble," a continuity based upon his persistent vision of linguistic and spiritual evolution in America. But within that continuity we find variations in the poet's view of the relationship between American English and its antecedents. These are actually variations in emphasis, however, rather than absolute differences in conception or principle. It would seem, then, that during the 1870s—at some point around the publication of *Democratic Vistas* in 1871 and the publication of *As a Strong Bird on*

Pinions Free in 1872—Whitman begins to stress the cumulative, retrospective qualities of the "ensemble" of American English. This theory helps to explain the seemingly radical changes in Whitman's poetic language after the publication of *Passage to India* in 1871. For the poet's increasing use of archaic, formal, abstract diction enacts the cumulative quality of American English, blending the ancient and the modern to form a linguistic "ensemble." And that "ensemble" is, in its effects, more conservative and retrospective than the language experiments of the 1855–56 editions of *Leaves of Grass*. Still, there remains the important, fundamental commitment throughout all six editions of *Leaves:* the commitment to the "vista" of future linguistic and spiritual developments. Both the continuities and the changes in emphasis lead us to the stylistic, rhetorical performances of the last four editions.

5

"The New Bible": Programmatic Style in the 1860 *Leaves of Grass*

In June 1857 Whitman wrote a famous self-admonition headed *"The Great Construction* of the *New Bible,"* in which he formally dedicated himself to "the principal object—the main life work—the Three Hundred & Sixty five" (*NUPM*, I, 353). That same month he outlined the poetic project in somewhat different terms:

> I wish now to bring out a third edition—I have now *a hundred* poems ready (the last edition had thirty-two). . . . In the forthcoming Vol. I shall have, as I said, a hundred poems, and no other matter but poems. . . . It is, I know well enough, that *that* must be the *true* Leaves of Grass—and I think it has an aspect of completeness, and makes its case clearer. The old poems are all retained. The difference is in the new character given to the mass, by the additions.[1]

1. *The Correspondence of Walt Whitman,* ed. Edwin Haviland Miller (New York: New York University Press, 1961), I, 44. Miller points out Whitman's incorrect dating of the letter, a fact which makes the numerical discrepancy between the manuscript

The difference between the two notions is one of quantity rather than quality, for in both documents Whitman is clearly announcing a "new character" to *Leaves of Grass*, one which is explicitly religious and didactic.[2] This suggests that the "efflux of the soul," a strong undercurrent in many of the poems of 1855–56, will surface more obviously in the poems of the 1860 edition.

One of the clearest embodiments of the "new character" is "Starting from Paumanok," which serves as the proem to Whitman's "programme of chants" (39).[3] The title of one manuscript draft of the poem, "Premonition," is richly polysemic, mixing the sense of a private feeling with that of a public notice, or warning, concerning future events.[4] Moreover, an 1856 notebook containing draft lines for "Premonition" suggests that Whitman associated the "programme" with his studies concerning language. On one leaf of the notebook the poet writes the title "Primer of words and Thoughts Ideas Principles" (*DBN*, III, 781); only fifteen leaves later, he drafts the verses that would eventually become Section 2 of "Starting from Paumanok" (*DBN*, III, 784). The collocation of title and verse indicates a close relationship between the linguistic notebooks, such as *Primer of Words*, and the "language experiment" of the new *Leaves of Grass*.[5] In

---

note and the letter—365 as opposed to 100—even more intriguing than it would otherwise be.

2. Grier argues that in *Whitman's Manuscripts: "Leaves of Grass" (1860), A Parallel Text* (Chicago: University of Chicago Press, 1955), pp. xxxv–xxxvi, editor Fredson Bowers "worries the text" of the manuscript note (*NUPM*, I, 353). Despite occasional worrying, Bowers's introduction to the "Growth of the Third Edition" (pp. xxxiii–li) remains invaluable.

3. Following the method employed in Part 1, I cite the 1881 edition of "Starting from Paumanok" as printed in the *Variorum*.

4. The etymological sense of "premonition" as a forewarning is, in fact, the only definition given by the *Shorter Oxford English Dictionary*: "The action of premonishing; a previous notification or warning of subsequent events; a forewarning." *Webster's* (1847) defines it as "previous warning, notice, or information. Christ gave to his disciples *premonitions* of their sufferings."

The text of "Premonition" is edited and printed in Bowers, *1860 Manuscripts*, pp. 2–36. Two appendixes also print earlier trial lines for "Premonition." Appendix I gives lines contained in the Valentine-Barrett manuscripts at the University of Virginia (pp. 36–39), while Appendix II gives parts of the important notebook contained in the Feinberg Collection at the Library of Congress (pp. 40–56). The entire notebook is edited in *DBN*, III, 777–803, from which I quote.

5. The notebook can be dated to September–October 1856 because of Whitman's notes on the inside front cover and flyleaf (*DBN*, III, 777–78). The date of the notebook indicates that Whitman was drafting "Premonition" shortly after the publication both of "America's Mightiest Inheritance" in April 1856 and of the second edition of *Leaves of Grass* in September 1856. For paleographical connections of these two texts to the *Primer* notebook, see "Dating Whitman's Language Studies," pp. 2–3.

other parts of the "Premonition" notebook, Whitman drafts lines that eventually form Section 14 of "Starting from Paumanok." On two leaves the poet sketches four ideas: "Endless Announcements," "Words of America," "The mother's, father's, husband's, wife's, son's, daughter's words," and the admonition, *The Proem must have throughout a strong saturation of America. The West, the Geography, the representative American man*" (*DBN*, III, 792). The four notebook entries yield, in exact sequence, the four stanzas of Section 14. So it is clear that Whitman associates his "programme of chants" with the linguistic vista of a "Primer of words."

Equally important is the notion of a "Primer," an introductory book on any subject. Whitman's "Proto-Leaf" serves as the "Primer of words and Thoughts Ideas Principles" that introduces the reader of *Leaves of Grass* to the terms and ideas of the poetic "programme." Not surprisingly, I would argue that the "programme" of the "*New Bible*," while multifaceted, focuses sharply on linguistic and spiritual evolution. And "Starting from Paumanok" functions as the verbal embodiment of Whitman's progressivist vision. For example, Section 1 of the poem begins the initiation of the reader with dynamic agential nouns. The poet portrays himself as a "*lover* of populous pavements" (3) and a "*dweller* in Mannahatta my city" (4), and he calls the Missouri River "the free fresh *giver*" (9). Whitman characteristically mixes these ad hoc nouns with established ones like "soldier" and "miner" (5), and the mixture emphasizes the dynamic quality of the speaker, who is actively "tallying, vocalizing all" (5[2]). Other instances of dynamic agential nouns are *language-shapers* (56), *satisfier* (67), *offenders* (161), *corpse-cleaners* (182), and, in the penultimate line of the poem, *desirer* and *lover* (270). In general the nouns are deverbal and dynamic, and they tend to emphasize the creative act of naming. As in the poems of 1855–56, the deverbal style blurs any distinction between flowing activity and stable identity, just as the dynamic quality of Whitman's poetics blurs the distinction between the one poet and his many readers.

The continuities between "Starting from Paumanok" and the earlier poems deepens when we turn to foreign borrowings. In the proem, Whitman employs many of the key words in his poetic vocabulary: *kosmos* (17), *debouch* (27), *Americanos* (32, 37), *Libertad* (38), *programme* (39), *philosoph* (54), *finalè* (66), *evangel-poem* (92), *en-masse* (96; 1860 edition only), *omnes* (98), *camerado* (123, 266), *ma femme* (157), *ensemble* (173), *adobie* (198), *sierras* (203), *dolce affettuoso* (233), *vistas* (248), and *arriere* (254). Perhaps the most surprising fact about the words in this list is that none is bound by the subject treated. At first glance, *adobie* seems determined by the context of the line within which it appears ("Land of the herd, the garden, the healthy house of adobie"), but there is no inherent connection between the general terms "herd," "garden," and "house" and the more specific term "adobie." In the same catalogue, Whitman praises the "land of sierras and peaks," and the use of the Spanish word is once again a matter of stylistic choice, especially since the notebook admonition specifically mentions "The West" as a necessary part of the "strong saturation of America" needed in the proem. Like the majority of the ad hoc, temporary agential nouns, foreign borrowings in "Starting from Paumanok" emphasize the freedom of the poet in using "the master's words" (*DBN*, III, 792).

A second feature of the words in the list is that many are used to express "new political and social relations" (*Rambles*, p. 273). One set of such terms includes the Spanish words *Americanos*, *Libertad*, and *camerado*. Whitman's vision of political democracy entails the dissemination of liberty to the West and to Latin America:

> See revolving the globe,
> The ancestor-continents away group'd together,
> The present and future continents north and south, with the
>   isthmus between.
>
> (22–24)

Within the framework of syntactic parallelism, the United States occupies the "present" continent of the North America, whereas the countries of Latin America occupy the "future" continent of South America. The poet's use of Spanish terms for "Americans," "Liberty," and "comrades" reflects his vision of the future audience of his "evangel-poem," an audience that will merge within a new political and social ensemble.

An equally important set of such terms is French, and it includes the two key words of Section 12, *ma femme* and *ensemble*. As we have seen in the poems of 1855–56, the latter term evokes a vision of an evolving spiritual and linguistic totality. The first term is new to the 1860 edition, and it occurs in two other poems first published there, "[States]" and "France, the 18th Year of these States."[6] In "Starting from Paumanok," the phrase creates the image of a spiritual marriage

---

6. The poem "[States]" appeared only in the 1860 edition of *Leaves of Grass*, as part of the "Calamus" cluster, but it served as the source of two later poems—"Over the Carnage Rose Prophetic a Voice" (first printed in *Drum-Taps* in 1865 and included in the "Drum-Taps" cluster in later editions), and "For You O Democracy," which became part of the "Calamus" cluster in 1867. For all three poems, see *Variorum*, II, 371–75.

between the poet and a personified "Democracy" (156). In "France,"
the image of a spiritual spouse is applied to "Liberty," which the poet
calls a "mate for me" (12). Finally, in "[States]," the spouse is once
again "Democracy."

Both "Starting from Paumanok" and "[States]" connect the image of "ma femme" to the future of America. In the proem, for instance, the direct address to Democracy leads to the vista of Democracy's offspring:

> Ma femme! for the brood beyond us and of us,
> For those who belong here and those to come,
> I exultant to be ready for them will now shake out carols
>   stronger and haughtier than have ever yet been heard upon
>   earth.
>
> (157–59)

The "brood" of future readers seems to spring from the ideal union of
the poet and Democracy, but in "[States]" the union is itself the result
of the ideal of manly love:

> I will make the continent indissoluble,
> I will make the most splendid race the sun ever yet shone upon,
> I will make divine magnetic lands.
>
> I will plant companionship thick as trees along all the rivers of
>   America, and along the shores of the great lakes, and all over
>   the prairies,
> I will make inseparable cities, with their arms about each
>   other's necks.
>
> For you these, from me, O Democracy, to serve you, ma femme!
> For you! for you, I am trilling these songs.
>
> (36–42)

Here the power to transform America into a spiritual democracy re-
sides with the poet, whereas Section 12 of "Starting from Paumanok"
represents that transformation as a natural, organic outcome of the
union of the poet with "ma femme." In both poems, however, Whitman's belief in the wholeness of the "ensemble"—in "ma femme"—
depends upon the "vista" of future "camerados," which he calls "an
audience interminable" (30).

A third category of programmatic diction is the American place-name.[7] Geographical features figure prominently throughout "Starting from Paumanok," beginning in the title, but they are especially striking in the catalogues of sections 3, 14, and 16. The 1860 version of the first catalogue suggests a reason for this "strong saturation of America":

> Chants of the prairies,
> Chants of the long-running Mississippi,
> Chants of Ohio, Indiana, Illinois, Wisconsin, Iowa, and
>   Minnesota,
> Inland chants—chants of Kanzas,
> Chants away down to Mexico, and up north to Oregon—
>   Kanadian chants,
> Chants of teeming and turbulent cities—chants of mechanics,
> Yankee chants—Pennsylvania chants—chants of Kentucky and
>   Tennessee,
> Chants of dim-lit mines—chants of mountain-tops,
> Chants of sailors—chants of the Eastern Sea and the Western
>   Sea,
> Chants of Mannahatta, the place of my dearest love, the place
>   surrounded by hurried and sparkling currents,
> Health chants—joy chants—robust chants of young men,
> Chants inclusive—wide reverberating chants,
> Chants of the Many In One.

(40–44[10])

The catalogue illustrates the principle of the "Many In One" through the variety of place names. The apparent randomness of the names adds to this effect of variety, but there is a loose structure to the catalogue. Whitman begins with "The West" and western states of the mid-nineteenth century, then expands to the territory of Kansas and to such future territories as Mexico, Oregon, and Canada. When he introduces the image of "teeming and turbulent cities," the poet begins to focus more upon human inhabitants than upon the places they inhabit. Likewise, his vision contracts, focusing upon the eastern states and ending the list of place names with "Mannahatta, the

7. For a survey of Whitman's notes on place-names, see Michael R. Dressman, " 'Names are Magic': Walt Whitman's Laws of Geographic Nomenclature," *Names* 26 (1978): 68–79. See also C. Carroll Hollis, "Names in *Leaves of Grass*," *Names* 5 (1957): 129–58.

Recently edited manuscript material on names includes *Words* (*DBN*, III, 705–6, 718), the *Primer* notebook (*DBN*, III, 735, 743, 747, 753–57), and scattered notes, most from the Harned Collection at the Library of Congress (*NUPM*, V, 1663–1709).

place of my dearest love." The catalogue thus enacts a rhythm of expansion and contraction to suggest a double inclusiveness: first, the inclusiveness of America, which will expand to the "Western Sea" and "away down to Mexico, and up north to Oregon"; second, the inclusiveness of Whitman's own "programme of chants," which will provide the linguistic and spiritual expansion to parallel the projected political and social expansions.

If Whitman's "programme of chants" seems too unbendingly trained upon the future, his use of place names in Section 16 of the poem presents an effective countermovement:

> On my way a moment I pause,
> Here for you! and here for America!
> Still the present I raise aloft, still the future of the States I
>   harbinge glad and sublime,
> And for the past I pronounce what the air holds of the red
>   aborigines.
>
> The red aborigines,
> Leaving natural breaths, sounds of rain and winds, calls as of
>   birds and animals in the woods, syllabled to us for names,
> Okonee, Koosa, Ottawa, Monongahela, Sauk, Natchez,
>   Chattahoochee, Kaqueta, Oronoco,
> Wabash, Miami, Saginaw, Chippewa, Oshkosh, Walla-Walla,
> Leaving such to the States they melt, they depart, charging the
>   water and the land with names.
>
> (237–45)

This is the retrospective, cumulative position on linguistic and spiritual expansion. Whitman does not advance far beyond the nostalgic view of aboriginal Americans as "children of the forest" held by such earlier writers as Freneau, Cooper, and Bryant. Yet there is progress, for Whitman focuses upon the linguistic inheritance bequeathed to the advancing "Americanos," and his emphasis implies that the names give Americans close contact with "natural breaths, sounds of rain and winds, calls as of birds and animals in the woods." Even in "teeming and turbulent cities," the spirit of a place is figured in the name the place bears.

Much of the background of this notion is contained in Whitman's *Primer* notebook, especially in a section of eighteen leaves devoted to *"American Names" (DBN,* III, 753–57). On two leaves, for example, Whitman makes the following point about the connection between names and the spirit of the nation that employs them:

All lies folded in names

I have heard it said that when the spirit arises that does not brook submission and imitation, it will throw off the ultramarine names.—That spirit already walks the streets of the cities of These States—I, and others, illustrate it.—I say America too shall be commemorated—shall stand rooted in the ground in names—shall flow in the water in names and be diffused in time, in days, in months, in their names.—Now the days signify extinct gods and goddesses—the months half-unknown rites and emperors—and the chronology with the rest is all foreign to America—All exiles and insults here. (*DBN*, III, 755)

Section 16 of "Starting from Paumanok" is a concrete realization of the abstract principles laid down in the *Primer* passage. Indeed, the imagery of the section strongly parallels that of the *Primer*, for in both Whitman connects names to the water and soil of the native place. The poet insists that his readers recognize a continuity between their own spirits and the spirits of the "red aborigines" who have left, "charging the water and the land with names." In this regard, it is significant that throughout the poem Whitman almost always refuses to employ place names that owe any allegiance to "ultramarine" sources. Instead, by employing "aboriginal" names he seeks to illustrate the native spirit "that does not brook submission and imitation."

Whitman's programmatic use of American place-names raises the issue of his view of the relationship of past to present. And once again the *Primer of Words* gives an insight into the temporality of his poetics:

There is so much virtue in names, that a nation which produces its own names, haughtily adheres to them, and subordinates others to them, leads all the rest of the nations of the earth.—I also promulge that a nation which has not its own names, but begs them of other nations, has no identity, marches not in front but behind. (*DBN*, III, 756)

By pausing a moment to consider the native linguistic heritage of America, Whitman attempts to solidify the nation's claim to a significant past, even though it has effectively obliterated that past.[8] The

8. For Whitman's sense of the loss incurred by that obliteration, see the late poem "Yonnondio" (*Variorum*, III, 716–17), which was first published in the *Critic*, 26 November 1887, then appeared in *November Boughs* (1888), and finally in the "Sands at

programmatic diction of Section 16 recalls the curious blend of two opposed views of past and present that we have seen in *Rambles Among Words:* On the one hand, the poet asserts that America's identity must be absolutely discontinuous with any "ultramarine" past; on the other hand, however, he appropriates the names of Native Americans to create a supposedly organic connection between the past and the present. Indeed, the programmatic diction of the entire poem reveals the same merging of opposite viewpoints, for the conservative use of American place-names contrasts strongly with Whitman's willingness to import new terms from "ultramarine" languages. And this stylistic merging is directly related to the evolutionary view of American English as "lead[ing] all the rest of the nations of the earth."

When we move to the next level of stylistic analysis, Whitman's "programme of chants" becomes no less paradoxical, but the rhythmical frame of "Starting from Paumanok" places the paradoxes within a vistalike, temporal structure. The poem opens with a fourteen-line phrasal portrait of the genesis of the poet. Whitman employs a variety of qualifying phrases to create a composite picture of the poetic self. The self is both active and passive, as shown in the very first line: "*Starting* from fish-shape Paumanok where I *was born.*" It is both one and many: The autobiography of the first four lines gives way to a multitude of American identities, signaled by the anaphoric repetend "or" (4–7). It is both past and present:

> Having studied the mocking-bird's tones and the flight of the
>   mountain-hawk,
> And heard at dawn the unrivall'd one, the hermit thrush from
>   the swamp-cedars,
> Solitary, singing in the West, I strike up for a New World.
>
> (12–14)

The catalogue terminates in the present action of the speaking poet, and the thirteen lines of qualifying phrases deliver the poet's qualifying antecedents. In this respect, the opening section of the poem is close to Section 1 of "Vocalism," which presents the necessary antecedents to "the divine power to speak words." In both cases, moreover, the "divine power to speak words" is the temporal result of a

---

Seventy" annex to the 1891–92 *Leaves of Grass.* The "Sands at Seventy" annex displays the poet's abiding interest in "aboriginal" American names: The first two poems in the annex are "Mannahatta" and "Paumanok," while the third is "From Montauk Point" (*Variorum,* III, 695–96).

catalogue that mixes stative and dynamic forms.

Section 1 does not set the rhythmical frame in the same way as such earlier poems as "The Sleepers" and "Crossing Brooklyn Ferry," for Whitman begins his proem with a catalogue, which is more characteristic of the expansion beyond the frame. Still, the catalogue establishes a movement from past to present, and it is within the terms of this chronological movement that Whitman sets the rhythmical structure of "Starting from Paumanok." In Section 2, for instance, three stanzas establish the expected clausal frame, moving from past to present to future:

> See revolving the globe,
> The ancestor-continents away group'd together,
> The present and future continents north and south, with the
>   isthmus between.
>
> See, vast trackless spaces,
> As in a dream they change, they swiftly fill,
> Countless masses debouch upon them,
> They are now cover'd with the foremost people, arts,
>   institutions, known.
>
> See, projected through time,
> For me an audience interminable.
>
> (22–30)

The three stanzas perform a double transformation. On the one hand, Whitman presents a narrative of the settling of America, and he implies that such populating will continue. On the other, he represents the settling of the "present and future continents" as a prelude to the spiritual settlement his "programme of chants" will provide. The second transformation becomes clear in the final stanza of Section 2:

> With firm and regular step they wend, they never stop,
> Successions of men, Americanos, a hundred millions,
> One generation playing its part and passing on,
> Another generation playing its part and passing on in its turn,
> With faces turn'd sideways or backward towards me to listen,
> With eyes retrospective towards me.
>
> (31–36)

The first two sections of "Starting from Paumanok" place the poet at the center of the "successions of men" that Whitman would eventually call the "law of successions" in *Democratic Vistas*. And this central position helps explain Whitman's double vision of temporal change, for he wishes his "audience interminable" to look backward toward him as well as forward toward the future, just as the poet looks both backward and forward.

Whitman's double vision continues to inform the rhythmical structure of "Starting from Paumanok." In Section 4 and Section 5, for example, he addresses the America of his present and future as well as America's "precedents":

> Dead poets, philosophs, priests,
> Martyrs, artists, inventors, governments long since,
> Language-shapers on other shores,
> Nations once powerful, now reduced, withdrawn, or desolate,
> I dare not proceed till I respectfully credit what you have left
>   wafted hither,
> I have perused it, own it is admirable, (moving awhile among
>   it,)
> Think nothing can ever be greater, nothing can ever deserve
>   more than it deserves,
> Regarding it all intently a long while, then dismissing it,
> I stand in my place with my own day here.
>
>   (54–62)

The stative quality of the first four phrasal lines yields to the dynamic character of the clausal frame, and the mixture of verbal aspects parallels Whitman's combining of the two views of temporal change. The poet "respectfully credits" the past, but then he dismisses it in favor of the present. The ordering of the two attitudes shows that Whitman maintains the fundamentally discontinuous view that characterizes the poetry of 1855–56.

Whitman's reason for favoring the present and the future emerges in the final stanza of Section 5, where he announces the goal of temporal progress:

> Here lands female and male,
> Here the heir-ship and heiress-ship of the world, here the flame
>   of materials,
> Here spirituality the translatress, the openly-avow'd,
> The ever-tending, the finalè of visible forms,
> The satisfier, after due long-waiting now advancing,
> Yes here comes my mistress the soul.
>
>   (63–68)

The stanza portrays the soul as the inevitable outcome of the temporal progress of America: The "flame of materials" gives rise to "spirituality, the translatress." The diction of the stanza clarifies, moreover, Whitman's complex view of Democracy as "ma femme," since the soul becomes in this passage "my mistress." The two female figures thus form a single vision of the religious democracy that is the goal of Whitman's "*New Bible.*"

The arrival of the soul triggers one of the most extended catalogues of the poem. Four stanzas of Section 6 present the poet's "programme of chants," framed by the clausal repetend "I will." The first and shortest stanza reiterates the idea that the material is another term for the spiritual, that the mortal body translated is the immortal soul (71–73). The second stanza expands in a consideration of democracy and the relationship of the many to "the One," figured in this case as the union of the many states (74–81). The third contracts somewhat, establishing the categories of geography, employments, and heroism (82–85). Finally, the most developed of the four stanzas treats "companionship" as the source of the poet's "evangel-poem" (86–94). The four stanzas divide the "programme of chants" into separate categories, but the repetend "I will," appearing fifteen times in twenty-four lines, provides the progressivist, dynamic frame within which the poet announces the separate categories.

The clarity of the Section 6 catalogue by no means exhausts Whitman's "programme of chants." In treating such themes as evil (Section 7), ambition (Section 8), and love (Section 9), Whitman's constant answer is the ideal of a new religion. In each case the poet presents religion as both the solution and the result of the problems he considers. So, for instance, he figures evil as part of religion, the "real and permanent grandeur of these States" (110). The young man's ambition is figured as the fuel that will be "burnt up for religion's sake" (119). And the mixed pain and satisfaction of human love come within the temporal compass of the ultimate "satisfier," religion: "It, magnificent, beyond materials, with continuous hands sweeps and provides for all" (128).

Section 10 presents the synthesis of these various themes, as well as Whitman's attempt to reestablish the rhythmical frame. In one of his most striking organic metaphors, the poet asserts that his purpose in all of *Leaves of Grass* is "solely to drop in the earth the germs of a greater religion" (129). The "germs" are "two greatnesses, and a third one rising inclusive and more resplendent, / The greatness of Love and Democracy, and the greatness of Religion" (132–33). The organic imagery presents the marriage of private and public themes

(Love and Democracy) and their inevitable outgrowth, "the greatness of Religion."

In the final three stanzas of Section 10, Whitman mixes phrasal and clausal lines to represent the combination of "the unseen and the seen" (134). So, for instance, the first of the three stanzas treats the "melange" of the spiritual and the material (134–39) in phrases; the second compares the father's "daily kiss" to the foster fatherhood of "all the spiritual world" (140–44) in a series of dynamic clauses; the third presents the mixture of the poet's "warblings under the sun" with the "strains musical flowing through ages" in a joining of stative phrases and dynamic clauses: "I take to your reckless and composite chords, add to them, and cheerfully pass them forward" (147). In presenting the "melange," Whitman plays the "composite chords" of his rhythmical frame within the temporal structure of "passing them forward."

The temporal character of both the rhythmical frame and the catalogue expansions structures the next four sections, which alternate between frame and catalogue. In Section 11, Whitman meditates in short, delicate stanzas on the "warblings" of the mockingbird, an image he develops most fully in "Out of the Cradle Endlessly Rocking." Here, the song of the bird is represented as a song for the future, "for those being born" (155), and it therefore parallels Whitman's own "programme of chants." Section 12 returns to the rhetoric of Section 6, for the "I will" repetend appears in thirteen of twenty-one lines. As we have seen in chapter 4, the section treats in turn the themes of democracy, the individual, and poetry. And the repetition of "I will" presents the three themes within the vistalike, temporal structure of the dynamic clausal catalogue.

Section 13 returns to the rhythmical frame with five short stanzas based upon clausal structures. In a series of complicated figural turns, Whitman equates the soul with the "real body" and the "real body" with "real words":

Of your real body and any man's or woman's real body,
Item for item it will elude the hands of the corpse-cleaners and
    pass to fitting spheres,
Carrying what has accrued to it from the moment of birth to
    the moment of death.

Not the types set up by the printer return their impression, the
    meaning, the main concern,
Any more than a man's substance and life or a woman's

> substance and life return in the body and the soul,
> Indifferently before death and after death.
>
> (181–86)

The figural equations recall Whitman's other uses of the adjective "real," as in "Real Grammar," the "Real Dictionary," "real literature," and the "real real." They also recall the denial of language as a mediating force in "Song of the Rolling Earth," where the poet insists upon a direct, unmediated relationship between words and things: "Were you thinking that those were the words, those delicious sounds out of your friends' mouths? / No, the real words are more delicious than they" (5–6). Whitman's poetic "Primer of words" depends upon the "law of successions" in that the paradoxes he proposes are only to be resolved if we consider the spiritual consequences of any material occurrences. Thus the "real words" are "the meaning, the main concern," rather than the dots and lines on the printed page. Likewise, the "real body" is the soul itself, rather than the merely material body.

Though somewhat satisfying, the resolution is not ultimately satisfactory, for we live in the paradoxes Whitman presents. We are both body and soul, and language is both scratches on paper and meaning. Thus the poet returns to the conflicting realm of paradox in the last stanza of the section:

> Behold, the body includes and is the meaning, the main
>   concern, and includes and is the soul;
> Whoever you are, how superb and how divine is your body, or
>   any part of it!
>
> (187–88)

This final movement distinguishes Whitman's view of the soul from that of orthodox Christianity, and it provides the rationale for printing a book such as *Leaves of Grass*. In Whitman's conception of both religion and literature, the material is as important as the spiritual, for the material is also "divine." This idea is particularly striking here, since Whitman addresses the problem within the material structure of his rhythmical frame, emphasized by the typography of stanzaic form.

The dynamic aspect of Whitman's programmatic rhetoric gathers power in the longest catalogue of the poem. As we have seen, the four stanzas of Section 14 parallel exactly the four linguistic themes Whitman sketches out in the early notebook version of "Premonition." The catalogue mixes phrases and clauses in thirty-five lines of complicated verse. As in the long catalogue of chants that appeared in the 1860 version of Section 3, Whitman first presents a varied landscape and then peoples it with varied inhabitants. The landscape appears in a series of phrases:

> Interlink'd, food-yielding lands!
> Land of coal and iron! land of gold! land of cotton, sugar, rice!
> Land of wheat, beef, pork! land of wool and hemp! land of the apple and the grape!
> Land of the pastoral plains, the grass-fields of the world! land of those sweet-air'd interminable plateaus!
> Land of the herd, the garden, the healthy house of adobie!
> Lands where the north-west Columbia winds, and where the south-west Colorado winds!
> Land of the eastern Chesapeake! land of the Delaware!
> Land of Ontario, Erie, Huron, Michigan!
> Land of the Old Thirteen! Massachusetts land! land of Vermont and Connecticut!
> Land of the ocean shores! land of sierras and peaks!
>
> (194–203)

If we exclude the last line of the passage, the initial movement of the catalogue divides thematically into two parts. The first lists products of the land, while the second lists place names. In a passage from the *Primer* notebook, Whitman makes a similar division: "Geography, shipping, steam, the mint, the electric telegraph, railroads, and so forth, have many strong and beautiful words ... mines—iron works—the sugar plantations of Louisiana—the cotton crops and the rice crop—, Illinois wheat—Ohio corn and pork—Maine lumber— all these sprout in hundreds and hundreds of words, all tangible and clean-lined, all having texture and beauty" (DBN, III, 733). The "texture and beauty" of the catalogue are evident, but equally apparent is that they do not simply "sprout" organically from the words the poet employs. Instead, they are created by the play between the phrasal structure of the catalogue, which provides a potentially stative frame, and the insistent variation of the number and type of terms, which creates a dynamic effect of randomness.

Whitman continues the play between stative and dynamic elements in the second movement of the catalogue:

> Land of boatmen and sailors! fishermen's lands!
> Inextricable lands! the clutch'd together! the passionate ones!

The side by side! the elder and younger brothers! the bony-
    limb'd!
The great women's land! the feminine! the experienced sisters
    and the inexperienced sisters!
Far breath'd land! Arctic braced! Mexican breez'd! the diverse!
    the compact!
The Pennsylvanian! the Virginian! the double Carolinian!
O and all and each well-loved by me! my intrepid nations! O I
    at any rate include you all with perfect love!
I cannot be discharged from you! not from one any sooner than
    another!

(204–11)

Whitman varies the catalogue in order to avoid monotony, mixing the
list of inhabitants with more general images such as "inextricable
lands! the clutch'd together! the passionate ones!" In addition, he
varies the number of terms in each line, usually playing upon com-
binations of doublets and triplets but occasionally expanding beyond
those formulas, as in the line "Far breath'd land! Arctic braced! Mexican breez'd! the diverse! the compact!" Then, in the last two lines of
the movement, he shifts from the phrasal to the clausal, from the
many lands to the single poet.

The final shift in the second movement prepares for the overwhelmingly dynamic effect of the third movement of the catalogue.
Whitman first turns from the scenes of life and living to the ultimate
act:

O death! O for all that, I am yet of you unseen this hour with
    irrepressible love,
Walking New England, a friend, a traveler,
Splashing my bare feet in the edge of the summer ripples on
    Paumanok's sands,
Crossing the prairies, dwelling again in Chicago, dwelling in
    every town,
Observing shows, births, improvements, structure, arts,
Listening to orators and oratresses in public halls.

(212–17)

Whitman's direct address to death triggers a reflection upon his own
death ("I am yet of you unseen this hour"), but the poet's concern
with future readers engenders a rush of present participles, representing his own dynamic spirit. The participial phrases present the
poet as an all-inclusive actor, "a friend, a traveler" who moves beyond

death by virtue of the dynamic act of speaking.

The dynamic linguistic act of inclusion becomes yet more pronounced in the second segment of the movement, where the terms of the first two movements are framed by the dynamic, active poet:

> Of and through the States as during life, each man and woman
>   my neighbor,
> The Louisianan, the Georgian, as near to me, and I as near to
>   him and her,
> The Mississippian and Arkansian yet with me, and I yet with
>   any of them,
> Yet upon the plains west of the spinal river, yet in my house of
>   adobie,
> Yet returning eastward, yet in the Seaside State or in Maryland,
> Yet Kanadian cheerily braving the winter, the snow and ice
>   welcome to me,
> Yet a true son either of Maine or of the Granite State, or the
>   Narragansett Bay State, or the Empire State.
>
> (218–24)

The passage mixes the names of places with the names of people, and it merges the two with the active poet, who insists that he is "of and through the States as during life." As in the poems of 1855–56, the poet's act of identification figures identity as inherently dynamic and active, and Whitman insists that this dynamic identity will continue beyond death.

The final segment of the catalogue indicates that the ground for Whitman's mysticism is linguistic:

> Yet sailing to other shores to annex the same, yet welcoming
>   every new brother,
> Hereby applying these leaves to the new ones from the hour
>   they unite with the old ones,
> Coming among the new ones myself to be their companion and
>   equal, coming personally to you now,
> Enjoining you to acts, characters, spectacles, with me.
>
> (225–28)

The word "annex" in the first line is tantalizing, since it has both political and literary connotations in Whitman's work. But even if the word is strictly political in the 1860 edition, the next two lines mingle the literary and the political in a fruitful ambiguity. The "new ones" refers primarily to new citizens and readers, but it can also

refer to new poems, which will "unite with the old ones" to form the
"*New Bible.*" In addition, the poet represents himself as actively part
of the future, and he does so by returning to the use of the present
participle that characterized the first segment of the movement. The
Section 14 catalogue is thus reminiscent of both "The Sleepers" and
"Crossing Brooklyn Ferry," for in all three poems Whitman represents
himself as spiritually active in the "present-saying" of the poem. The
extravagant line from "The Sleepers" comes to mind: "The diverse
shall be no less diverse, but they shall flow and unite—they unite
now" (160). In Section 14, that extravagant rhetoric is repeated in the
image of the poet as "coming personally to you now."

Whitman's extravagance reaches its peak in the final catalogue
of the poem, which comprises all of Section 18. In the intervening
sections, the clausal frame structures the direct address to the reader
(Section 15), the momentary reflection on the "red aborigines" (Section 16), and the full turn to the future (Section 17). The last of these
three sections signals the poet's complete faith in the "vista" of the
future:

> Expanding and swift, henceforth,
> Elements, breeds, adjustments, turbulent, quick and audacious,
> A world primal again, vistas of glory incessant and branching,
> A new race dominating previous ones and grander far, with new
>   contests,
> New politics, new literatures and religions, new inventions and
>   arts.
>
> These, my voice announcing—I will sleep no more but arise,
> You oceans that have been calm within me! how I feel you,
>   fathomless, stirring, preparing unprecedented waves and
>   storms.
>
>   (246–52)

Whitman figures the present of America as analogous to the "world
primal" of the "red aborigines" in the preceding section. And, as in
the catalogue of Section 14, the "vistas of glory" the poet announces
depend upon the act of his "voice announcing." The figure of the voice
recalls the paradoxes of "Song of the Rolling Earth" and "Crossing
Brooklyn Ferry," for the figure denies the written text in order to establish the poet's personal presence within the text.

This paradoxical rhetoric, denying its own textual status at the
same time that it asserts it, becomes most pronounced in the catalogue of Section 18:

See, steamers steaming through my poems,

See, in my poems immigrants continually coming and landing,

See, in arriere, the wigwam, the trail, the hunter's hut, the flat-
boat, the maize-leaf, the claim, the rude fence, and the
backwoods village,

See, on the one side the Western Sea and on the other the
Eastern Sea, how they advance and retreat upon my poems
as upon their own shores,

See, pastures and forests in my poems—see, animals wild and
tame—see, beyond the Kaw, countless herds of buffalo
feeding on short curly grass,

See, in my poems, cities, solid, vast, inland, with paved streets,
with iron and stone edifices, ceaseless vehicles, and
commerce,

See, the many-cylinder'd steam printing-press—see, the electric
telegraph stretching across the continent,

See, through Atlantica's depths pulses American Europe
reaching, pulses of Europe duly return'd,

See, the strong and quick locomotive as it departs, panting,
blowing the steam-whistle,

See, ploughmen ploughing farms—see, miners digging mines—
see, the numberless factories,

See, mechanics busy at their benches with tools—see from
among them superior judges, philosophs, Presidents, emerge,
drest in working dresses,

See, lounging through the shops and fields of the States, me
well-belov'd, close-held by day and night,

Hear the loud echoes of my songs there—read the hints come at
last.

(253–65)

The catalogue returns to the "See" repetend employed in Section 2,
but here twelve successive lines present a dynamic expansion beyond
the rhythmic frame set in the earlier section. Whitman repeats the
present participle no less than eleven times in the twelve lines, adding to the dynamic quality of the passage. Finally, two strategic uses
of finite verb elements—"they advance and retreat" and "superior
judges, philosophs, Presidents, emerge"—complement the imperatives and participles. The three types of verb elements combine to
create a persuasive performance of Whitman's characteristic paradox: He claims to present *things* in his poems, denying the status of
those "things" as words.

Whitman disguises the paradox by employing the rhetoric of deferral. The images he employs appear in the present of the poem, but in the last three lines of the catalogue he projects those "things" into the future. Thus the "ensemble" of American people and places becomes the "vista" of future "superior judges, philosophs, Presidents," who will "emerge, drest in working dresses." Further, the poet presents himself as "well-belov'd, close-held by day and night," and this line moves from the personal to the literary, since we know that *Leaves of Grass* itself will be "close-held." The anaphora of the final line moves from the visual to the auditory, and the shift emphasizes the verbal, literary quality of the poet's rhetoric: "Hear the loud echoes of my songs there—read the hints come at last." Whitman's songs no longer exist on an equal plane with "things," for in this last line he promises only "loud echoes." The poet's final "announcement" is an ensemble of "hints." Because Whitman is so adamantly given to the double "vista" of his "audience interminable" and of the life of his soul in poetry, he inevitably presents nothing more—and nothing less—than "endless announcements." This doubleness helps to account for the seemingly extraneous Section 19, which closes the poem with the double appeal to the "camerado close" (266) and "a word to clear one's path ahead endlessly" (267).

If "Starting from Paumanok" furnishes a "Primer of words and Thoughts Ideas Principles," introducing many of the dictional, syntactic, and rhetorical devices that appear throughout *Leaves of Grass*, two other poems written during the years between the 1856 edition and the 1860 edition show how Whitman develops differing approaches to his "programme of chants." "Out of the Cradle Endlessly Rocking" and "As I Ebb'd with the Ocean of Life," both probably composed in 1859, are meditations upon the genesis of the poet, and in this respect they represent a strong continuity with the "Thoughts Ideas Principles" announced in "Starting from Paumanok."[9]

9. For the publication history of the two poems, see *CRE*, pp. 246–47, 252–53.

For approaches differing from mine, the reader should consult these important interpretations of the poem: Leo Spitzer, " 'Explication de Texte' Applied to Walt Whitman's 'Out of the Cradle Endlessly Rocking,' " *ELH* 16 (1949): 229–49; Chase, *Walt Whitman Reconsidered*, pp. 120–27; James E. Miller, Jr., *Critical Guide to "Leaves of Grass"* (Chicago: University of Chicago Press, 1957), pp. 104–10; Roy Harvey Pearce, "Whitman Justified: The Poet in 1860," *Minnesota Review* 1 (April 1961): 261–94, reprinted in *Walt Whitman*, ed. Harold Bloom (New York: Chelsea House, 1985), pp. 65–86; Stephen E. Whicher, "Whitman's Awakening to Death: Toward a Biographical Reading of 'Out of the Cradle Endlessly Rocking,' " *Studies in Romanticism* 1 (1961): 9–28, reprinted in *Walt Whitman*, ed. Arthur Golden (New York: McGraw-Hill, 1974), pp. 77–96; Waskow, *Whitman: Explorations in Form*, pp. 114–29; Edwin H. Miller, *Walt Whitman's Poetry: A Psychological Journey* (Boston: Houghton Mifflin, 1968), pp. 175–85; Stephen A. Black,

The connections between "Starting from Paumanok" and "Out of the Cradle Endlessly Rocking" are especially strong. In Section 11 of the proem, Whitman announces both the scene and the theme that he develops fully in "Out of the Cradle":

As I walk'd in Alabama my morning walk,
I have seen where the she-bird the mocking-bird sat on her nest
   in the briers hatching her brood.

I have seen the he-bird also,
I have paus'd to hear him near at hand inflating his throat and
   joyfully singing.

And while I paus'd it came to me that what he really sang for
   was not there only,
Nor for his mate nor himself only, nor all sent back by the
   echoes,
But subtle, clandestine, away beyond,
A charge transmitted and gift occult for those being born.

(148–55)

The "he-bird" figures the poet himself, who sings "for those being born" rather than for the sounds "sent back by the echoes." Whitman draws the parallel in the first line of Section 12, where he addresses his largest audience: "Democracy! near at hand to you a throat is now inflating itself and joyfully singing" (156). By repeating the phrasing of Section 11 ("I have paus'd to hear him near at hand inflating his throat and joyfully singing"), Whitman identifies himself as the voice of both nature and democracy.

In "Out of the Cradle Endlessly Rocking," Whitman alters the scene and the theme, but he maintains a strong connection with the introductory poem. The locale is no longer Alabama; instead, it is Paumanok itself. Nor is Democracy the "femme" for whom the poet joyfully sings. Rather, Whitman portrays himself as the "chanter of pains and joys, uniter of here and hereafter" (20). Despite these alterations, "Out of the Cradle" functions within the context set by the introductory poem. In both texts, the genesis of the poet is a central

"Radical Utterances from the Soul's Abysms: Toward a New Sense of Whitman," *PMLA* 88 (1973): 100–111; David Bromwich, "Suburbs and Extremities," *Prose* 8 (1974): 25–38; Rohn S. Friedman, "A Whitman Primer: Solipsism and Identity," *American Quarterly* 27 (1975): 443–60; Robin Riley Fast, "Structure and Meaning in Whitman's 'Sea-Drift,' " *ATQ* 53 (1983): 49–66; and Michael Vande Berg, " 'Taking All Hints to Use Them': The Sources of 'Out of the Cradle Endlessly Rocking,' " *WWQR* 2 (1985): 1–20.

concern, and in both he sings "for those being born," who are also those who will die. It is no wonder, then, that Whitman regarded "Out of the Cradle" as a suitable poem for recitation in the field hospitals of the Civil War (*NUPM*, II, 544).

An even deeper connection between "Starting from Paumanok" and "Out of the Cradle Endlessly Rocking" is the theme of language. The subject is of course central to Whitman's introductory poem, a poetic "Primer of words." And it is even more pronounced in "Out of the Cradle." The original title of the poem, "A Word out of the Sea," announces the theme, and the introductory stanza echoes the title with the pronounced use of anaphora:

> Out of the cradle endlessly rocking,
> Out of the mocking-bird's throat, the musical shuttle,
> Out of the Ninth-month midnight,
> Over the sterile sands and fields beyond, where the child
>   leaving his bed wander'd alone, bareheaded, barefoot,
> Down from the shower'd halo,
> Up from the mystic play of shadows twining and twisting as if
>   they were alive,
> Out from the patches of briers and blackberries,
> From the memories of the bird that chanted to me,
> From your memories sad brother, from the fitful risings and
>   fallings I heard,
> From under that yellow half-moon late-risen and swollen as if
>   with tears,
> From those beginning notes of yearning and love there in the
>   mist,
> From the thousand responses of my heart never to cease,
> From the myriad thence-arous'd words,
> From the word stronger and more delicious than any,
> From such as now they start the scene revisiting,
> As a flock, twittering, rising, or overhead passing,
> Borne hither, ere all eludes me, hurriedly,
> A man, yet by these tears a little boy again,
> Throwing myself on the sand, confronting the waves,
> I, chanter of pains and joys, uniter of here and hereafter,
> Taking all hints to use them, but swiftly leaping beyond them,
> A reminiscence sing.
>
> (1–22)

The long stanza opens the poem with a phrasal catalogue, featuring a series of prepositional repetends: "out of" becomes "out from," and then "from" structures the central portion of the passage. All of the prepositions denote a starting point, a point of departure, and they indicate a multitude of sources for the genesis of the poet. Out of this multitude Whitman creates an integral poetic self, and the key to the creation is "the word stronger and more delicious than any" (14). When the poet arrives at "the word," he moves from the simple past to a mixture of past and present, and he moves away from the prepositional phrases denoting origins, from "the word" to "from such as now they start the scene revisiting" (15). The punctuation of the 1860 edition clarifies the line, for it indicates that "they" refers to the dynamic words of Whitman's poems: "From such, as now they start, the scene revisiting."

The antecedent to the word "they" is purposely ambiguous, however, since it could refer to the "beginning notes" of the bird, to the "thousand responses" of the poet's heart, or to the "myriad thencearous'd words" of *Leaves of Grass*. All three possibilities remain in play as the stanza continues:

> As a flock, twittering, rising, or overhead passing,
> Borne hither, ere all eludes me, hurriedly,
> A man, yet by these tears a little boy again.

The key word here is "as," because it signals the figural quality of the lines. Words, responses, and the bird's notes function interchangeably, and all three constitute the poetic self, which is both "a man" and "a little boy again."

The poetic self is, as in all of Whitman's strongest poems, essentially dynamic. As the introductory stanza draws to a close, that dynamic quality is figured in a series of present participles and dynamic agential nouns. In the last four lines, Whitman employs no less than six dynamic deverbal forms: "throwing," "confronting," "chanter," "uniter," "taking," and "leaping." Then, as if the potentially endless nature of the catalogue threatened to overwhelm the poetic "I," Whitman halts the string of phrases with a syntactically inverted clause: "A reminiscence sing." The effect of this closural device is to maintain the opposition between the reminiscence and the "hereafter," between the clausal rhythmical frame and the catalogue expansion.

The dual opposition created by the opening stanza certainly affects the tone of the poem, which oscillates between the lyric and the programmatic poles. The overwhelming absence of the programmatic diction that marks "Starting from Paumanok" would seem to indicate that the poem leans more heavily toward the lyric tone. For instance, we find only two place names in the entire poem, "Alabama" and "Paumanok," and none of the foreign borrowings that figure so prominently in the introductory poem of the 1860 edition. Still, the choice of the two "aboriginal" place names is important, since it joins the South and the North in a poetic "ensemble."

Whitman hints at a third type of programmatic term when he says that "Fifth-month grass was growing" (24). The line echoes the image of "Fifth-month flowers" (11) in "Starting from Paumanok," and the centrality of the image of grass indicates that the use of the Quaker term is closely associated with the poet's "programme of chants." Both *Words* and the *Primer of Words* support this idea. In the former Whitman writes, "In These States, there must be new Names for all the Months of the year – They must be characteristic of America – The South, North, East, and West must be represented in them – What is the name January to us? – Or March to us? –January commemorates Janus – and March commemorates Mars – the bloody god of war, for the sake of War!" (*DBN*, III, 700–701). In the *Primer* Whitman makes a similar point: "Needed in American Nomenclature . . . Appropriate names for the Months . . . Those now used perpetuate old myths" (*DBN*, III, 754). By employing the Quaker names for the months, Whitman seeks to create a native mythology of peace. And this programmatic aim is all the more telling when we consider that "Out of the Cradle" was written as Whitman's beloved "femme," the United States, was about to be torn apart by "the bloody god of war."

Despite the resonance of place-names and Quaker terms, "Out of the Cradle" displays far less programmatic diction than a poem like "Starting from Paumanok." Part of the reason for this difference relates to the delicate, nostalgic tone of the reminiscence. Another has to do with the balance of tone throughout *Leaves of Grass*. If all of Whitman's poems were replete with foreign borrowings, geographical terms, and religious names for the months, the poems would quickly become too explicitly didactic. And this would run counter to Whitman's fundamental ideal of athletic reading, formulated most clearly in *Democratic Vistas*: "Books are to be call'd for, and supplied, on the assumption that the process of reading is not a half-sleep, but, in highest sense, an exercise, a gymnast's struggle; that the reader is to do something for himself, must be on the alert, must himself or herself construct indeed the poem, argument, history, metaphysical essay—the text furnishing the hints, the clue, the start or framework" (*PW*, II, 424–25). In "Out of the Cradle," the poet portrays himself as "taking all hints to use them, but swiftly leaping beyond them." The sparing use of programmatic words furnishes "the hints, the clue, the start or frame-work," but Whitman leaps "beyond them" to create an effective balance between the programmatic and the lyric.

The principal device for creating that balance is the dialogue between the poet and the "he-bird," which becomes a dialogue between programmatic and lyric styles. Whitman adumbrates the distinction between the two styles through typography and quality of voice. The use of italics to designate the bird's song sets it apart from the roman type of the poet's response. More subtly, the bird's song employs a distinctive stylistic trait, the triple repetition of key terms. So, for example, italicized stanzas begin with such lines as *"Shine! shine! shine!"* (32), *"Blow! blow! blow!"* (52), *"Soothe! soothe! soothe!"* (71), *"Loud! loud! loud!"* (81), and *"Land! land! O land!"* (90). These strategic placements culminate in the last stanza of the song:

> *O past! O happy life! O songs of joy!*
> *In the air, in the woods, over fields,*
> *Loved! loved! loved! loved! loved!*
> *But my mate no more, no more with me!*
> *We two together no more!*
>
> (125–29)

The insistent repetition emphasizes the loss of the bird's mate and the "pastness" of the love that held the "two together." Thus the triple exclamation of the first line moves into five past participles, which prefigure the five repetitions of the "word out of the sea." Then the stanza closes with the triple repetition of the phrase "no more."[10] The repeated terms point to the fundamental absence at the heart of the bird's song: More than love, it is the loss of the beloved that inspires the "beginning notes."

The figure of the poet functions as both a parallel and a contrast to that of the bird. Like the bird, the poet sings for an irretrievable past, and the only retrieval the poet is able to make is a translation of the bird's song into words. The parallel is thus one of absence, and this is especially clear when the bird exclaims *"Shake out carols!"* (99). The line strangely echoes Section 12 of "Starting from Paumanok," which, as we have seen, stresses the parallel between the bird and the poet: "I exultant to be ready for them will now shake out carols stronger and haughtier than have ever yet been heard upon earth" (159). The phrase "shake out carols" parallels that of "Out of

---

10. The phrase tempts one to speculate about Poe's influence on the lyric style of the bird's song. For Whitman's view of Poe's poetry as morbid but musical, see *PW*, I, 230–33.

the Cradle," but the tone of the line from "Starting from Paumanok" contrasts sharply with that of the bird's *reckless despairing carols* (104). This difference in tone points toward a fundamental dissimilarity between the bird and the poet, for the absence at the heart of the poet's song relates not only to the past but to the future of "those being born" ("Starting from Paumanok," 155).

Whitman furnishes the start or framework for this interpretation through his use of the present participle:

> The aria sinking,
> All else continuing, the stars shining,
> The winds blowing, the notes of the bird continuous echoing,
> With angry moans the fierce old mother incessantly moaning,
> On the sands of Paumanok's shore gray and rustling,
> The yellow half-moon enlarged, sagging down, drooping, the face of the sea almost touching,
> The boy ecstatic, with his bare feet the waves, with his hair the atmosphere dallying,
> The love in the heart long pent, now loose, now at last tumultuously bursting,
> The aria's meaning, the ears, the soul, swiftly depositing,
> The strange tears down the cheeks coursing,
> The colloquy there, the trio, each uttering,
> The undertone, the savage old mother incessantly crying,
> To the boy's soul's questions sullenly timing, some drown'd secret hissing,
> To the outsetting bard.
>
> (130–43)

The repetition of present participles recalls the dynamic style of "Song of the Broad-Axe," but here their terminal placement signals a more programmatic framework. This is one of Whitman's longest and most effective catalogues based upon the present participle, and it presents a dynamic image of "the outsetting bard." The bird's "aria" sinks into echoes, but the poet's voice awakes. And it does so in the form of nineteen present participles, which create a linguistic and conceptual movement toward activity and temporal process. Thus the backward-looking, nostalgic lyricism of the bird engenders the forward-looking, progressivist song of the poet.

The contrast becomes sharper in one of Whitman's most famous stanzas:

O you singer solitary, singing by yourself, projecting me,
O solitary me listening, never more shall I cease perpetuating
   you,
Never more shall I escape, never more the reverberations,
Never more the cries of unsatisfied love be absent from me,
Never again leave me to be the peaceful child I was before what
   there in the night,
By the sea under the yellow and sagging moon,
The messenger there arous'd, the fire, the sweet hell within,
The unknown want, the destiny of me.

(150–57)

The stanza begins with the basic parallel between the two solitary
singers, but the style of the poet's song stresses the future instead of
the past. The repeated phrase "never more" recalls the bird's "*no
more,*" but instead of a sense of loss the phrase creates a sense of
promise or destiny. The two figures are parallel in their yearning,
their "unknown want," but the "outsetting bard" sees his yearning in
terms of the "vista" of the future. Moreover, the repetition of the future tense in the stanza clearly contrasts with the "pastness" of the
aria.

The image of the outsetting bard, as distinct from that of the
bird, sharpens in the closing stanzas of the poem, for the poet is not
satisfied with what the "messenger" has delivered. He hears "the
word final, superior to all" not from the bird, but from the sea, the
"savage old mother." And the word out of the sea comes, once again,
in the form of present participles:

Whereto answering, the sea,
Delaying not, hurrying not,
Whisper'd me through the night, and very plainly before
   daybreak,
Lisp'd to me the low and delicious word death,
And again death, death, death, death,
Hissing melodious, neither like the bird nor like my arous'd
   child's heart,
But edging near as privately for me rustling at my feet,
Creeping thence steadily up to my ears and laving me softly all
   over,
Death, death, death, death, death.

(165–73)

Eight present participles combine with ten repetitions of the word "death" to point toward the goal of temporal process. And in this respect "Out of the Cradle Endlessly Rocking" functions perfectly within the programmatic context set by "Starting from Paumanok." Just as the proem portrays the soul as continually progressing, continually active, so "Out of the Cradle" enacts that temporal and spiritual progression through the mixture of verbal and nominal forms in its penultimate stanza.

The two texts are also similar in the poet's characteristic use of the rhetoric of deferral. Just as the introductory poem delivers only "endless announcements," so Whitman's most effective lyric of poetic genesis delivers, finally, merely the word "death." The meaning of the word is implied by the comforting tone of the stanza, but it remains a translation of an unknown tongue. The central absence of defined meaning is the source of more words, more songs. Thus Whitman closes the poem with a coda, but the coda returns both to the word and to the initial image of the rocking cradle:

> Which I do not forget,
> But fuse the song of my dusky demon and brother,
> That he sang to me in the moonlight on Paumanok's gray beach,
> With the thousand responsive songs at random,
> My own songs awaked from that hour,
> And with them the key, the word up from the waves,
> The word of the sweetest song and all songs,
> That strong and delicious word which, creeping to my feet,
> (Or like some old crone rocking the cradle, swathed in sweet
> garments, bending aside,)
> The sea whisper'd me.
>
> (174–83)

The meaning of the word "death" is suggested rather than defined, for the key to the meaning is that the word "starts" more words. It therefore functions as a hint, a clue, rather than as a final answer. The key to Whitman's songs, then, is the fact that the human spirit is always "outsetting," always being reborn. He stresses the point in the penultimate line of the poem, which must rank as one of his most judicious additions to the 1881 edition of *Leaves of Grass*. The image of the "old crone rocking the cradle" returns us to the first line of the poem, creating a circular pattern of closure. In the "gymnast's struggle" of "Out of the Cradle Endlessly Rocking," the reader must continually be "outsetting," actively moving between the poles of the past and the future, the lyric and the programmatic, the word and what the word signifies.

"As I Ebb'd with the Ocean of Life" is closely connected to "Starting from Paumanok" and "Out of the Cradle Endlessly Rocking" in date of composition, scene, and theme. The poem was probably written in the autumn of 1859, and it was first published as "Bardic Symbols" in the April 1860 issue of the *Atlantic Monthly*.[11] The dramatic scene of the poem is once again the shores of Paumanok, "where the fierce old mother endlessly cries for her castaways" (5). And the theme is Whitman's "programme of chants" itself.

Although the fifth line of "As I Ebb'd" strongly echoes "Out of the Cradle Endlessly Rocking," the two poems differ markedly in tone, for in "As I Ebb'd" Whitman places his "programme of chants" in doubt. The two poems relate to one another in much the same way that "The Sleepers" relates to "Song of Myself." Just as "Song of Myself" portrays the genesis of the poetic self in overwhelmingly celebratory terms, so "Out of the Cradle" moves toward a celebration of the "programme of chants." And just as "The Sleepers" takes full account of limitation in the capricious "efflux of the soul," so "As I Ebb'd with the Ocean of Life" figures the human spirit as "capricious, brought hither we know not whence" (69).

Whitman establishes the tone of "As I Ebb'd" in the first two sections by employing the syntax of clauses:

> As I ebb'd with the ocean of life,
> As I wended the shores I know,
> As I walk'd where the ripples continually wash you Paumanok,
> Where they rustle up hoarse and sibilant,
> Where the fierce old mother endlessly cries for her castaways,
> I musing late in the autumn day, gazing off southward,
> Held by this electric self out of the pride of which I utter poems,
> Was seiz'd by the spirit that trails in the lines underfoot,
> The rim, the sediment that stands for all the water and all the
>   land of the globe.
>
>   (1–9)

Whereas "Out of the Cradle" begins with the prepositional phrases of origin and the dynamic effects of the present participle, "As I Ebb'd" features the simple past tense. The poem portrays an active poetic self, but as in "The Sleepers" the self is "ill-assorted, contradictory."

11. *CRE*, pp. 252–53.

The contradictory nature of the opening stanza rests in the play between direction and lack of direction. For instance, the archaic word "wended" implies etymologically a turn or change of direction, and Whitman's transitive use of the verb calls upon the nautical meaning of "to turn (a ship's bow or head) to the opposite tack." But the more current meaning of the word, revived in the early nineteenth century, is "to go or journey in a certain way or direction. Now only *to wend one's way*."[12] Whitman's choice of an archaic verb exploits both meanings in order to create a fundamental ambiguity. Similarly, the simple past tense of the opening clauses plays against the present-tense images of continuing action—"where the ripples continually wash you Paumanok," and "where the fierce old mother endlessly cries." Finally, the active voice of the past and present tense plays against the passive voice of the last few lines: "Held by this electric self," and "Was seiz'd by the spirit." Even though the opening stanza of the poem does not portray the confusion of the poetic self as explicitly as does "The Sleepers," it implies confusion nonetheless.

The opening stanza prompts the poet's "old thought of likenesses" (14), and the fundamental "likenesses" of the poem are reductive and ascetic. The most basic likeness is that "I too but signify at the utmost a little wash'd-up drift" (22). This likeness is connected to a second, that between what Whitman calls in "Starting from Paumanok" the "unseen and the seen" (134). The second metaphor appears in Section 2 of "As I Ebb'd" as a reduction of knowledge:

> As I wend to the shores I know not,
> As I list to the dirge, the voices of men and women wreck'd,
> As I inhale the impalpable breezes that set in upon me,
> As the ocean so mysterious rolls toward me closer and closer,
> I too but signify at the utmost a little wash'd-up drift,
> A few sands and dead leaves to gather,
> Gather, and merge myself as part of the sands and drift.
>
> (18–24)

The change from simple past to present tense signals the poet's movement from the known to the unknown. The passage figures the movement as one from life to death, from the palpable to the impalpable. And the movement reduces the significance of Whitman's poetry: The

---

12. *SOED Webster's* (1847) treats "wend" only as an intransitive verb and gives two definitions: "To go; to pass to or from [Obsolete except in poetry; but its preterit, *went*, is in common use.] 2. To turn round. *Obs.* [*Wend* and *wind* are from the same root.]" Whitman's use of the word differs from the dictionary in both form and function.

image of "dead leaves" contrasts sharply with the "myriad thence-arous'd words" that death engenders in "Out of the Cradle." In the final line of the stanza, the image of "merge myself as part of the sands and drift" contrasts with the "electric self out of the pride of which I utter poems." The present-tense movement toward the unknown enacts a journey toward "the spirit that trails in the lines underfoot," and that journey is figured as a voyage of reduction.

Whitman makes the voyage of reduction in the first two sections of the poem through the absence of programmatic diction and syntax. There are none of the foreign borrowings, word formations, place names, or religious terms that mark "Starting from Paumanok" and "Out of the Cradle Endlessly Rocking." Nor do we find any of the dynamic catalogue expansions of the other two poems. Instead, the dynamic poetic self seems to "trail in the lines underfoot," imprisoned by the clausal frame. The only effects approaching catalogue technique are limited to the list of "chaff, straw, splinters of wood, weeds, and the sea-gluten, / Scum, scales from shining rocks, leaves of salt-lettuce, left by the tide" (11–12). The stative quality of the concrete nouns parallels the "baffl'd, balk'd, bent" quality of the poetic self, which reaches a nadir in the last two stanzas of Section 2:

> O baffl'd, balk'd, bent to the very earth,
> Oppress'd with myself that I have dared to open my mouth,
> Aware now that amid all that blab whose echoes recoil upon me
>   I have not once had the least idea who or what I am,
> But that before all my arrogant poems the real Me stands yet
>   untouch'd, untold, altogether unreach'd,
> Withdrawn far, mocking me with mock-congratulatory signs
>   and bows,
> With peals of distant ironical laughter at every word I have
>   written,
> Pointing in silence to these songs, and then to the sand beneath.
>
> I perceive I have not really understood any thing, not a single
>   object, and that no man ever can,
> Nature here in sight of the sea taking advantage of me to dart
>   upon me and sting me,
> Because I have dared to open my mouth to sing at all.
>
> (25–34)

The first stanza of the passage approaches the limits of the rhythmical frame, for it presents seven phrasal lines, but the stanza can hardly be called a dynamic expansion. The past participle controls the phrasing, and the single deverbal noun—"the blab"—conveys none of the joy of the poet's characteristic "barbaric yawp."

In the last two sections of the poem, Whitman escapes the reduction to silence by returning to the rhetoric of "Crossing Brooklyn Ferry." In the 1856 poem, Whitman resolves the opposition between limitation and expansion by finding the positive within the negative, and the resolution depends upon the poet's approach to his future readers. In Section 3 of "As I Ebb'd" he makes a similar approach:

> You oceans both, I close with you,
> We murmur alike reproachfully rolling sands and drift,
>   knowing not why,
> These little shreds indeed standing for you and me and all.
>
> (35–37)

The "oceans both" could refer to "Nature here in sight of the sea," to the past of Section 1 and the present of Section 2, or to the known and the unknown. But the most fundamental equation in the stanza is between the material, exterior ocean and the spiritual, interior ocean. The figure of the ocean as spiritual and interior is supported by Section 17 of "Starting from Paumanok," where the poet exclaims, "You oceans that have been calm within me! how I feel you, fathomless, stirring, preparing unprecedented waves and storms" (252). When the poet tentatively asserts that "we murmur alike reproachfully," he reveals that language mediates between the two terms of the basic equation.

Section 3 emphasizes the approach of the poet to the exterior world through the direct address to Paumanok as the poet's father:

> I too Paumanok,
> I too have bubbled up, floated the measureless float, and been
>   wash'd on your shores,
> I too am but a trail of drift and debris,
> I too leave little wrecks upon you, you fish-shaped island.
>
> (41–44)

Here Whitman echoes Section 3 and Section 5 of "Crossing Brooklyn Ferry," where he makes such statements as "I too many and many a time cross'd the river of old" (27) and "I too had been struck from the float forever held in solution / I too had receiv'd identity by my body" (62–63). The father image also recalls Section 10 of "Starting from Paumanok," where the father is "all the spiritual world." The mixture of material and spiritual engenders poetic power, for now Whitman begins to employ his most characteristic diction and syntax. Dynamic verbs—"throw," "cling," "hold," "kiss," "touch," and "breathe"—frame the last six lines of the section.

The 1860 version of the poem shows that Whitman addresses the "father land" in order to renew his language. The last two stanzas in the 1860 edition of *Leaves of Grass* read as follows:

> Kiss me, my father,
> Touch me with your lips, as I touch those I love,
> Breathe to me, while I hold you close, the secret of the
>   wondrous murmuring I envy,
> For I fear I shall become crazed, if I cannot emulate it, and
>   utter myself as well as it.
>
> Sea-raff! Crook-tongued waves!
> O, I will yet sing, some day, what you have said to me.
>
> (48–50[3])

The three deleted lines make the explicit connection between the material, exterior world of nature and the spiritual, interior world of the poet, and they do so by appealing to the mediating power of language. Thus the poet seeks to "utter myself as well as it," and he closes the appeal to the father by turning to the "fierce old mother," the "crooked-tongued waves." The turn delivers to the poet the "word out of the sea," for he can now promise that he "will yet sing, some day, what you have said to me." The future tense of the poet's promise figures the turn from the limiting effects of past and present. In the "vista" of the future "programme of chants," Whitman finds the true source of his linguistic power.

As in "Crossing Brooklyn Ferry," the poet's renewed sense of poetic power is performed in a dynamic style. Section 4 of "As I Ebb'd" opens in the same manner as the catalogue expansion of Section 9 of "Crossing Brooklyn Ferry":

> Ebb, ocean of life, (the flow will return,)
> Cease not your moaning you fierce old mother,
> Endlessly cry for your castaways, but fear not, deny not me,
> Rustle not up so hoarse and angry against my feet as I touch
>   you or gather from you.
>
> (51–54)

The tone here is not nearly so expansive as that of the 1856 poem, and the sense of limitation lingers in the brevity of the stanza. But Whitman employs six dynamic verbs in the imperative mood, and the promising image of "the flow will return" recalls the initial line of the 1856 catalogue: "Flow on, river! flow with the flood-tide, and ebb with the ebb-tide!" (101). The poet's renewed linguistic power is further revealed in the dynamic rhetoric of performance: "as I touch you or gather from you."

The penultimate stanza of "As I Ebb'd" develops the linguistic power of the poet by focusing upon the future readers of Whitman's poetry. The poet is no longer "seiz'd by the spirit that trails in the lines underfoot." Instead, he expresses a renewed sense of confidence in his "programme of chants": "I gather for myself and for this phantom looking down where we lead, and following me and mine" (56). In a moment of "present-saying," the poet now surpasses the "phantom," which is in the position of "following me and mine."

Whitman's vision of the union of the one and the many recalls the rhetoric of "The Sleepers" and "Crossing Brooklyn Ferry," and the last stanza mirrors that vision in its style:

> Me and mine, loose windrows, little corpses,
> Froth, snowy white, and bubbles,
> (See, from my dead lips the ooze exuding at last,
> See, the prismatic colors glistening and rolling,)
> Tufts of straw, sands, fragments,
> Buoy'd hither from many moods, one contradicting another,
> From the storm, the long calm, the darkness, the swell,
> Musing, pondering, a breath, a briny tear, a dab of liquid or
>   soil,
> Up just as much out of fathomless workings fermented and
>   thrown,
> A limp blossom or two, torn, just as much over waves floating,
>   drifted at random,
> Just as much for us that sobbing dirge of Nature,
> Just as much whence we come that blare of the cloud-trumpets,
> We, capricious, brought hither we know not whence, spread out
>   before you,
> You up there walking or sitting,
> Whoever you are, we too lie in drifts at your feet.

(57–71)

The mixed catalogue begins with the reductive images of death that baffled and balked the poet in Section 2. But then the parenthesis presents the graphic death of the poet himself in dynamic terms. The deverbal noun "ooze" combines with the present participles "exuding," "glistening," and "rolling" to portray death as a process, and the repeated command "See" recalls the programmatic style of "Starting from Paumanok." Whitman returns to the more stative style of the opening in the next two lines, but then deverbal nouns and present participles enact the process of dying: "the swell," "musing," "pondering," "a dab," "workings," "floating," "sobbing," "that blare," "walking," and "sitting" play against such stative phrases as "a briny tear" and "a limp blossom or two." The play creates a positive tone to close the poem, despite the sense of limitation that remains. Whitman balances expansion and limitation in much the same way that he balances the programmatic and the lyric, or the "vista" of the future and the reductive fact of death. He balances between "many moods, one contradicting another," and in doing so he creates one of his most effective "gymnast's struggles," one which moves through limitation and doubt to affirm the poet's faith in the future of "me and mine." That faith makes the reader into a nearly divine figure in the 1860 version of the poem, for Whitman capitalizes the "You" of the closing direct address (69–71). The poem suggests, finally, that *The Great Construction of the New Bible*" is itself an ongoing process, a process that depends upon the spiritual activity of both the one poet and his many readers.

6

"A Growth Out of the Past": Continuity and Succession in *Leaves of Grass*, 1860–1892

Writing to William D. O'Connor on 6 January 1865, Whitman made the surprising assertion that his new volume, *Drum-Taps*, then ready for the press, was "superior to *Leaves of Grass*—certainly more perfect as a work of art, being adjusted in all its proportions, & its passion having the indispensable merit that though to the ordinary reader let loose with wildest abandon, the true artist can see it is yet under control."[1] Later in the letter, Whitman distinguished further between the two books. *Drum-Taps*, he asserted, "delivers my ambition of the task that has haunted me, namely, to express in a poem (& in the way I like, which is not at all by directly stating it) the pending action of this *Time & Land we swim in*" (p. 246). By contrast, in *Leaves of Grass* the poet sought to express "by sharp-cut self assertion, *One's-Self* & also, or may be still more, to map out, to throw together for American use, a gigantic embryo or skeleton of

---

1. *Correspondence*, I, 246; subsequent quotations from the letter refer to the page numbers of this edition and appear in my text.

Personality, fit for the West, for native models—but there are a few things I shall carefully eliminate in the next issue, & a few more I shall considerably change" (p. 247).

The letter to O'Connor provides several insights into Whitman's changing poetics. First, the poet regards his earlier poems as full of "perturbations" (p. 247), whereas *Drum-Taps* keeps the passions "under control." Second, the *"New Bible"* will undergo careful pruning in the next edition, and Whitman asserts that he will excise all "verbal superfluity" (p. 247). Third, the earlier emphasis on *"One's-Self"* is to be replaced by an emphasis on "this *Time & Land we swim in*," so that the poet appears to be turning away from the interior, subjective experiences of the 1850s in favor of the exterior, objective events of the Civil War and its aftermath. In sum, the letter suggests that in 1865 Whitman has reconceived his poetic project, and the new volume *Drum-Taps* should be the first step toward a new "programme of chants."

This clearly overstates the case, of course, since *Leaves of Grass* continues to occupy the center of Whitman's attention for the rest of his career. The 1865 letter foreshadows the great work of revision and rearrangement that is the fundamental emphasis of the editions of 1867, 1871, and 1881.[2] And *Drum-Taps* itself would eventually become a part of the "ensemble" of *Leaves of Grass*. In addition, the poems of the 1865 *Drum-Taps* and the 1865–66 *Sequel to Drum-Taps* reveal deep continuities with the programmatic style of the 1860 edition. Whitman wishes to apply the "law of successions" to the volumes of his poetry, but ultimately the poetry reveals that continuity and the cumulative are as important as succession to the poet's postwar "thought of the ensemble."

The play between continuity and succession is already important in "A Broadway Pageant," published just three months after the 1860 edition.[3] The occasion of the poem is the arrival of "the nobles of Niphon, the errand-bearers" (6) in Manhattan and their procession through the city. The poem thus affords Whitman the opportunity to record the meeting of East and West, ancient and modern:

Superb-faced Manhattan!
Comrade Americanos! to us, then at last the Orient comes.

2. For the definitive account of revisions in the 1867 edition, see Arthur Golden, *Walt Whitman's Blue Book*, II (Textual Analysis).

3. The poem appeared in the *New York Times*, 27 June 1860; see *CRE*, pp. 242–43.

To us, my city,
Where our tall-topt marble and iron beauties range on opposite
    sides, to walk in the space between,
To-day our Antipodes comes.

The Originatress comes,
The nest of languages, the bequeather of poems, the race of eld,
Florid with blood, pensive, rapt with musings, hot with passion,
Sultry with perfume, with ample and flowing garments,
With sunburnt visage, with intense soul and glittering eyes,
The race of Brahma comes.

(21–31)

The diction of the passage recalls the programmatic style of the 1860
edition, especially in the use of foreign borrowings like "Americanos,"
innovative suffixes like "Originatress," and deverbal nouns like "bequeather." Still, the tone of the poem is not nearly so optimistically
progressivist as that of the 1860 edition. The poet represents the Orient as paying its due respects to the new civilization of America, but
he also pays his own respects to the "nest of languages, the bequeather of poems, the race of eld."

Whitman's respect for the past becomes ecstatic in the catalogue
rhetoric that closes Section 2:

For I too raising my voice join the ranks of this pageant,
I am the chanter, I chant aloud over the pageant,
I chant the world on my Western sea,
I chant copious the islands beyond, thick as stars in the sky,
I chant the new empire grander than any before, as in a vision
    it comes to me,
I chant America the mistress, I chant a greater supremacy,
I chant projected a thousand blooming cities yet in time on
    those groups of sea-islands,
My sail-ships and steam-ships threading the archipelagoes,
My stars and stripes fluttering in the wind,
Commerce opening, the sleep of ages having done its work,
    races reborn, refresh'd,
Lives, works resumed—the object I know not—but the old, the
    Asiatic renew'd as it must be,
Commencing from this day surrounded by the world.

(54–65)

The insistent repetition of "I chant" creates a dynamic clausal catalogue, and it echoes the "programme of chants" in "Starting from

Paumanok." But the dynamic catalogue rhetoric does not enact an exclusively progressivist, discontinuous view of time and change. Instead, the poet portrays America as a composite of past and present, ancient and modern, and the arrival of the Japanese "errand-bearers" signals the renewal of the ancient civilization within the modern. Whitman's cumulative vision crystallizes in the word "resumed," which denotes both a recapitulation and a recommencement of work (SOED).

In the final section of "A Broadway Pageant," the poet addresses "America the mistress" as "Libertad of the world" (66), but he insists upon the continuity between past and present:

> The sign is reversing, the orb is enclosed,
> The ring is circled, the journey is done,
> The box-lid is but perceptibly open'd, nevertheless the perfume
>   pours copiously out of the whole box.
>
> Young Libertad! with the venerable Asia, the all-mother,
> Be considerate with her now and ever hot Libertad, for you are
>   all,
> Bend your proud neck to the long-off mother now sending
>   messages over the archipelagoes to you,
> Bend your proud neck low for once, young Libertad.
>
> (70–76)

Whitman figures "Libertad" as "all," but Asia is the "all-mother," the "Originatress" of all. When the poet calls upon the young mistress to bend her "proud neck to the long-off mother," a clear figure of the respect owed the ancient world by the modern world, the sign is indeed reversing. Instead of the defiant tone of the earlier editions of *Leaves*, Whitman strikes a note of balance, implying that America is the respectful daughter of the "long-off mother."

The last two stanzas of the poem develop the maternal imagery in terms that recall the ethnological studies of Christian C. J. Bunsen:

> Were the children straying westward so long? so wide the
>   tramping?
> Were the precedent dim ages debouching westward from
>   Paradise so long?
> Were the centuries steadily footing it that way, all the while
>   unknown, for you, for reasons?
>
> They are justified, they are accomplish'd, they shall now be
>   turn'd the other way also, to travel toward you thence,

> They shall now also march obediently eastward for your sake
> Libertad.
>
> (77–81)

The passage figures the westward journey of races as being now accomplished, with America, or "Libertad," as the goal of the journey.
The temporal structure of the two stanzas enacts a recapitulation of
the journey, for it moves from the past tense in the first stanza of
questions to the present tense and future tense in the second stanza
of answers. The poem figures "Libertad" as the cumulative, composite product of eons of "straying" and "tramping," and it closes by
promising the "vista" of the ancient world marching "obediently
eastward" toward the modern world of America. Whitman's programmatic style is similar to that of the 1860 *Leaves of Grass*, but it
mingles the conflicting categories of "ensemble" and "vista" in a new
way.

Other poems from *Drum-Taps* reveal many of the characteristics
of the 1860 "programme of chants." In "First O Songs for a Prelude,"
originally the title poem of the volume, the poet addresses his native
city in native terms:

> And you lady of ships, you Mannahatta,
> Old matron of this proud, friendly, turbulent city,
> Often in peace and wealth you were pensive or covertly frown'd
>   amid all your children,
> But now you smile with joy exulting old Mannahatta.
>
> (55–58)

"Mannahatta" is figured as the mother of New York City, and the war
causes the poet to invoke the "spirit . . . that does not brook submission and imitation" (*DBN*, III, 755). As in Section 16 of "Starting from
Paumanok," the aboriginal name evokes the retrospective, cumulative view of linguistic and spiritual change, and it is within the context of this view that Whitman can regard the outbreak of war as a
joyous event.

A second poem from *Drum-Taps*, "From Paumanok Starting I Fly
like a Bird," echoes the 1860 proem, but it emphasizes the union of
the United States more than the sovereignty of the individual states:

> To sing first, (to the tap of the war-drum if need be,)
> The idea of all, of the Western world one and inseparable,
> And then the song of each member of these States.
>
> (9–11)

The poem announces a cumulative view of progress, framed by the ideal of the "ensemble," the "idea of all." Taken together, the image of the mother in "First O Songs" and the image of "the all" in "From Paumanok Starting I Fly like a Bird" echo the "all-mother" of "A Broadway Pageant," and the two "reveille" poems strike a similar balance between continuity and succession. The political crisis of the Civil War exercises a profound influence upon Whitman's progressivist vision, rendering it less naively optimistic and shifting it from *"One's-Self"* to the cumulative "ensemble" of the United States, to the *"Land & Times we swim in."*

Whitman's use of geographical names in *Drum-Taps* reflects the new emphasis on the union of the states. In "Eighteen Sixty-One," for example, he employs a catalogue technique that is reminiscent of the programmatic poems of 1860, but the catalogue produces an effect that is strikingly different from the earlier poems:

> As I heard you shouting loud, your sonorous voice ringing
>   across the continent,
> Your masculine voice O year, as rising amid the great cities,
> Amid the men of Manhattan I saw you as one of the workmen,
>   the dwellers in Manhattan,
> Or with large steps crossing the prairies out of Illinois and
>   Indiana,
> Rapidly crossing the West with springy gait and descending the
>   Alleghanies,
> Or down from the great lakes or in Pennsylvania, or on deck
>   along the Ohio River,
> Or southward along the Tennessee or Cumberland rivers, or at
>   Chattanooga on the mountain top,
> Saw I your gait and saw I your sinewy limbs clothed in blue,
>   bearing weapons, robust year,
> Heard your determin'd voice launch'd forth again and again,
> Year that suddenly sang by the mouths of the round-lipp'd
>   cannon,
> I repeat you, hurrying, crashing, sad, distracted year.
>
>   (6–16)

At first glance the catalogue appears to repeat the westward expansion announced in Section 14 of "Starting from Paumanok," but here the place names are associated with Union soldiers, troop movements, and military victories. The image of the "sonorous voice" becomes that of "your determin'd voice," and the innocent progressivism of "Starting from Paumanok" becomes a more tragic vision. Thus

Whitman characterizes the year as "hurrying, crashing, sad, distracted," joining two dynamic present participles with two stative adjectives. Finally, the poem enacts the mingling of *"Time & Lands,"* for it mixes the geographical names with the direct address to the year.

Place names figure prominently in three other poems from *Drum-Taps:* "Song of the Banner at Daybreak," "From Paumanok Starting I Fly like a Bird," and "Pioneers! O Pioneers!" In all three poems, the names gesture toward the diversity and individuality of the states, but in each case Whitman subordinates diversity to unity, the "Identity formed out of thirty-eight spacious and haughty States" ("Banner," 75). Nor do the lists of names create a dynamic "vista" of the future, for the war figures as the terminating goal of American progress. So, for instance, the fifth stanza of "Pioneers! O Pioneers!" can assert that "all the past we leave behind, / We debouch upon a newer mightier world, varied world" (16–17), but the final stanza closes the poem with the image of impending battle:

> Till with sound of trumpet,
> Far, far off the daybreak call—hark! how loud and clear I hear it
> wind,
> Swift! to the head of the army!—swift! spring to your places,
> Pioneers! O pioneers!
>
> (100–103)

Whitman still employs the dynamic rhetoric of performance, but the performance halts at a moment of crisis. The closing image presents the image of soldiers rather than the image of future readers "hasting on" with the poet.

Despite the mixed tone of the "reveille" poems, *Drum-Taps* marks its continuity with the 1860 "programme of chants" in several programmatic poems. In "Turn O Libertad," for example, the poet returns to the diction of "Starting from Paumanok," and the rhetoric of the poem strongly echoes the 1860 proem:

> Turn O Libertad, for the war is over,
> From it and all henceforth expanding, doubting no more,
> resolute, sweeping the world,
> Turn from lands retrospective recording proofs of the past,
> From the singers that sing the trailing glories of the past,
> From the chants of the feudal world, the triumphs of kings,
> slavery, caste,

Turn to the world, the triumphs reserv'd and to come—give up
  that backward world,
Leave to the singers of hitherto, give them the trailing past,
But what remains remains for singers for you—wars to come
  are for you,
(Lo, how the wars of the past have duly inured to you, and the
  wars of the present also inure;)
Then turn, and be not alarm'd O Libertad—turn your undying
  face,
To where the future, greater than all the past,
Is swiftly, surely preparing for you.

                                                            (1–12)

The word "Libertad" signals the poet's progressivist vision of the future, and Whitman combines that dictional signal with the catalogue
elements of anaphoric repetition, imperative verbs, and present participles. The optimistic rhetoric of performance is tempered by the
parenthesis, in which the poet recalls the "wars of the past," and the
parenthesis gestures toward the cumulative, retrospective view of
progress. But the poem effectively represents the past as "that backward world," and in the word "slavery" it associates the "feudal
world" with the defeated Confederacy. Whitman is able to turn toward the future because "the war is over," but the turn is actually a
return to the optimistic, programmatic style of the 1860 *Leaves of
Grass*.

If "Turn O Libertad" appears to reestablish the fundamental progressivism of Whitman's vision and style, the most important poem
of *Drum-Taps*, "The Wound-Dresser," presents a strong countercurrent
of elegy. The poem begins in the active, performative mode of "The
Sleepers," and it also displays close affinities with the vision of the
cumulative expressed in "A Broadway Pageant." The poet is "an old
man bending," and instead of looking toward the future he figures
himself as "years looking backward resuming in answer to children"
(1–2). The poetic act of "resuming" the past creates a mixed tone of
loss and joy, a tone which clearly recalls "The Sleepers." The connections with the 1855 poem become yet stronger in these central stanzas from Section 2:

But in silence, in dreams' projections,
While the world of gain and appearance and mirth goes on,
So soon what is over forgotten, and waves wash the imprints off
  the sand,

With hinged knees returning I enter the doors, (while for you up
    there,
Whoever you are, follow without noise and be of strong heart.)

Bearing the bandages, water and sponge,
Straight and swift to my wounded I go,
Where they lie on the ground after the battle brought in,
Where their priceless blood reddens the grass the ground,
Or to the rows of the hospital tent, or under the roof'd hospital,
To the long rows of cots up and down each side I return,
To each and all one after another I draw near, not one do I miss,
An attendant follows holding a tray, he carries a refuse pail,
Soon to be fill'd with clotted rags and blood, emptied, and fill'd
    again.

I onward go, I stop,
With hinged knees and steady hand to dress wounds,
I am firm with each, the pangs are sharp yet unavoidable,
One turns to me his appealing eyes—poor boy! I never knew
    you,
Yet I think I could not refuse this moment to die for you, if that
    would save you.

                                                              (20–38)

As in "The Sleepers," the poet represents himself as actively engaged
in an ongoing process, and he actifies himself by means of "dreams'
projections." The three stanzas mingle the imagery of the active self
with that of the dying, and they enact the poet's return to the past by
representing the past as present. Thus the present tense dominates
the hospital scene, reaching its sharpest focus in the image of the
soldier's "appealing eyes" and the poet's promise, "I think I could not
refuse this moment to die for you."

The dynamic rhetoric of performance continues to dominate in
Section 3 of the poem, but Whitman's use of five short stanzas creates
a dreamlike, delicate tone. The delicate quality also figures in the
mixture of past and present, which reaches a fragile balance in the
final section:

Thus in silence in dreams' projections,
Returning, resuming, I thread my way through the hospitals,
The hurt and wounded I pacify with soothing hand,
I sit by the restless all the dark night, some are so young,
Some suffer so much, I recall the experience sweet and sad,

(Many a soldier's loving arms about this neck have cross'd and
    rested,
Many a soldier's kiss dwells on these bearded lips.)

                          (59–65)

The image of the poet pacifying the restless wounded with soothing
hand recalls the opening section of "The Sleepers," where he passes
his "hand soothingly to and fro a few inches from them, / The restless
sink in their beds, they fitfully sleep" (24–25). But "The Wound-
Dresser" does not present the divine "efflux of the soul" or the "invigoration of the night." Instead, it dwells upon the past and upon the
poet's act of "resuming" the past. In the final line of the poem, Whitman associates the act of "resuming" with an image of the cumulative, for the poet's lips bear "many a soldier's kiss." In addition, the
image of the poet's lips gestures toward his role as spokesman for the
dying soldiers, and it therefore suggests that language is the mediating force between the many soldiers and the one poet. In parallel
fashion, the line suggests that language mediates between past and
present, and the mixture of past and present tenses in the final stanza
performs the act of mediation.

Although "The Wound-Dresser" has clear connections with "The
Sleepers," the style of the Civil War elegy more strongly recalls that
of "As I Ebb'd with the Ocean of Life." For Whitman employs none of
the programmatic diction and catalogue rhetoric that mark his progressivist mode of poetry. Instead, he strikes the chord of doubt
through the absence of programmatic rhetoric. "The Wound-Dresser"
is focused more resolutely upon the past than is "As I Ebb'd," and it
is concerned more with the *"Time & Lands we swim in"* than with
"this electric self out of the pride of which I utter poems." The elegy
thus moves toward the objective, cumulative vision announced in the
1865 letter to O'Connor, and it strikes the "undertone of sweetest com-
radeship & human love" with which Whitman sought to balance the
"perturbations" of *Leaves of Grass*.

In *Drum-Taps* the poet tends to keep the programmatic and elegiac
modes in separate compartments, and the balance between them is
suggested rather than fully developed. But in the most important
poem of *Sequel to Drum-Taps*, "When Lilacs Last in the Door-yard
Bloom'd," he succeeds in bringing the two modes to bear upon one
another, and the mixture of the programmatic and elegiac strikes a
balance between continuity and succession of poetic form. "Lilacs"
represents a fundamental shift in Whitman's poetics, but it also reveals a deep continuity with the 1860 "programme of chants."

The shift is immediately recognizable in the increased spatialization of form. In earlier poems like "The Sleepers," "Song of Myself," "As I Ebb'd with the Ocean of Life," "Out of the Cradle Endlessly Rocking," and even "A Broadway Pageant," a temporal structure imposes a kind of pseudonarrative upon the variety of poetic moods and modes that Whitman employs. Even in "Starting from Paumanok" the temporally dynamic, progressivist relationship between the poet and his future reader governs the variety of themes and performances. In "Lilacs," on the other hand, the sixteen sections do not function in a clear temporal structure akin to monodrama; instead, each section creates its own imaginative space, and the poem is more like music than narrative in its structure.[4]

These critical analogies, while helpful, do not suffice to explain the structure of "Lilacs," for the poem depends upon opposition rather than analogy. The three principal images of the poem, for example, do not readily function as symbols to which the reader can assign an abstract meaning. He or she associates the "powerful western fallen star" (7) with President Lincoln, the "shy and hidden bird" (19) with the poet, and the "lilac blooming perennial" (4) with the poem itself, but these associations are neither absolute nor restrictive. Whitman himself shows how "floating and movable" the three images can be in his reminiscence of the spring of 1865 in *Specimen Days*:

> *Night of March 18, '79.*—One of the calm, pleasantly cool, exquisitely clear and cloudless, early spring nights—the atmosphere again that rare vitreous blue-black, welcom'd by astronomers. Just at 8, evening, the scene overhead of certainly solemnest beauty, never surpass'd. Venus nearly down in the west, of a size and lustre as if trying to outshow herself, before departing. Teeming, maternal orb—I take you again to myself. I am reminded of that spring preceding Abraham Lincoln's murder, when I, restlessly haunting the Potomac's banks, around Washington city, watch'd you, off there, aloof, moody as myself. (*PW*, I, 187)

4. The editors of *CRE* note that the poem creates "a structure which resembles music in that it is its own being, its own experience of emotion that matters,—not its 'meaning' " (p. 328). The most thorough attempt to tie Whitman's poetry to the analogy of music is Robert Faner's *Walt Whitman and Opera* (Philadelphia: University of Pennsylvania Press, 1951). For a more recent attempt, see Robert E. Carlile, "Leitmotif and Whitman's 'When Lilacs Last in the Door-yard Bloom'd,' " *Criticism* 13 (1971): 329–39.

For an interpretation of the poem that argues against critical analogies, see Miller, *Critical Guide*, pp. 111–19. The most important recent essay on the poem is Mutlu Konuk Blasing, "Whitman's 'Lilacs' and the Grammars of Time," *PMLA* 97 (1982): 31–39.

The star calls up three different associations: First it is "maternal," then it reminds Whitman of the spring before Lincoln's assassination, and finally it is "aloof, moody as myself."

The "floating and movable" quality of Whitman's imagery applies equally well to the "trinity sure" he introduces in the first section of the poem. The trinity comprises the "lilac blooming perennial," the "drooping star in the west," and the "thought of him I love" (5–6). Conspicuously absent is the image of the hermit thrush. Moreover, the trinity appears to distinguish the star from "him I love," thus blurring the edges of a symbolic correspondence between the star and Lincoln. Finally, the "trinity sure" does not remain stable and well-defined, for it reappears in Section 14 as the poet, the "knowledge of death," and the "thought of death" (120–22).

Rather than present the reader with a one-to-one correspondence between image and meaning, Whitman employs the principal images in a dramatic, dynamic structure of opposition. In the first four sections, he introduces the three images and sets the rhythmical frame of the poem. Section 2 verges upon catalogue rhetoric because the apostrophe "O" is repeated eight times in just five lines, but the stanzaic form of the first four sections insists upon the mixture of phrases and clauses in units from two to six lines long. Even Section 2 reveals how Whitman balances between the rhythmical frame and catalogue expansion:

> O powerful western fallen star!
> O shades of night—O moody, tearful night!
> O great star disappear'd—O the black murk that hides the star!
> O cruel hands that hold me powerless—O helpless soul of me!
> O harsh surrounding cloud that will not free my soul.
>
> (7–11)

The section is structured like a phrasal catalogue, and that syntactic mode figures the "powerless" and "helpless" quality of the poet. Whitman opposes the stative quality of the phrases with three relative clauses containing three dynamic verbs—"hides," "hold," and "will not free"—and the opposition enacts the contrast between the helpless, passive poet and the threatening, active darkness. The section mixes phrases and clauses in a drama of opposition, just as the short, five-line stanza form opposes the exclamatory rhetoric of the repeated apostrophes.

The most fundamental structure of the poem opposes the programmatic and elegiac modes, and that opposition is figured in both the diction and the syntax of "Lilacs." The programmatic diction of the poem takes the form of dynamic verbal forms, American place names, and Quaker terms. The last of the three is the least important, for in only one instance does Whitman employ a Quaker name: "Pictures of growing spring and farms and homes, / With the Fourth-month eve at sundown" (81–82). The Quaker name for April resonates within the poet's mythology of peace, and it is particularly important in the historical context of the poem. But the single use of a Quaker term gestures almost imperceptibly at the mythology.

More important to the tone of the poem is the use of place names, and Whitman employs two sorts of geographical terms to balance the programmatic and the elegiac. The first are invented names, which the poet introduces in Section 10: "Sea-winds blown from east and west, / Blown from the Eastern sea and blown from the Western sea, till there on the prairies meeting" (74–75). By substituting invented names for the Atlantic and Pacific oceans, Whitman represents the native spirit of America, corresponding to the geographical boundaries of the United States. The winds significantly blow inland, toward the prairies that gave birth to Lincoln, Whitman's representative man.

The second type of geographical name develops this double representation:

> Lo, body and soul—this land,
> My own Manhattan with spires, and the sparkling and hurrying tides, and the ships,
> The varied and ample land, the South and the North in the light, Ohio's shores and flashing Missouri,
> And ever the far-spreading prairies cover'd with grass and corn.
> (89–92)

The stanza echoes the 1860 "programme of chants" in a number of ways. First, the theme of "body and soul" recalls the arrival of the soul in Section 6 of "Starting from Paumanok," and the image of the soul is especially appropriate to the elegiac mode. Second, Whitman joins the elegiac with the programmatic through the use of place names. The aboriginal name for New York City is hinted at in "Manhattan." Next, the two warring regions are represented as equally "in the light," composing the "varied and ample land." Finally, the two rivers figure as tributaries of the Mississippi, the "spinal river" of "Starting from Paumanok" (221), and they join in the "far-spreading prairies cover'd with grass and corn." The stanza moves toward an image of union or "ensemble," and the dynamic quality of present participles like "sparkling," "hurrying," "flashing," and "far-spreading" renders the "ensemble" active and temporal. The final image of the prairie echoes the meeting-place of the sea-winds in Section 10, blending the elegiac and the programmatic modes.

The final category of programmatic diction in "Lilacs" is the dynamic verbal form, and the most persistent form is that of the present participle. Whitman employs the present participle programmatically in sections 5, 6, 11, 12, 14, and 16, and in most cases it functions within the poet's catalogue rhetoric. As in the poems of the first three editions of *Leaves of Grass*, then, the present participle joins the stylistic levels of diction and syntax.

Sections 5 and 6 treat indirectly the journey of Lincoln's coffin to Springfield, but Whitman represents the journey as an ongoing process. The first section begins as a catalogue of prepositional phrases and ends with an inverted clause, thus echoing the initial stanza of "Out of the Cradle Endlessly Rocking." The image of the coffin appears only in the final line, and the phrasal segment of the passage emphasizes the union of the *"Time & Lands we swim in"* by mixing dynamic present participles with more stative nouns:

> Over the breast of the spring, the land, amid cities,
> Amid lanes and through old woods, where lately the violets
>   peep'd from the ground, spotting the gray debris,
> Amid the grass in the fields each side of the lanes, passing the
>   endless grass,
> Passing the yellow-spear'd wheat, every grain from its shroud
>   in the dark-brown fields uprisen,
> Passing the apple-tree blows of white and pink in the orchards,
> Carrying a corpse to where it shall rest in the grave,
> Night and day journeys a coffin.
>
>   (26–32)

The five present-participial phrases oppose images like "yellow-spear'd wheat," "apple-tree blows," and "corpse," and the structure of opposition renders the journey of the coffin as a present-tense, perpetually occurring event.

Section 6 takes up the image of the coffin presented in Section 5, but Whitman alters the style to create a self-enclosed passage, one which opposes the previous section. The poet shifts from objective presentation to the rhetoric of direct address, and the phrasal catalogue enacts the slow passing of the funeral train:

Coffin that passes through lanes and streets,
Through day and night with the great cloud darkening the land,
With the pomp of the inloop'd flags with the cities draped in
  black,
With the show of the States themselves as of crape-veil'd
  women standing,
With processions long and winding and the flambeaus of the
  night,
With the countless torches lit, with the silent sea of faces and
  the unbared heads,
With the waiting depot, the arriving coffin, and the sombre
  faces,
With dirges through the night, with the thousand voices rising
  strong and solemn,
With all the mournful voices of the dirges pour'd around the
  coffin,
The dim-lit churches and the shuddering organs—where amid
  these you journey,
With the tolling tolling bells' perpetual clang,
Here, coffin that slowly passes,
I give you my sprig of lilac.

(33–45)

Nine present participles, as well as the sound-symbolic deverbal
noun "clang," appear in just thirteen lines, and they contrast with the
synecdochic images of the "silent sea of faces and the unbared heads,"
"the mournful voices," and "the dim-lit churches." The mixture of dynamic and stative forms creates a fundamental opposition between
action and stasis, between grieving and grief. On a higher stylistic
level, the programmatic, progressivist rhetoric of the future opposes
the elegiac, backward-looking rhetoric of the past.

The elegiac mode dominates Section 7 through Section 10, where
Whitman reestablishes the rhythmical frame based upon clausal
lines and short stanzas. Even in Section 8, which presents a clausal
expansion beyond the rhythmical frame, the elegiac rhetoric recalls
the first four sections of the poem. Significantly, Section 8 begins
with the rhetoric of direct address and moves into a sequence of past-
tense clauses:

O western orb sailing the heaven,
Now I know what you must have meant as a month since I
  walk'd,
As I walk'd in silence the transparent shadowy night,

As I saw you had something to tell as you bent to me night after
    night,
As you droop'd from the sky low down as if to my side, (while
    the other stars look'd on,)
As we wander'd together the solemn night, (for something I
    know not what kept me from sleep,)
As the night advanced, and I saw on the rim of the west how
    full you were of woe,
As I stood on the rising ground in the breeze in the cool
    transparent night,
As I watch'd where you pass'd and was lost in the netherward
    black of the night,
As my soul in its trouble dissatisfied sank, as where you sad orb,
Concluded, dropt in the night, and was gone.

                                                        (55–65)

Here the poet focuses upon the image of Venus, the "western orb,"
and the image becomes associated with the poet's own soul, which
sinks in the same way as the "sad orb." The passage presents one of
Whitman's most moving enactments of the sense of loss and grief,
and it concentrates exclusively on the elegiac mode of the past tense.

    In Section 11, the present participle once again functions pro-
grammatically. Even though the catalogue presents "pictures" that
the poet will "hang on the walls" of Lincoln's "burial-house," the pictures move from the elegiac mode of grief and death to the programmatic mode of renewal and life:

Pictures of growing spring and farms and homes,
With the Fourth-month eve at sundown, and the gray smoke
    lucid and bright,
With floods of the yellow gold of the gorgeous, indolent, sinking
    sun, burning, expanding the air,
With the fresh sweet herbage under foot, and the pale green
    leaves of the trees prolific,
In the distance the flowing glaze, the breast of the river, with a
    wind-dapple here and there,
With ranging hills on the banks, with many a line against the
    sky, and shadows,
And the city at hand with dwellings so dense, and stacks of
    chimneys,
And all the scenes of life and the workshops, and the workmen
    homeward returning.

                                                        (81–88)

The phrasal nature of the catalogue of pictures would seem to imply a stative, grief-stricken tone, but Whitman strategically places the present participle to take the catalogue beyond the elegiac. Such dynamic forms as "growing," "sinking," "burning," "expanding," "the flowing glaze," "a wind-dapple," "ranging," and "returning" insist upon the temporally progressive aspect of the pictures. The catalogue thus discovers beauty within grief, "scenes of life" within the fact of death, and it effects a shift in tone from the elegiac to the programmatic. Section 12 develops that shift, both in the use of programmatic place names in the first stanza and in the present participles of the second stanza: "spreading," "bathing," "coming," "shining," "enveloping" (96–98).

In Section 13 the poet returns to the rhythmical frame, echoing the direct addresses to the hermit thrush in Section 4 and Section 9. But the elegiac return is only temporary, and Section 14 performs a more significant return on Whitman's part, a return to the rhetoric and insight of "Out of the Cradle Endlessly Rocking." The section shows how completely Whitman is the master of stanzaic form, for it modulates effortlessly from the programmatic to the elegiac and back again. The first stanza appears to be programmatic, presenting images of "the large unconscious scenery of my land" that recall sections 11 and 12. The poet employs present participles to further the effect, delivering images of "farmers preparing their crops" (109), "the arching heavens of the afternoon swift passing" (112), "the summer approaching" (114), and "the streets how their throbbings throbb'd" (116). But the stanza then returns to the elegiac image of the "black murk" of Section 2:

> And the streets how their throbbings throbb'd, and the cities
>   pent—lo, then and there,
> Falling upon them all and among them all, enveloping me with
>   the rest,
> Appear'd the cloud, appear'd the long black trail,
> And I knew death, its thought, and the sacred knowledge of
>   death.
>
> (116–19)

The image of the cloud "enveloping me with the rest" reverses the positive image of the sun "enveloping man and land" in Section 12. And the active, dynamic quality of the present participles appears to be invested, here, in the elegiac mode rather than the programmatic mode. Life is figured as the victim or prisoner of death. But the final line of the stanza modulates yet again, uniting the elegiac and the programmatic in Whitman's triple assertion of knowledge: "And I knew death, its thought, and the sacred knowledge of death."

The remaining stanzas of Section 14 perform a double function. First, they tell the narrative of the poet's journey with his two companions, the "knowledge of death" and the "thought of death," to the "solemn shadowy cedars and ghostly pines so still" (120–25). Second, they reestablish the rhythmical frame. The six-line stanza of the journey becomes three tercets focusing upon the poet's reaction to the "carol" of the hermit thrush (126–34). Then the bird's song finally appears in seven measured quatrains (135–62). The two functions work within the structure of opposition, for the emergence of the bird's carol of death disrupts the narrative sequence that frames it. Thus the section opposes the past-tense narrative to the present-tense lyric.

The temporal opposition of past and present brings about a parallel shift in tone. The poet's narrative, though it asserts the knowledge of death announced in "Out of the Cradle," is fundamentally elegiac and backward-looking. When Whitman delivers the song of the thrush in words, however, the tone shifts to celebration and to the future:

> *Approach strong deliveress,*
> *When it is so, when thou hast taken them I joyously sing the dead,*
> *Lost in the loving floating ocean of thee,*
> *Laved in the flood of thy bliss O death.*
>
> *From me to thee glad serenades,*
> *Dances for thee I propose saluting thee, adornments and feastings*
> *   for thee,*
> *And the sights of the open landscape and the high-spread sky are*
> *   fitting,*
> *And life and the fields, and the huge and thoughtful night.*
>
> *The night in silence under many a star,*
> *The ocean shore and the husky whispering wave whose voice I*
> *   know,*
> *And the soul turning to thee O vast and well-veil'd death,*
> *And the body gratefully nestling close to thee.*
>
> *Over the tree-tops I float thee a song,*
> *Over the rising and sinking waves, over the myriad fields and*
> *   the prairies wide,*
> *Over the dense-pack'd cities all and the teeming wharves and*
> *   ways,*
> *I float this carol with joy, with joy to thee O death.*
>
> (147–62)

The thrush and the poet merge in the verbal translation of the song, which stresses the deferred arrival of the "deliveress." The style of the song becomes more and more dynamic, moving toward a crescendo in the last two stanzas, where six present participles appear in eight lines. The tone of celebration and the rhetoric of deferral combine to invest the song of the thrush with Whitman's programmatic power, though the song remains tinged with the effects of the elegiac narrative.

The mixture of tone and form continues to provide Whitman with power in Section 15, which shifts from the song of the thrush to the tallying song of the poet. The first three stanzas feature the three-line and two-line stanzas of the rhythmical frame, and within them Whitman returns to his narrative exposition. But in the last two stanzas the narrative expands to become a lyrical vision, where the sounds of the bird become the catalogued sights of the visionary:

> And I saw askant the armies,
> I saw in noiseless dreams hundreds of battle-flags,
> Borne through the smoke of the battles and pierc'd with
>   missiles I saw them,
> And carried hither and yon through the smoke, and torn and
>   bloody,
> And at last but a few shreds left on the staffs, (and all in
>   silence,)
> And the staffs all splinter'd and broken.
>
> I saw battle-corpses, myriads of them,
> And the white skeletons of young men, I saw them,
> I saw the debris and debris of all the slain soldiers of the war,
> But I saw they were not as was thought,
> They themselves were fully at rest, they suffer'd not,
> The living remain'd and suffer'd, the mother suffer'd,
> And the wife and the child and the musing comrade suffer'd,
> And the armies that remain'd suffer'd.
>
> (171–84)

The combination of past participles and the repetend "I saw" creates a stative effect in the first stanza, where the "thought of death" controls the steady diminution of the battle flags into "a few shreds." But then the anaphoric "I saw" merges with the terminal repetition of the finite verb "suffer'd," and the "knowledge of death" governs the more dynamic style of the final stanza. The tone of the passage balances between the thought of death and the knowledge of death, be-

tween the elegiac and the programmatic. Without belittling the suffering of the war's survivors, Whitman manages to celebrate the
necessary opposition of life and death.

In the opening stanza of Section 16, Whitman employs the present participle in its most concentrated form, enacting the "passing"
of the poet from the elegiac to the programmatic:

> Passing the visions, passing the night,
> Passing, unloosing the hold of my comrades' hands,
> Passing the song of the hermit bird and the tallying song of my
>   soul,
> Victorious song, death's outlet song, yet varying ever-altering
>   song,
> As low and wailing, yet clear the notes, rising and falling,
>   flooding the night,
> Sadly sinking and fainting, as warning and warning, and yet
>   again bursting with joy,
> Covering the earth and filling the spread of the heaven,
> As that powerful psalm in the night I heard from recesses,
> Passing, I leave thee lilac with heart-shaped leaves,
> I leave thee there in the door-yard, blooming, returning with
>   spring.
>
> (185–94)

The ten-line stanza contains twenty-two present participles, and this
astounding rush of dynamic forms figures both the poetic self and
the poem itself as inherently active and "ever-altering." It implies,
moreover, that the suffering and grief are to be left behind, for now
the poet appears to embrace the present-tense world of temporal
change.

If the poem were to end here, it would create a dynamic, programmatic effect of closure, one that is familiar to us from such
poems as "Starting from Paumanok." But the final section of the
poem returns to the rhythmical frame in the penultimate stanza,
where the poet bids yet another farewell to the star, the "comrade
lustrous with silver face" (197). And the final stanza of the poem,
though it expands beyond the rhythmical frame, evokes the circular
structure of "Out of the Cradle Endlessly Rocking":

> Yet each to keep and all, retrievements out of the night,
> The song, the wondrous chant of the gray-brown bird,
> And the tallying chant, the echo arous'd in my soul,

> With the lustrous and drooping star with the countenance full
>   of woe,
> With the holders holding my hand nearing the call of the bird,
> Comrades mine and I in the midst, and their memory ever to
>   keep, for the dead I loved so well,
> For the sweetest, wisest soul of all my days and lands—and this
>   for his dear sake,
> Lilac and star and bird twined with the chant of my soul,
> There in the fragrant pines and the cedars dusk and dim.
>
> (198–206)

Like the coda of "Out of the Cradle," the stanza mixes the dynamic present participle with the imagery of the poem's opening sections. Significantly, the dynamic verbal forms disappear four lines before the end of the poem. In those final four lines, the poet returns to "the dead I loved so well" and to the place where "lilac and star and bird twined with the chant of my soul." The past tense of the lines opposes the programmatic use of the present participles and present-tense finite verbs, and it strongly echoes the elegiac tone with which the poet opens "Lilacs." Thus Whitman re-creates the mixture of the programmatic and the elegiac modes in the closing coda, and the effect of the closure is to return the reader to the beginning of the poem, where the "retrievements out of the night" begin their inevitable oppositions over and over again.

"When Lilacs Last in the Door-yard Bloom'd" represents the pinnacle of Whitman's poetic achievement. The mixture of the elegiac and the programmatic modes of poetry creates parallel mixtures of private and public personae, of stative and dynamic styles, and of backward-looking and forward-looking visions of human experience. But after the publication of the *Sequel to Drum-Taps*, Whitman suffers, according to the foremost critics of his work, a significant falling off of poetic power.[5] With a few notable exceptions, including "Passage to In-

5. The negative view of Whitman's late poetry is pervasive. Representative critics are Chase, pp. 146–52; Roy Harvey Pearce, *The Continuity of American Poetry* (Princeton: Princeton University Press, 1961), pp. 164–74; Hyatt Waggoner, *American Poets from the Puritans to the Present* (Boston: Houghton Mifflin, 1968), pp. 179–80; Waggoner, *American Visionary Poetry* (Baton Rouge: Louisiana State University Press, 1982), pp. 60–65; E. H. Miller, *Psychological Journey*, pp. 210–21; Jerome Loving, *Emerson, Whitman, and the American Muse* (Chapel Hill: University of North Carolina Press, 1982), pp. 145–91; and David Cavitch, *My Soul and I: The Inner Life of Walt Whitman* (Boston: Beacon, 1985), p. xv–xvi.

The major criticism of Whitman's late style appears in Roger Asselineau, *The*

dia" and "Song of the Red-wood," I would agree that Whitman's strength no longer finds a focus in individual poems. But poetic power is not therefore absent; rather, it makes itself felt on a new formal level in the postwar editions of *Leaves of Grass*. In the 1860 *Leaves* Whitman begins to organize the poems into "clusters," groupings that change continually through the editions of 1867, 1871, and 1881.[6] After the 1881 edition, moreover, the aging poet adds two "annexes" to the "ensemble," and only death prevented him from making yet a third addition.[7] In Whitman's cluster arrangements we can see once again the play of continuity and succession, so that *Leaves* becomes a growth out of its own past. And, like "Lilacs," that growth depends largely upon the spatialization of form.

Several manuscript notes show that the cluster arrangements of the 1860 edition spring from an intensely personal twelve-poem sequence called "Live Oak with Moss."[8] The twelve poems record, as

---

Evolution of Walt Whitman (Cambridge, Mass.: Belknap Press, 1962), pp. 225–38. For a statistical analysis of the changes in Whitman's style, see Hollis, *Language and Style*, pp. 211–32, 253–56.

6. For an introduction to "Cluster Arrangements in *Leaves of Grass*," see *Variorum*, I, lvii–lxxv. Important earlier attempts at defining a structure in *Leaves of Grass* are W. S. Kennedy, *Reminiscences of Walt Whitman* (London: Alexander Gardner, 1896), pp. 100–102; Irving C. Story, "The Structural Pattern of *Leaves of Grass*," *Pacific University Bulletin* 38:4 (1942): 2–12; Miller, *Critical Guide*, pp. 165–261; Thomas Edward Crawley, *The Structure of "Leaves of Grass"* (Austin: University of Texas Press, 1971), pp. 80–226.

7. The first annex, "Sands at Seventy," was published in *November Boughs* (1888) and added to the 1891–92 edition of *Leaves* (*CRE*, pp. 506–7). The second annex, "Good-Bye My Fancy," was separately published in 1891 and then added to the 1891–92 edition (*CRE*, pp. 536–37). "Old Age Echoes," comprised of thirteen poems, was apparently to form a third annex; see Horace Traubel's "Executor's Diary Note, 1891" (*CRE*, p. 575).

8. For an introduction to the "Live Oak" sequence, see Bowers, pp. lxiii–lxiv, and Golden, II, xxii–xxvii. The twelve poems of the sequence are as follows:

"Live Oak"	1860	1881 title
I.	"Calamus," 14	"Not Heat Flames up and Consumes"
II.	20	"I Saw in Louisiana a Live-Oak Growing"
III.	11	"When I Heard at the Close of the Day"
IV.	23	"This Moment Yearning and Thoughtful"
V.	8	"[Long I Thought . . .]"
VI.	32	"What Think You I Take My Pen in Hand?"
VII.	10	"Recorders Ages Hence"
VIII.	9	"[Hours Continuing Long]"
IX.	34	"I Dream'd in a Dream"
X.	43	"O You whom I Often and Silently Come"

Fredson Bowers points out, "an artistically complete story of attachment, crisis, and renunciation."⁹ "Live Oak with Moss" is significant because it is the kernel of the 1860 "Calamus" cluster, which expanded from twelve to forty-five poems. In the process of transforming the "Live Oak" sequence into the "Calamus" cluster, Whitman made two other important changes. First, the narrative plot and temporal progression of "Live Oak" are dispersed, so that the "Calamus" cluster does not tell a recognizable story of homosexual love. Second, the additional poems in the 1860 cluster shift the emphasis of the group from private to public, from the lyric to the programmatic style.

These two stylistic alterations come together in several manuscript notes. In the first, Whitman considers a series of poems on the theme of heterosexual love as a necessary counterbalance to the "Live Oak" sequence:

> A string of Poems, (short, etc.) embodying the amative love of woman—the same as *Live Oak Leaves* do the passion of friendship for man. (*NUPM*, I, 412)

The word "string" implies the kind of temporal, linear sequence that marks the arrangement of poems in the first two editions of *Leaves of Grass* and in the twelve-poem "Live Oak with Moss." Furthermore, the title Whitman uses ("*Live Oak Leaves*"), while it differs from that of the twelve-poem sequence, shows that the poet still considers the live oak as the central image of the "string." Finally, the heterosexual theme is only vaguely outlined. The first note suggests, then, that in the early stages of altering the "Live Oak with Moss" sequence, Whitman was still thinking in terms of a linear, temporal progression, a "string" instead of a "cluster," but he was also beginning to seek a more balanced, inclusive representation of human sexuality than would be present in the "Live Oak Leaves" alone.

A second note focuses upon the "Calamus" theme and alters the sequential image of the "string":

> Poems. A Cluster of Poems, Sonnets expressing the thoughts, pictures, aspirations, &c., fit to be perused during the days of the

---

XI.	36	"Earth, My Likeness"
XII.	42	"To a Western Boy"

9. P. lxvi.

approach of Death. that I have prepared myself for that purpose.
Remember now——— Remember the———. (*NUPM*, IV, 1361)

The word "cluster" signals the movement from a linear sequence to
a more spatialized form. And the language of the note parallels that
of "Scented Herbage of My Breast," which appeared as the second
poem in the "Calamus" cluster in 1860:

> Scented herbage of my breast,
> Leaves from you I glean, I write, to be perused best afterwards,
> Tomb-leaves, body-leaves growing up above me above death.
>
> (1–3)

The parallels in language reveal that "Scented Herbage" is a key to
the "Calamus" cluster, for the poem negotiates the passage from the
image of the "live oak leaves" to that of the sweet flag root. For instance, the draft version of the phrase "perennial roots" (4) is "perennial leaves," and the draft of the line "Do not fold yourself so in your
pink-tinged roots timid leaves" (19) does not contain the phrase
"pink-tinged roots." On the other hand, both the draft version and the
printed text employ the image of the root, suggestive of the calamus
plant, in the line "Yet you are beautiful to me you faint tinged roots,
you make me think of death" (10).[10]

The alteration of imagery parallels alterations in theme and
form. "Scented Herbage" associates the theme of manly love with the
"real reality" (33) of death and the soul, so the poem moves toward
the programmatic treatment of the "Calamus" theme that marks Section 6 of "Starting from Paumanok."

> Emblematic and capricious blades I leave you, now you serve
>   me not,
> I will say what I have to say by itself,
> I will sound myself and comrades only, I will never again utter
>   a call only their call,
> I will raise with it immortal reverberations through the States,
> I will give an example to lovers to take permanent shape and
>   will through the States,
> Through me shall the words be said to make death exhilarating.
>
> (22–27)

10. See Bowers, pp. 68–75, for both texts.

Whitman's programmatic style is apparent in the repeated phrase "the States" and in the dynamic clausal catalogue, featuring the repetend "I will." The rhetoric of future realization allows the poet to spiritualize homosexual love, and in doing so he negotiates the passage from private to public love, from lyric to programmatic style. Despite the negotiated passage, however, both aspects of the theme and form are present in the poem. As Whitman says, "I see that you belong to me now above all, and are folded inseparably together, you love and death are" (29).

The poet's tendency to mix modes of representation emerges clearly in the next manuscript note, where homosexual and heterosexual themes mingle:

> Theory of a Cluster of Poems the same *to the Passion of Woman-Love* as the "Calamus-Leaves" are to adhesiveness, manly love. /
> Full of animal-fire, tender, burning,—the tremulous ache, delicious, yet such a torment,
> The swelling, elate and vehement, that will not be denied, / Adam, as a central figure and type. /
> one piece
> Presenting a vivid picture, (in connection with the spirit,) of a fully-complete, well-developed, man eld, bearded, swart, fiery—as more than rival of the youthful type-hero of novels and love poems (*NUPM*, I, 413)

The note repeats the idea of a heterosexual group of poems as a counterpart to the poems of manly love, but here the term "cluster" replaces the earlier word "string" and "Calamus" replaces the earlier "Live Oak Leaves." Furthermore, the "Woman-Love" cluster is associated with the "central figure" of Adam. It would seem, then, that Whitman's plans for the "Enfans d'Adam" cluster date from the same period in which he was expanding the "Live Oak with Moss" sequence into the "Calamus" cluster of forty-five poems. And the language of the note, concentrating on the male figure and evoking exclusively male sexuality, suggests that "Enfans d'Adam" is mainly concerned with spiritualizing and generalizing the poet's own sexual feelings: "Presenting a vivid picture, (in connection with the spirit,) of a fully-complete, well-developed, man eld, bearded, swart, fiery."

The notes relating to the "Calamus" and "Enfans d'Adam" clusters indicate that, even in the earliest stages of preparing the third edition of *Leaves of Grass*, Whitman was attempting to combine a personal, private source of inspiration with a programmatic, public expression. Three manuscript notes dating from the same period clarify the attempt. In the first, the poet is close to the imagery of the note concerning "Enfans d'Adam":

> A cluster of poems, (in the same way as "Calamus Leaves") expressing the idea and sentiment of Happiness, Extatic life, (or moods,) Serene Calm Infantum Juvenatum Maturity—a young mans [*sic*] moods. . . . Middle-age   Strong, well-fibred, bearded, athletic, full of love, full of pride & joy   Old Age   Natural Happinesses   Love, Friendship (*NUPM*, IV, 1360)

Although the words "cluster" and "Calamus" indicate the poet's movement away from the sequential, private narrative of "Live Oak with Moss," the note still displays a rough chronological order of the stages of life, running from "Infantum" to "Old Age." But in focusing upon "moods," Whitman alters the earlier meditations concerning sexuality, and the dominant mood is one of joy rather than the brooding tone of the notes for "Scented Herbage."

The shifts in tone and focus become yet more pronounced in the second manuscript note. Whitman proposes "A cluster (same style as of Sonnets like, as "Calamus Leaves,") of poems, verses, thoughts, etc. embodying religious emotions" (*NUPM*, IV, 1362). The word "Sonnets" recalls the "Scented Herbage" note, as does the connection of "religious emotions" to the theme of death. But the focus also looks forward to the religious theme of the "Whispers of Heavenly Death" cluster in the 1881 edition of *Leaves*, and the tone of the note is dispassionate and general. In the final note, these shifts are clear:

Cluster of Sonnet-Poems.

Leading *trait-idea*
The splendor & copiousness of
    These Days:
    ? (Would not that be a good name for them viz: "These Days."
(*NUPM*, IV, 1363)

Whitman's proposed cluster forecasts both the 1865 letter to O'Connor, where the poet emphasizes "this *Time & Land we swim in*," and the prose collection *Specimen Days*. By the time we come to this final note, then, the "*trait-idea*" of a given cluster no longer springs from the personal sexuality of the poet. Instead, the "*trait-idea*" focuses upon two of the poet's most characteristically programmatic themes—"religious emotions" and "These Days."

My description imposes a kind of narrative upon the manuscript notes, and this narrative raises at least two problems. First, the notes are difficult to date, so the plot of spiritualization depends upon an assumed chronological order, which in turn depends upon the general shape of Whitman's poetic career. Second, and more serious, the plot itself disguises a fundamental contradiction in Whitman's poetry. By narrating a movement from the private, lyric source of the clusters to the public, programmatic form of expression, the description implies that the programmatic mode resolves any difficulties encountered either in the lyric mode or in the clash between the two modes themselves. But while my narrative may depict Whitman's changing conception of the cluster form accurately, it does not necessarily resolve the fundamental opposition between Whitman's two modes of poetic expression.

An important cluster from the 1860 edition provides a focus for analyzing the play of Whitman's contradictory impulses and poetic modes. This is the "Leaves of Grass" cluster, a title Whitman retains through the editions of 1867 and 1871.[11] At the most fundamental level, this cluster would seem to function as a synecdochic figure for the entire "New Bible," where the cluster represents the architectural "ensemble." The 1860 "Leaves of Grass" cluster invites this interpretation, for ten of the first twelve poems originally appeared in the 1855 and 1856 editions of *Leaves*.[12] It is as if the poet were summarizing the first two editions, regarding the earlier work as only part of the now larger, more comprehensive "ensemble."

The spatial figure of the synecdoche is partially undercut by the nearly chronological, sequential arrangement of the first twelve poems in the cluster. The order mixes five poems from each of the first two editions of *Leaves*, and in two cases Whitman uses the exact

11. The "Leaves of Grass" cluster title is used in the editions of 1860, 1867, and 1871; it also appears in the *Songs Before Parting* annex (1867) and in the *Passage to India* supplement (1871). For a list of poems in these clusters, see *Variorum*, I, lxx–lxxii.

12. The first twelve poems in the 1860 "Leaves of Grass" cluster are as follows:
1. "As I Ebb'd with the Ocean of Life" (1860)
2. "Great are the Myths" (1855)
3. "Song of the Answerer," 1 (1855)
   ("Morning's Romanza")
4. "This Compost" (1856)
5. "Song of Prudence" (1856)
6. "Song of the Answerer," 2 (1855)
   ("The Indications")
7. "Assurances" (1856)
8. "Miracles" (1856)
9. "There Was a Child Went Forth" (1855)
10. "Myself and Mine" (1860)
11. "Who Learns My Lesson Complete?" (1855)
12. "On the Beach at Night Alone" (1856)

arrangement he hit upon in the 1856 edition. First, three poems in the 1856 edition appear in sequence in the 1860 cluster: "Song of Prudence," "The Indications," and "Assurances" ("Leaves of Grass" 5–7). Second, "Miracles" and "There Was a Child Went Forth" ("Leaves of Grass" 8–9) appear together in both editions, and in both they follow closely the three-poem sequence. The first half of the cluster represents the first two editions of *Leaves*, while the second half features more recent poems. Thus the 1860 "Leaves of Grass" enacts the oppositions of continuity and succession, temporal and spatial form.

The contradictory connection between the spatial "ensemble" and the temporal "vista" is apparent in the arrangements of the "Leaves of Grass" clusters in the 1867 edition. Whitman emphasizes the spatial aspect of the new edition by creating four short "Leaves of Grass" clusters to replace the twenty-four-poem group of 1860. But two of the four clusters partially retain the order used in the 1860 edition. In the first 1867 "Leaves" cluster, for instance, three consecutive poems from the 1860 arrangement appear: "There Was a Child Went Forth," "Myself and Mine," and "Who Learns My Lesson Complete" ("Leaves of Grass," 9, 10, and 11 in the 1860 edition). Similarly, the third "Leaves" cluster in the 1867 edition includes, in their 1860 order, "Unfolded Out of the Folds," "Night on the Prairies," "The World Below the Brine," and "I Sit and Look Out" ("Leaves of Grass" 14, 15, 16, and 17 in 1860). The 1867 edition thus retains, in part, the sequential, consecutive arrangements of the 1860 "Leaves of Grass" cluster, but at the same time it disperses the grouping of 1860, placing it within a new spatial "ensemble."

The arrangements of "Leaves of Grass" in the 1860 and 1867 editions reveal the characteristic merging of "ensemble" and "vista." In the 1860 cluster, the themes of spiritual and linguistic progress appear in nearly every one of the twenty-four poems, and the thematic persistence tends to create the expectation that the form, too, will follow a model of development. But the method Whitman in fact employs seems to follow the order of composition more closely than any narrative progression inherent in the arrangement itself. The problem with the 1860 "Leaves" is that it straddles uneasily between the temporal model of the "string," or sequence, and the spatial model of the "cluster."

In the 1867 edition, on the other hand, the split between the temporal "vista" and the spatial "ensemble" is not so wide, for each of the four "Leaves of Grass" clusters creates a sense of progression or development. In the first of the clusters, "There Was a Child Went Forth" ("Leaves of Grass" 9 in 1860) presents the birth of the poet in private and in public terms, combining lyric and programmatic rhetoric. The next two poems, "Myself and Mine" and "Who Learns My

Lesson Complete?" ("Leaves of Grass" 10 and 11 in 1860) focus more sharply upon the programmatic theme of perpetual development, a theme that becomes even more pronounced in the poems of the third and fourth "Leaves of Grass" clusters. The fourth cluster is the most programmatic, and it features three poems drawn from the 1860 "Chants Democratic" cluster: "To Oratists" (Section 1 of "Vocalism"), and "Laws for Creations" and "Poets to Come" ("Chants Democratic," 12, 13, and 14). In all three poems Whitman addresses the question of future poets and poems, delivering his "programme" to the poets of the deferred future. In a rough way, then, the four "Leaves of Grass" clusters move from the personal birth of the poet to the public "programme of chants" that he bequeaths to his followers. In parallel fashion, they move from mixed modes, which combine the lyric and the programmatic, to the more purely programmatic.

The problem with this progression, however, is that it once again effaces the opposition between the two rhetorical modes. The element of progression is certainly present, but equally evident are such lyric, or antiprogrammatic, expressions as "O Sun of Real Peace," "Tears," and "Aboard at a Ship's Helm," which form the second "Leaves of Grass" cluster in the 1867 edition. The first of the three poems is perhaps the most interesting, for Whitman created it by taking eleven lines from the 1860 poem "Apostroph."[13] A more urgently programmatic expression than "Apostroph" would be difficult to find, but "O Sun of Real Peace" takes the vision of "Libertad" and presents it as a threat to the poet:

O heights too swift and dizzy yet!
O purged and luminous! you threaten me more than I can
    stand!
(I must not venture—the ground under my feet menaces me—it
    will not support me:
O future too immense,)—O present, I return, while yet I may, to
    you.

(10–13)

By returning to the present, Whitman rejects the bright vision of the future "programme," and as a result he concentrates in "Tears" upon his solitary sense of death as "all dark and desolate" (4). "Aboard at a Ship's Helm" does little to relieve the dark lyricism of the cluster. Although it presents the "ship of the body, ship of the soul, voyaging,

13. For the texts of both poems, see *Variorum*, II, 290–93. I quote here from the 1871 text of "O Sun of Real Peace."

voyaging, voyaging" (11), the poem functions "to warn the ship from its wreck-place" (6), and the tone never rises to the characteristic optimism of Whitman's programmatic rhetoric.

The dispersal of the "Leaves of Grass" poems in the 1867 edition accomplishes several purposes. First, it clearly represents an increased spatialization of poetic form. By scattering the twenty-four poems of the 1860 "Leaves of Grass" cluster, Whitman complicates the temporal, sequential model of progression. In this regard, it is significant that the 1867 edition also saw the first use of section numbers in "Song of Myself." They create a spatializing effect, one that makes the work into a "cluster" of fifty-two poems rather than a narrative sequence or progression.[14] Second, the dispersal allows Whitman to retain progressive elements in a shorter sequence of poems. So, for example, the third and fourth "Leaves of Grass" clusters retain, in part, the sequential arrangement of the 1860 cluster, but by limiting the number of poems within each cluster Whitman increases the effect of coherence and unity. Thus the spatialization of form paradoxically enhances the temporal model of progressivist development. Third, the dispersal creates an interpenetration of the lyric and the programmatic modes of expression. Neither is privileged, and each resonates throughout the 1867 edition. The cluster arrangements of the 1867 *Leaves of Grass* therefore repeat the structure of opposition that Whitman develops in "When Lilacs Last in the Door-yard Bloom'd."

The cluster arrangements of the 1871 edition assume a more complicated form, and the salient features of the edition are the greater number and wider dispersal of the "Leaves of Grass"clusters. After the new cluster "Inscriptions" and the established "Children of Adam" and "Calamus," seven "Leaves of Grass" clusters alternate reg-

---

14. See the editors' note to "Song of Myself," *Variorum*, I, 1.

There have been several important attempts to read "Song of Myself" through phases or stages, and each attempt creates a pseudonarrative "plot" of development. See, for instance, Carl F. Strauch, "The Structure of Walt Whitman's 'Song of Myself,' " *English Journal* 27 (1938): 597–607; Miller, *Critical Guide*, pp. 6–35; Malcolm Cowley, "Introduction," in *Walt Whitman's "Leaves of Grass." The First (1855) Edition* (New York: Penguin, 1976), pp. vii–xxxvii; Harold Bloom, *Poetry and Repression* (New Haven, Conn.: Yale University Press, 1976), pp. 235–66.

For an essay arguing against the "phasal" structure, see V. K. Chari, "Structure of Whitman's Catalogue Poems," *Walt Whitman Review* 18 (1972): 3–17. In "A Backward Glance O'er Travel'd Roads," Whitman himself seems to argue against the idea of "Song of Myself" as a unified long poem: "I was repaid in Poe's prose by the idea that (at any rate for our occasions, our day) there can be no such thing as a long poem. The same thought had been haunting my mind before, but Poe's argument, though short, work'd the sum out and proved it to me" (*CRE*, p. 569).

ularly with such clusters as "The Answerer," "Drum-Taps," "Marches Now the War is Over," "Bathed in War's Perfume," "Songs of Insurrection," and "Songs of Parting." The alternation reveals a fundamental opposition between the spatial arrangement of the "Leaves of Grass" clusters and the chronological arrangement of the Civil War clusters. But the opposition between the poles of "ensemble" and "vista" does not create the sense of balance attained in the 1867 edition. Instead, the dispersal of the "Leaves of Grass" clusters diffuses both the programmatic vision of the future and the lyric vision of the past and present.

The failure of the 1871 edition is due, in large part, to Whitman's choice of poems for the seven "Leaves of Grass" clusters. Of the twenty-seven poems, only eleven are present in the "Chants Democratic" and "Leaves of Grass" clusters of 1860, and only six appear in the "Leaves of Grass" clusters of 1867. Furthermore, none of the seven clusters creates the dynamic sense of programmatic change that Whitman managed to forge in the third and fourth "Leaves of Grass" clusters of 1867. The poems appearing in the seven clusters of 1871 thus do little to provide a programmatic context for the unfolding account of the poet's Civil War experiences.

The failure of the 1871 *Leaves of Grass* stems from Whitman's interest in creating a new volume of poems—as if he wished to escape the confines of his own project. Whitman hints at the wish by adding three supplements—*Drum-Taps, Sequel to Drum-Taps,* and *Songs Before Parting*—to the 1867 edition, and he makes the wish more explicit in the *Passage to India* supplement annexed to the 1872 issue of *Leaves.* In the 1876 preface to *Leaves of Grass,* the poet clarifies the status of *Passage to India* as his "special chants of death and immortality":

> It was originally my intention, after chanting in "Leaves of Grass" the songs of the body and existence, to then compose a further, equally needed volume, based on those convictions of perpetuity and conservation which, enveloping all precedents, make the unseen soul govern absolutely at last. I meant, while in a sort continuing the theme of my first chants, to shift the slides, and exhibit the problem and paradox of the same ardent and fully appointed personality entering the sphere of the resistless gravitation of spiritual law, and with cheerful face estimating death, not at all as the cessation, but as somehow what I feel it must be, the entrance upon by far the greatest part of existence, and something that life is at least as much for, as it is for itself. (*PW,* II, 466)

Here Whitman attempts to reconstruct his project in several ways. First, the earlier distinction between individuality and nationality now shifts to that between the body and the soul, so that the spiritual quality of the poet's democratic vision becomes the focus of the "further, equally needed volume." Second, Whitman's cumulative vision of spiritual and linguistic evolution is evidenced in the "convictions of perpetuity and conservation ... enveloping all precedents." But Whitman does not seem to see that his vision of the cumulative could apply equally well to *Leaves of Grass*. He thus speaks of "spiritual law" as if it were a completely new concept in his poetry, disregarding the spiritual aspect of the 1860 and 1867 "programme of chants." Despite the peculiar blindness of the reconstruction, however, this passage suggests that *Passage to India* is not a new volume of poems but a cumulative reformation of the poet's essential lifework.

The cumulative nature of the *Passage to India* supplement is apparent in the "Leaves of Grass" cluster, its most prominent formal feature. The first three poems here are new, but most of the remaining twenty-one poems first appeared in the "Leaves of Grass" and "Chants Democratic" clusters of 1860. "Excelsior," "Mediums," and "On Journeys Through the States," for example, are "Chants Democratic" 15, 16, and 17 in the 1860 edition. "Miracles," "Myself and Mine," "Who Learns My Lesson Complete," "Night on the Prairies," "What Am I After All," and "Locations and Times" are "Leaves of Grass" 8, 10, 11, 15, 22, and 23 in 1860. Of these six poems, moreover, three appear in "Leaves of Grass" clusters in the 1867 edition. The form of the 1871 "Leaves of Grass" cluster, with its twenty-four poems, recalls the cluster of the 1860 edition, and the poems themselves create the programmatic "thread-voice" that runs so clearly through the 1860 "programme of chants." The 1871 supplement thus represents a return to the poet's earlier conception of the cluster, for the block of programmatic poems consolidates the programmatic vision of spiritual evolution that was obscured by the dispersals in the 1871 edition of *Leaves of Grass*.[15]

15. The first three poems in the cluster are new, but most of the remaining twenty-one come from the 1860 "Chants Democratic" and "Leaves of Grass" clusters.

The *Passage to India* supplement includes the following poems in other clusters: "As I Ebb'd With the Ocean of Life" ("Leaves of Grass," 1), "On the Beach at Night Alone" ("Leaves of Grass," 12), and "The World Below the Brine" ("Leaves of Grass," 16) appear in the "Sea-Shore Memories" cluster; "Assurances" ("Leaves of Grass," 7) appears in the "Whispers of Heavenly Death" cluster; and "To the Reader at Parting" ("Leaves of Grass," 24) appears in the "Now Finale to the Shore" cluster. In sum, the supplement features eleven of the 1860 "Leaves of Grass" poems, many of which also figure prominently in the "Leaves of Grass" clusters of the 1867 edition.

The cluster arrangements of the 1881 edition of *Leaves of Grass* might seem, at first glance, to signal Whitman's final defeat. The "Leaves of Grass" clusters, which function in the volumes of 1860–72 as a synecdoche for the entire poetic "ensemble," disappear completely. It is therefore tempting to interpret the disappearance as the ultimate dispersal both of the poet's programmatic vision and of his poetic self. That is the view taken by Gay Wilson Allen, one of the most sympathetic and penetrating of Whitman's critics: "Since Whitman's avowed purpose was to put on record his own life, which he regarded as typical and representative, we would expect the poems of his life-record to be arranged either in chronology of their composition (which is to say, the chronology of his poetic and emotional development) or classified so that their subject-matter at least suggests a natural biographical sequence. . . . [But] the life-allegory arrangement is still quite general and unsystematic, and there is little visible attempt at chronology inside the groups."[16]

The problem with this view of the 1881 cluster arrangements is that it assumes two versions of a temporal model. The poems should be arranged either according to the date of composition or according to a "natural biographical sequence." But this is to ignore the spatialization of form that marks Whitman's attempts at creating an architectural "ensemble" in the editions of 1860, 1867, and 1871. The architectural ideal is still the poet's goal in the 1881 edition, as an interview with Whitman indicates:

> In a small inner room connected with the printing establishment of Rand, Avery, & Co., Walt Whitman the poet was reading by a table yesterday. Near by was a pile of corrected proof-sheets bearing the heading "Leaves of Grass." His ruddy features were almost concealed by his white hair and beard. When he laid down his book on the intrusion of the writer, his eye, still bright and keen, glowed with a genuine good nature. No, he had no objections to entering into a conversation which should be given to the public, provided there was any interest in what he might say. He was here, he said, to look over the proofs for his new "Leaves of Grass," which James R. Osgood & Co. are to issue. "It is a long time," remarked the reporter, "since the book by that name was first given to the world." "Yes," replied the poet, leaning back comfortably in his chair, and looking reflectively across

16. *Handbook*, pp. 148–49. For contrasting views of the 1881 cluster arrangements, see Miller, *Critical Guide*, pp. 188–261, and Crawley, pp. 80–164.

the table at the writer, who had seated himself opposite, "it is now, I believe, twenty-five years since I began to work upon the structure; and this edition will complete the design which I had in my mind when I began to write.

"The whole affair is like one of those old architectural edifices, some of which have been hundreds of years building, and the designer of which has the whole idea in his mind from the first. His plans are pretty ambitious, and, as means or time permits, he adds part after part, perhaps at quite wide intervals. To a casual observer it looks in the course of its construction odd enough. Only after the whole is completed, one catches the idea which inspired the designer, in whose mind the relation of each part to the whole has existed all along. That is the way it has been with my book. It has been twenty-five years building. There have been seven different hitches at it. Seven different times have parts of the edifice been constructed,—sometimes in Brooklyn, sometimes in Washington, sometimes in Boston, and at other places. The book has been built partially in every part of the United States; and this Osgood edition is the completed edifice." [17]

Whitman's statements are clearly an exercise in creative reconstruction, a revising of his shifting, contradictory visions of the poetic lifework. They also revise the poet's usual rhetoric of deferral, for now he proclaims the 1881 edition to be "the completed edifice," the full realization of the original "whole idea." The architectural figure emphasizes, moreover, the spatial character of the book, though Whitman's interest is also drawn to the "twenty-five years building," the process of construction itself rather than the completed product of the construction. So the interview suggests that the 1881 edition is the completed edifice, but it also suggests that the architectural "ensemble" cannot be separated from the temporal "vista," even when the "vista" is essentially retrospective.

The cluster arrangements of the 1881 edition create, as in "When Lilacs Last in the Door-yard Bloom'd," a structure of opposition. Perhaps the most fundamental of several oppositions is that between

17. The interview appeared in the *Boston Globe* on 24 August 1881, and it was reprinted in the Osgood advertising prospectus for the 1881 edition of *Leaves of Grass*. A copy of the prospectus, from which I quote, is in Container 21 of the Feinberg Collection.

spatial and temporal form, and several of the new clusters in the 1881 edition combine both formal elements. Four new clusters, for instance, gesture toward both spatial and temporal elements: "Birds of Passage," "Sea-Drift," "By the Roadside," and "Autumn Rivulets." All four titles emphasize change or transition, and the transition can be either spatial or temporal. "By the Roadside," for instance, figures both a resting place and a journey; "Autumn Rivulets" combines the temporal figure of the season with the more spatial figure of water flowing into a larger stream.

The figure of transition controls the cluster arrangements of 1881, combining the opposed elements of "Body and Soul." This strategy of incorporation is most clearly evident in "Sea-Drift." The cluster joins the poems included in the "Sea-Shore Memories" cluster of the *Passage to India* supplement with such later poems as "To the Man-of-War-Bird," "Song for All Seas, All Ships," "Patroling Barnegat," and "After the Sea-Ship." Moreover, it incorporates several poems from the 1860 and 1867 "Leaves of Grass" clusters: "As I Ebb'd with the Ocean of Life," "Tears," "Aboard at a Ship's Helm," "The World Below the Brine," and "On the Beach at Night Alone." The eleven poems of the cluster represent the full range of Whitman's poetic career, from the 1856 "On the Beach at Night Alone" to the 1880 "Patroling Barnegat." They thus represent a cumulative gathering of poems treating the central images of sea and shore.

More important, the eleven poems reveal Whitman's strong tendency to mix modes of representation. "Out of the Cradle," for example, combines the lyric and programmatic rhetorical modes, while its dark twin, "As I Ebb'd with the Ocean of Life," places the programmatic rhetoric in doubt in order to renew it. This kind of pairing, or twinning, also explains other parts of the cluster. "Tears" and "To the Man-of-War-Bird" present the opposed tones of desolation and joy, though both poems treat the image of a storm. Similarly, "Aboard at a Ship's Helm" combines the programmatic image of the voyaging soul with the "loud admonition" (7) concerning a storm's potential danger to the soul, while "On the Beach at Night" reassures the reader (as well as the dramatized child in the poem) that the "ravening clouds shall not long be victorious" (16). For not only the stars, but also the soul, will endure:

Something there is,
(With my lips soothing thee, adding I whisper,
I give thee the first suggestion, the problem and indirection,)
Something there is more immortal even than the stars,
(Many the burials, many the days and nights, passing away,)

Something that shall endure longer even than lustrous Jupiter,
Longer than sun or any revolving satellite,
Or the radiant sisters the Pleiades.

                                                    (25–32)

Though reassuring, the poet gives us a "problem and indirection" rather than a direct solution to the question of mortality. The "something" is the enduring, immortal soul, but as in "Aboard at a Ship's Helm" he refuses to deliver the image of the soul in a pure, unadulterated form.

The mixture of representational modes continues in two important poems from earlier "Leaves of Grass" clusters: "The World Below the Brine" and "On the Beach at Night Alone." The controlling structure of opposition is registered, first of all, in the style of the two poems. "The World Below the Brine" is an eleven-line phrasal catalogue, whereas "On the Beach at Night Alone" is a mixed catalogue, employing both phrasal and clausal lines. We might expect "The World Below the Brine" to create a stative representation, but the opposite is the case. The present participle functions to blend movement and stasis, actions and objects, within the poet's vision of the "change onward" of all worlds. Likewise, the mixed catalogue of "On the Beach at Night Alone" functions to join part and whole within the poet's vision of "a vast similitude." The style of "The World Below the Brine" enacts the temporal "vista," whereas that of "On the Beach at Night Alone" enacts the spatial "ensemble."

In "Song for All Seas, All Ships" and "Patroling Barnegat," Whitman once again shows his predilection for pairing poetic modes. The first of the two poems moves from the many to the one, from "ships sailing the seas, each with its special flag or ship-signal" (2) to "a pennant universal, subtly waving all time, o'er all brave sailors, / All seas, all ships" (22–23). The poem inclines toward a restatement of the spatial theme presented in "On the Beach at Night Alone," and both poems tend to produce a programmatic tone. But Whitman is careful to avoid any single mode of representation. In "Patroling Barnegat," therefore, he once again exploits the combination of the phrasal catalogue and the present participle, and the combination produces one of his most effective late lyrics:

Wild, wild the storm, and the sea high running,
Steady the roar of the gale, with incessant undertone
     muttering,
Shouts of demoniac laughter fitfully piercing and pealing,
Waves, air, midnight, their savagest trinity lashing,

Out in the shadows there milk-white combs careering,
On beachy slush and sand spirts of snow fierce slanting,
Where through the murk the easterly death-wind breasting,
Through cutting swirl and spray watchful and firm advancing,
(That in the distance! is that a wreck? is the red signal flaring?)
Slush and sand of the beach tireless till daylight wending,
Steadily, slowly, through hoarse roar never remitting,
Along the midnight edge by those milk-white combs careering,
A group of dim, weird forms, struggling, the night confronting,
That savage trinity warily watching.

(Variorum, III, 684)

The fourteen-line form and the regular terminal repetition of the present participle combine to create a stable rhythmical frame, one that approaches the tradition of the sonnet. But within that frame, the poet presents a host of fragmented sounds and actions, displacing the sonnet tradition with a fluid movement from the natural to the human. The first six lines focus upon the "demoniac" trinity of "waves, air, midnight," but the seventh line presents the subtle volte face through the indirect representation of human beings "breasting" the "easterly death-wind." In the "sestet," the terminal participle modifies images of nature, but in the "octave" it modifies images of the human. Thus the demoniac, purposeless quality of such participles as "running," "muttering," "pealing," and "lashing" yields to the human, purposive quality of "breasting," "advancing," "wending," "confronting," and "watching." Perhaps the most subtle example of the shift appears in the repetition of the participle "careering" (5, 12), which shifts from the chaotic movement of the "milk-white combs" to the purposive movement of the patrolers "along the midnight edge by those milk-white combs." As in "Aboard at a Ship's Helm" and "On the Beach at Night," however, Whitman employs the image of the storm in order to deliver, not an answer or a programme, but "the problem and indirection." The opposition between the natural and the human is not resolved; instead, the poet leaves us with an enduring, perpetual purpose: "That savage trinity warily watching."

"After the Sea-Ship," the final poem of "Sea-Drift," serves as a poetic coda, summarizing the oppositions that structure the entire cluster by combining the programmatic and lyric modes of representation. The image of the "sea-ship" figures the purposive, progressivist world of human beings, and it echoes the image of the "ship of the soul" presented in "Aboard at a Ship's Helm." In contrast, the "myriad myriad waves hastening, lifting up their necks" figure the more nostalgic, lyric vision of nature and the body. The clear opposition is complicated by further figuration in the poem. The waves are "emulous," an adjective evoking both rivalry and imitation. The evocation implies both the human and, more specifically, the literary, and the latter becomes yet clearer in the image of the waves as "a motley procession with many a fleck of foam and many fragments" (11). The "motley procession" figures the complicated mixture of "ensemble" and "vista," of lyric and programmatic modes. The cluster of poems forms a "procession," but it is "motley," including "many a fleck of foam and many fragments." Despite this possible undercutting of the "procession," however, Whitman ends the poem with the image of the waves "following the stately and rapid ship, in the wake following."

The double figure of ship and wake closes the "Sea-Drift" cluster with an image of dynamic transition. And that image includes the opposed elements of, on the one hand, body and soul, and, on the other, temporal and spatial form. In its incorporating power, "After the Sea-Ship" echoes the codas of such poems as "Out of the Cradle Endlessly Rocking" and "When Lilacs Last in the Door-yard Bloom'd." In addition, the poem can stand as a final suggestion that from 1860 to 1892 Whitman's "language experiment" continues, in a cumulative fashion, to succeed.

Index